Loving and Learning

Lc

ving and Learning

Interacting with Your Child from Birth to Three

Norma J. McDiarmid

Mari A. Peterson

James R. Sutherland

 Harcourt Brace Jovanovich, New York and London

Printed in the United States of America

The quotation on p. 7 is from *Love Is Not Enough*, by Bruno Bettelheim,
copyright © 1950 by The Free Press, a corporation, and is used
by permission of The Macmillan Publishing Co. Inc. "Slowly, Slowly,
Very Slowly" is from *Games for the Very Young*, by Elizabeth Matterson,
copyright © 1969, and is used with permission of McGraw-Hill Book
Company and Penguin Books Ltd. "If You're Happy and You Know It" is
from the book *Sally Go Round the Sun*, by Edith Fowke, copyright © 1969
by McClelland and Stewart Limited, and is reprinted by permission of the
Canadian Publishers, McClelland and Stewart Limited, Toronto, and also
of Doubleday & Company, Inc. "The Wheels of the Bus Go Round and
Round" is from the book of that title by Nancy Larrick, published by
Childrens Press. The Exercises on pages 33–36 are adapted from *How to
Keep Your Child Fit from Birth to Six*, by Bonnie Prudden, copyright ©
1964 by Bonnie Prudden, and are used by permission of Harper & Row,
Publishers, Inc. The game described on page 175 is from Ira J. Gordon's
Child Learning Through Child Play, published by St. Martin's Press, Inc.

Library of Congress Cataloging in Publication Data

McDiarmid, Norma J
    Loving and learning.

    Bibliography: p.
    1. Parent and child. 2. Child study. 3. Love.
I. Peterson, Mari A., joint author. II. Sutherland,
James R., joint author. III. Title.
HQ769.M15   649'.12'2   74–19395
ISBN 0–15–154730–0

First edition
B C D E

3/21/75- Di

Dedicated to the Canadian Mothercraft Society

Contents

Foreword

During the past few years, there has been a renewed interest in the first few years of life on the part of behavioral scientists, educators, social planners, and to some extent parents as well. From a scientific point of view, much has been added to our understanding of the competencies and characteristics of infants and toddlers, and there have been many studies concerned with the effects of environmental as well as biological influences on development in the first three years of life. From the point of view of social policy and programs, there has been a special concern with remediation of the adverse socioeconomic and health conditions of many low-income groups, particularly to ensure that during the important early years of life the young child's environment is supportive of optimal physical and psychological development.

Partly as a result of this movement, partly because of the growing number of working mothers at all income levels, efforts are being made to provide more broadly available, high quality group care outside the home for infants and toddlers, either in day-care centers or in family day-care homes. In connection with such efforts, many manuals concerned with group care for infants and toddlers have recently appeared, often with guidelines for providing learning experiences and stimulation likely to promote the very young child's growth and development. At the same time, a number of programs have been concerned with helping low-income parents to encourage the development of their infants and toddlers, in part through visits by home "teachers." These efforts, also, have led to a number of general manuals or guidelines for home visitors and for parents as well.

This book represents a welcome addition to the literature available to parents interested in gaining a greater understanding of the development of their young children during the first three years of life, and of some of the ways in which they can help foster that development. The book attempts to communicate a sense of the pleasure and joy that parents can derive from a more perceptive understanding of their infant's and toddler's behavior. It contains many examples of ways in which parents can share meaningful and pleasurable experiences with their very young child—experiences that will at the same time facilitate the child's development.

The title of the book, Loving and Learning, reflects the authors' conviction that it is the sphere of early human relationships which is paramount, and that learning and intellectual development readily thrive in a context of warm and loving interactions between the infant or toddler and his parents. The authors express considerable concern about what may be seen as a contemporary overemphasis on intellectual stimulation, particularly through automated "gadgets," and sometimes at the expense of adequate opportunities for close social interaction with parents. This emphasis on the importance of warm and affectionate adult-child interrelationships from the point of view of both the infant and the parents represents an important contribution of this volume.

These general views are set forth in the authors' introductory chapter, which is followed by chapters dealing with successive six-month periods of life from birth to age three. Each of these six chapters begins with an overview of what the infant is like at this stage of his development, and of the major changes that have taken place during the period under consideration. The remaining portions of each chapter focus on suggested play activities and learning experiences that parents can set up to aid the infant's or toddler's development during the period in question. These discussions are rich with examples from the authors' own experience, and they clearly communicate the pleasure and joy a parent or other care-giver can derive from observing, sharing in, and supporting the young child's early attempts to understand and enjoy his world. Great stress is placed on active participation by the parent, from making toys and play materials or creating enjoyable situations, to becoming involved in these activities with the infant or toddler. Many of the interchanges and games are suggested as natural parts of such routine care-giving activities as feeding, bathing, diaper changing, and so on.

The authors place considerable emphasis on the importance of the father's participation in caring for and playing with his infant or toddler. Also, they stress the fact that spending much time playing with and caring for one's own baby provides much gratification and important learning opportunities for the parent as well as the infant or toddler. The authors suggest, quite appropriately, that having such time together is particularly valuable in those instances where an infant or toddler may be spending a good bit of time in the care of someone other than the parents—as, for example, in day care.

Since so much of the volume deals with detailed suggestions for carrying out various specific activities with the infant or toddler, the casual reader may get the impression that good parenting depends heavily on mother and father engaging in many carefully scheduled, formally planned learning experiences with their very young child. The authors wisely caution against such an interpretation of their book at several points, but particularly in the final chapter, which might usefully be scanned by the reader immediately after the Introduction, and read again at the conclusion of the volume. They remind the reader that the many activities described are offered primarily as illustrations of ways parents can participate in pleasurable interactions with their very young child that may at the same time promote the child's development. However, they caution, the infant or toddler is an active explorer of his world who learns much independently, particularly in an affectionate and supportive environment, so that he needs some quiet time, some time when he is on his own. Also, there is much value in spontaneity and naturalness in parent-child interactions, so parents should not be overly rigid about scheduling and formal presentations of the various experiences and activities suggested in the book. These are important points that deserve the emphasis placed upon them by the authors.

All in all, this should be an informative and helpful book not only for parents, to whom it is primarily addressed, but also for a variety of other people who have some responsibility for the care of infants and toddlers either in the child's own home, in family day-care settings, or in day-care centers.

Henry N. Ricciuti
*Professor, Human Development
and Family Studies*
Cornell University

Acknowledgments

We would like to thank the staff of the Canadian Mothercraft Society Infant Day Nursery for their enthusiastic interest in trying out new activities and games with the children in the center. Special thanks must go to the children who willingly participated in new ventures and so gave the authors the clues as to whether or not these ventures were enjoyable and interesting. We would also like to thank Mrs. Eva Stevens and Mrs. Mary Holland for typing much of the preliminary manuscript and last but not least Drs. Garnet McDiarmid and Rein Peterson, who supported and encouraged the authors with understanding and sensitivity throughout the writing of this book.

Loving and Learning

1

A New Life

Loving and learning are two vital ingredients in the mixture of social, emotional, physical, and intellectual growth that takes place during the early years. Our book on loving and learning is based on the premise that love is the most important ingredient, since learning is most productive when it takes place in an atmosphere of warmth and love. A baby who is loved is usually a happy baby and fun to be with. A loved baby reaches out to his parents with smiles and gestures of delight when he is with them. In turn, parents who are responded to in this loving way feel more secure in their handling of the baby, and the family together can thus weather any unsettled times that are part of growing up because they have a strong base of love and understanding to guide them.

Loving and learning go hand in hand, partners in the struggle to adapt to the rapid changes that occur in modern living. Learning can take place without love, but lacking its partner this learning is often unproductive and self-defeating. For example, an unloved baby learns that his unhappy cries are met by loud words, indifference, or spanking, and that the world is a harsh place, not conducive to exploration and adventure. Indeed, he learns that he is the only one concerned with his unhappiness. He must turn inward and seek assurance in himself. But he is too young to cope all by himself, so he cries some more, confused and lonely, his energies wasted on yet more tears. A loved baby in the same situation learns that his cries are soon met with a reassuring hug, soft words, and an attempt by the loved one to help him solve his problem. He does not have to waste his energies on more tears but can turn his attention to exploring his world, secure in the knowledge that if he needs help it is forthcoming.

The early years are ones of great growth and change equaled only by the almost miraculous changes that occur after the time of conception, when a baby grows from one cell to trillions of cells. When egg and sperm unite to begin a new life the baby's heredity is already determined, but whether or not he reaches his full potential depends to a large extent on his environment. Even before birth, the attitude of the parents, especially of the mother, can have an effect on the baby's development. A mother and father who anticipate the birth of their baby with joy will do everything to see that the mother has adequate rest, good nutrition, and the supervision of a qualified doctor. Concern during pregnancy is a forerunner of the care the parents will show at the birth of the baby, and a baby with such a head start is well on the way to the adventures of learning about his world.

At birth, sounds, light, hunger, and uneven temperatures are all new to the baby. Even the ability to move around freely and really stretch is a new experience. From his comfortable home in the womb he is thrust into a new, confusing, and sometimes frightening world that will shape and mold his inherited characteristics. This unique little baby will react in his own special way to what his environment offers him. Since this new environment is strange to the baby, parents as well as other people act rather like interpreters, communicating with the baby what this big, bewildering world is all about. Right from the very beginning a two-way system of communication is already working, and because it is the mother who cares for the baby most intimately during the early months, it is usually the mother who sends and receives the first communicative signals that indicate to the baby that he is loved and wanted.

As this communicative system develops, the baby learns to feel good or bad about himself as a person and in this way his basic outlook for the rest of his life may be positively or negatively focused. The early years are a time for the development of trust and self-esteem, as well as a time for the development of independence. From those around him he learns that he is loved and wanted and that he can depend on people and his environment. A baby who is loved learns to love in return and the channels of communication remain open. However, a baby may also learn that he is not liked and cannot trust anyone, and his world remains confusing, making him feel insecure. The channels of communication become blocked in some areas and he cannot develop fully to become self-reliant and independent in the same way as the baby who trusts his world. Love, care, understanding, and appropriate stimulation act as steppingstones to a solid foundation on which to build a rewarding future for the baby.

Learning to trust develops at a time of life when a baby is more helpless than he will ever be again, dependent on others to nurture, protect, and reassure him. If at this time in his life the infant is left in a world where he is mostly responded to by gadgets that whirl and click and give him feedback, then he will grow to depend on them, rather than on human contact, for comfort. While feedback toys and gadgets are great for brief periods of time and can teach a baby that his actions result in interesting happenings, the gadgets cannot always respond to the baby's needs appropriately since they are limited in the responses that they can make. They amuse and interest the baby but teach him little about human contact and how to cope with his emotions and feelings. On the other hand, if an infant is never given the opportunity to express himself on his own terms but is always smothered and overwhelmed by overprotective and hovering parents, he will grow up to cling to them and depend on them for everything. He will not realize that he can do things for himself, that he is an independent being capable of having an

5

effect on the world. Indeed, a child needs warmth, security, and support as he explores his world, but he should not have to cling to his mother and depend on her for everything. Somewhere there is a balance for each baby between independent learning and exploring, and gentle, loving, warm contact with others that blends to develop a healthy foundation for human relationships and future growth.

Until fairly recently, parents have rested secure in the knowledge that until an infant is nearly two and starts showing signs of verbal communication, his needs are primarily physical. Baby-care books are written and used that focus mainly on the physical needs of the baby—the feeding, sleeping, and toilet routines. Some reference is made to emotional, intellectual, and social needs, but these are often fleeting and nonspecific. As long as the baby is kept clean, dry, and warm, well fed and safe, all his needs are taken care of and the parents are assured that they are doing their job well. This attitude has prevailed even though we have known for some time now that infants in institutions, whose physical needs were met in a reasonably satisfactory manner, failed to thrive as healthy, happy babies. Margaretha Ribble, Rene Spitz, John Bowlby, and Betty Flint among others have written poignantly about those babies who survived the institutional experience, and those who died. (For works by these authors, see the bibliography.) It is interesting to note that very often death was not due to initial physical illness, but came about simply because the babies seemed to lose their will to live. It is almost as though they gave up on the world, which is most unusual since babies fight tenaciously to live and learn, provided they experience love and the comfort of being held close.

We know now that to grow into healthy babies and caring, productive adults, infants need more than just good physical care. While basic good health practices and sound nutrition are extremely important in contributing to the well-being of a baby, babies also need warm, loving, face-to-face personalized attention geared specifically to their needs and level of maturity at any given time. They need to be held and cuddled and talked to; they need to be stroked and patted, nuzzled and rocked with positive emotion; they need "contact comfort" that can come only from another person (and not another thing) to be maximally effective. Nothing seems to soothe an upset, crying infant as much as being picked up and held close. Tender words and gentle rocking usually calm the baby, and mother can then go on to find the cause of the baby's initial discomfort. Home-reared babies generally receive much of this kind of caring and attention during routine caretaking interactions with their parents as well as during playtimes.

There is a well-worn cliché that if you love your baby, everything else will automatically fall into place. But as Bruno Bettelheim points out in his book of that title, love is not enough. Parents in our increasingly complex world must make a conscious effort to structure it in such a way that it becomes meaningful and coherent for the baby.

Modern living conditions have made it much more difficult for parents to create a setting in which both their own legitimate needs and the needs of their children can be satisfied with relative ease. That is why *love alone is not enough* [our italics] and must be supplemented by deliberate efforts on the part of the parent. Fortunately most parents love their children and conscientiously strive to be good parents. But more and more of them become weary of the struggle to arrange life sensibly for their children, while modern pressures create more and more insensible experiences which are added to the life of the child. More and more they are exposed to crowded living quarters, to over-stimulating and incomprehensible experiences through radio and television, and have to face almost daily some new gadget they must learn to master or avoid.

In this day of gadgetry, it is too easily assumed that one can keep a child amused with mechanized, moving, and sound-making toys and objects that reverberate and respond to the baby's

touch. All around him there are kaleidoscopes of sound, movement, and color created by special see-through plastic bumpers
for the crib, some with colorful inserts, mobiles overhead, baby
gyms, brightly colored sheets, an abundance of pictures on the
walls, busy boxes within easy reach, and numerous objects to
help the baby move, sit up, and take notice on his own. Brightly
colored objects entice the child to touch, feel, and explore, first
visually and then tactually, as he tries to make sense of his busy,
mixed-up world.

It is a deep concern of the authors that all these wonderful
and interesting gadgets that occupy the baby's time may tend to
detract somewhat from the face-to-face contact the baby may
otherwise be getting from his mother or another loving person.
Thus, the emphasis of this book is on activities that parents and

babies can engage in *together*, giving them a better opportunity to learn together and understand each other as they interact. To understand each other is to know each other, and knowing can lead to much enjoyment. It is easy for a busy mother to say, "Oh, the baby is quiet and amusing himself so I'll just leave him alone a little longer." But we should ask ourselves the question, "What are we depriving the infant of when we are providing him with nonhuman stimulation?" We are depriving him of human contact and the warmth and security that goes along with knowing that mother is very close, to touch him, to smile at him, to help him out if he gets stuck and frustrated. She is there to pick him up for just a quick hug and a kiss on the spur of the moment because she loves him and cares for him. This is not to say that babies should never be left alone to play and learn to do things independently, and that gadgets and feedback toys are bad, it is just to point out that the onus is on us, as caring adults, to moderate and interpret the environment to the babies in a human-oriented, warm and loving way.

Modern conveniences and gadgets have freed the harried housewife and mother not only from some of the drudgery of cooking and housework but also from some of the drudgery of child care. Along with these conveniences we have, as a society, inherited infant day-care centers, preschool programs, and junior kindergartens. These centers may be stimulating and caring environments in which babies and toddlers come into contact with other children of their own age and experience activities that are not readily available in the average home situation. These developments make it easier for parents to spend as much or as little time as they want with their infants. But whatever time parents choose to be with their children, they should be filled with the enjoyment of being parents of a wonderful, unique child. They should take time to sit back and observe their children as they master the environment and glow with little triumphs—that first fantastic grin, the first time baby manages to sit up all by him-

9

self, the first big step, and all those achievements that endear infants to our hearts as they struggle to become independent.

Researchers and psychologists are stressing the importance of the first five years in laying down a good foundation and groundwork for future development. To lay a solid groundwork, parents must provide for the infant's physical, emotional, and intellectual needs. We know that infants are capable of a lot more than we ever dreamed possible. Lee Salk and Rita Kramer in their book *How to Raise a Human Being* point out that infants are very vulnerable to early experiences and that learning starts in the first days of life, and in some ways even before birth. Benjamin Bloom, in *Stability and Change in Human Characteristics*, feels that the child's environment has a maximum impact on a developing characteristic during that characteristic's period of most rapid development. For example, when a baby is learning to crawl, keeping him confined in a crib, playpen, infant seat, or stroller is not going to encourage the baby to fulfill this need, but providing an open and safe place, verbal encouragement, and activities that will help him fulfill his need to crawl *when he is ready* will develop this new mobility at an optimal time. Also, since human intelligence increases most rapidly during the first five years of life, this is the time when the environment can influence it most easily. Old habits are· hard to break once they have become deeply entrenched, and thus these early environmental experiences are crucial to the well-being of the baby.

In the past we have tended to think of babies as passive creatures who do little else but sleep away the time with a few active interludes for feeding, changing, and bathing. We have tended to classify babies as good or bad depending on their level of irritability and how much time they demand from us. A good baby sleeps a lot, a bad baby annoys us with his crying. We have not tended to think of babies as problem solvers, active from the time of birth. Babies do not learn by passively absorbing their environment but by actively being involved with it. They are, from the start, like sophisticated scientists posing silent questions about their environment and seeking to find out all the possible solutions. A little baby will observe, mouth, feel, and listen to objects and sounds over and over again; he will bang and tap the objects on surfaces and on himself; he will twist and turn them to see what happens. From his many separate explorations and experiences he will eventually be able to piece the information together to correctly identify the objects.

Babies are adventurers. They discover themselves and the world through sensory experiences. In other words, they learn by doing, by experiencing and physically getting involved with their world, be it through the sense of smell, touch, sight, hearing, or taste. As they experience things they store them away for future use and reference, building a fund of knowledge from the very beginning of life. Notice how quickly a baby learns to adjust to sucking from a nipple, be it breast or bottle. The sucking reflex is there, but the baby must adjust to the size of the nipple and suck smoothly and strongly to get the milk. Thus, not only does the infant absorb information, but he is constantly and efficiently involved in an effort to bring order and meaning to these experiences. We, as adults, can provide him with many new experiences, but it is the baby who must work through them and impose his own order and logic on what he is experiencing.

It is difficult to understand how complex little babies really are without spending a lot of time observing them very closely and being deeply involved with them. Just as babies learn about the world by being involved with it, we can only learn about babies by being deeply involved with them. It is through just this kind of intimate involvement and careful observation that the Swiss psychologist Jean Piaget developed his theories of intellectual development in children from birth through adolescence. His theories, always based on actual, empirical observation of children's behavior, have become subject to much research and consideration, and many of the activities we present in this   11 book have been guided by the principles set forth by Piaget.

We all know that babies learn to adjust to their environment, but the question is: "How do they make this adjustment?" Piaget postulates that all living species inherit two basic tendencies (along with physical structures and reflexes)—an ability to *adapt* and to *organize*. Organization refers to a tendency that is common to all forms of life to integrate their physical and psychological structures into higher-order systems or structures. That is, a very young infant has available a system for looking at objects and a system for grasping objects, but it takes a while for him to integrate (or put together) these two separate systems into a higher-order system that enables him to grasp an object and look at it at the same time in a deliberate fashion.

As with organization, all species are born with a tendency to adapt to their particular environment. Adaptation occurs through two complementary processes, assimilation and accommodation. Assimilation refers to the way in which a person deals with the environment in terms of structures that he already has available. Babies do not have very many structures at birth and so deal with the world in very uncomplicated and direct ways. It is a process by which the person tries to integrate new material into what he already knows. On the other hand, its partner, accommodation, involves the transformation and changing of these old structures to take account of the demands that the environment is making on him. Thus, upon being confronted with a new experience or stimulus, a baby tries to assimilate it into an existing idea (behavior pattern, or understanding). Sometimes this is not possible; he has never had an experience quite like this before. So the baby can do one of two things: he can either create a whole new category in his mind to take this new experience into consideration and store it away for next time, or he can somehow modify an already existing idea that he has and fit it into his mental image of the world that way. This is true not only of mental structures but of physical behavior as well.

Piaget refers to the first two years of life as the sensorimotor period, since the baby lives through experiences rather than thinks through them. Once language is established, this frees the child to think through activities and consequences of his actions. By doing things over and over again, with slight variations, a baby's actions become part of him and he can perform actions without thinking about them—they become habitual and automatic. It is just like someone learning to type; at first the process is painfully slow, with many errors, setbacks, and frustrations. After much practice, eyes read words off a page and fingers fly over the keys without a thought on the part of the typist. The actual typing has become reflexive—habitual. An adept typist can now adjust to typing in any language and any combination of letters and numbers—she has adapted. However, she would never have learned to type by just sitting and staring at the keyboard of the typewriter—she had to be actively, physically involved with what she was doing. And so too it is with the infant. His eyes move in search of his surroundings, his hands move in search of something to touch. At first action is random, but very quickly it becomes organized, complex, and purposeful.

Each baby will organize and adapt (assimilate and accommodate) his world in his own special way, depending on his temperament and the kinds of experiences he is exposed to. As S. Chess, A. Thomas, and H. G. Birch point out in *Your Child Is a Person*, there are eight main ways that babies can be different from one another. In *activity level*, some babies take life very slowly, others are go-getters from the start. In terms of *regularity* mothers are always comparing notes as to how easy or difficult it was for baby to accept routines. Some babies are so regular that you can almost set your clocks by them, others wake at odd hours and never seem to be ready for meals when you are. Some babies are very *adaptable* if their routine is changed, others get cranky and fuss. Some babies are predominantly happy, others seem quiet and serious, a difference in *mood*. Some babies always laugh and cry lustily and react to everything with great gusto, others are timid and respond in a more quiet way, a tentative smile perhaps or a gentle tap instead of a vigorous bang, indicating variability in the *intensity* with which they respond. Some babies seem to react to the slightest noise, the gentlest touch, whereas others sleep through anything and it is necessary to rub their backs quite hard should they have to be wakened (this is called *difference in sensory threshold*). Babies vary in how *distractible* they are. Some concentrate so hard on what they are doing that should their concentration be broken by an unintentional interruption, they are really startled, others look up at the slightest distraction, finding it hard to concentrate. And finally, closely related to distractibility is *persistence*, with some babies never giving up until they are quite satisfied with their efforts and others having to be coaxed and enticed to stick to an activity for even a short while.

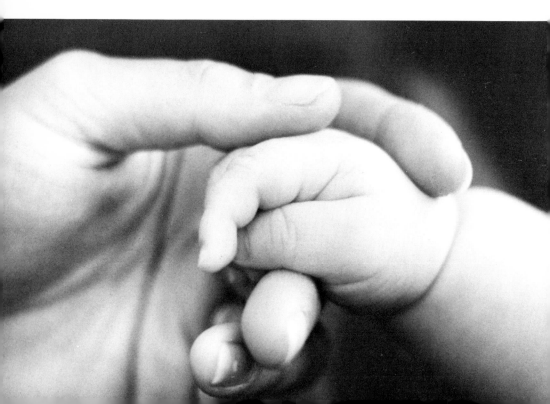

Not only do infants differ in these areas but so do parents, and it is the unique combination of individual parents interacting with their babies that helps to shape the baby's feelings about the world around him. Since each baby has his own style, the variations in "normal" or "average" infant development are enormous, each baby influencing his environment as much as it influences him. T. Berry Brazelton points this out in his book *Infants and Mothers: Differences in Development*, in which he compares how three different babies interact with their parents and their environment and how their parents respond to them. The babies are characterized as being average, quiet, and active and their individuality is clearly exhibited. A crying baby receives a different response from those around him, depending on their tolerance for crying, their experience with babies, and their interpretation of why the baby is crying.

As we have already mentioned, rather than being passive creatures who lie in their cribs and let things happen to them, infants are active from the time of birth and even prenatally (as any mother who has carried a moving, kicking fetus will attest). Infants are born with a set of reflexes that they very quickly modify and adjust, adapting them relative to their experience. The symbiotic interaction between parent and child does not happen accidentally; one learns from the other to accommodate so that they will both be comfortable. While a newborn's senses may be a bit dull at first, from the very moment of birth he is feeling and responding to his environment and learning from it.

In most cases, mothers intuitively respond to their babies by softly talking to them, cuddling them, and touching them. Early signs of recognition on the part of the baby that something is happening to him bring delighted smiles and coos from mother, which in turn excites and stimulates the baby. He watches her face closely as it changes expression, listens to her voice, and eventually will smile, change his own expression, and perhaps demonstrate his delight and excitement by moving his arms and legs. The baby soon learns that sounds from himself almost always elicit cooing and sound responses from his mother. When he realizes this he will continue to coo for longer periods in order to prolong this pleasant exchange. Not only is the baby learning to respond to his mother, but he is also learning that he has some control over what he does. Even though during the earliest weeks his sound production may be random and uncontrolled, it soon becomes purposeful. He gets feedback from others and also from himself as he listens to the sounds he makes and then tries to repeat them or move on to a new sound as his vocal cords and tongue dexterity mature. The infant needs to reach a certain level of maturity before he tries out new-found skills, but he also needs the opportunity and freedom to practice these skills.

In much the same way, mother responds to her baby during the caretaking routines of feeding, changing, and bathing. During these tasks a mother may cuddle and fondle her infant, gently stroke his face and frequently sing the many time-worn nursery songs that have been sung to infants for centuries. At times she may imitate faces and sounds the baby makes, spontaneously developing a give-and-take relationship with him. The baby's response to his mother's attention is usually one of satisfaction and comfort, knowing his is a safe, loving, and stimulating world.

We will continue to speak mainly to a loving person called "mother," but we cannot stress strongly enough the important role that a loving father plays in the healthy development of his baby. It takes two people to produce a baby, and it takes two people to help him grow up to be healthy and strong in body and spirit. A father's strong hands can be as gentle and supporting at feeding, bathing, and playtime as those of a mother. A father's voice and tender hug can quiet a fretful child as well as a mother's can, and the baby learns he has two caring people he can always depend on. Maria Montessori recounts an anecdote of a Japanese father who showed a deep comprehension of children. As she watched, he was standing with his legs apart so that his child could run in and out between them. On a busy street he did this with an air of dignity, indicating his realization that children need to be childlike. She goes on to note that we seem anxious only that the child become an adult in society and conform to our moods of the moment, but we are reluctant to consider the moods of our children. All too often, father is delegated the role of disciplinarian, when his role should really be as tender and warm as that of mother. Parents are as unique in their partnership as their baby is in his individuality, each contributing together and individually to the family's well-being.

In their desire to give their children the best possible start in life, in not only a physical sense but also in an emotional and intellectual sense, many parents have looked for specific information in order to give their child that good start. It is an unfortunate fact, as Fitzhugh Dodson says in his book *How to Parent*, that producing a child does not automatically provide wisdom and effectiveness in the art of being a parent. Our book is an attempt to help parents understand how their baby grows and develops, in what ways the child-parent bond can be strengthened, and in what ways a baby can be stimulated so that he gains knowledge about his world in a pleasant way, along with a loving relationship with his parents and caretakers. Loving and learning is a two-way process, and as the baby learns about his world, so too the parent learns about his baby and learns to delight in his growth and antics.

This book is not intended to be a panacea for problems a parent may encounter, and should not be used as an all-inclusive reference work on infant stimulation. It is intended to be a guide, a jumping-off point to help parents develop their own personal and intuitive ways of interacting with their baby. We do not present facts as ends in themselves, but as means to ends, whereby parents can encourage their babies and themselves to grow *together*. While intellectual development is important, we believe that any intellectual gains that occur because of increased stimulation should be by-products of a warm, loving interaction between parents and children, and not the focus of the interaction.

While the activities and chapters in the book are age-related, it should be remembered that each infant is an individual who will grow and develop at his own pace. Some infants are much more precocious in their physical development than others; some take longer to develop head control, start babbling, and so on, and thus the activities suggested at each age level may or may not be appropriate for any particular infant. Only you can judge that, and the two of you will have to work out which activities you enjoy doing together and when you will do them. Some babies are much more ready for new experiences and can adapt very quickly, while others take a while to get used to new places, faces, sounds, and activities. In the concluding chapter we will reiterate some of the overall aspects of parent-child interaction that we feel. are important, since underlying the uniqueness of each infant is a general pattern of development that is the same for all humans.

Unfortunately, the English language provides no word to encompass both the male and female genders, so we will bow to tradition, using the pronoun "he" to refer to both male and female babies. Similarly, while we refer mostly to "mother" throughout the text for ease of reference, it is most appropriate and important that fathers and other caring people should participate actively in a warm, loving way with their infants. Indeed, we would encourage this since it provides great benefit to both the child and to the participating adult.

Finally, in this world of ours with its ever-accelerating pace of life, its rapidly expanding horizons of knowledge, its mobility, and its new techniques for handling human relationships, one of the most precious commodities we have that we can share with our child is *time*. Time to let him grow and mature at his own pace; time to let him explore and learn on his own; time to be with him and wonder about things; time to be spontaneous and silly; time to cuddle; time to teach, experience, and grow with him. Time in the early years is very precious since the dramatic changes that take place from the moment the child is born to the time when he becomes an upright, steady, mobile. talking being pass like an eyeblink in a lifetime.

Beginning

Birth to Six Months

While it is true that the infant who is only a few weeks old must of necessity spend a lot of time sleeping, there are several periods during the day when he is awake for necessary caretaking, such as feeding, bathing, and diaper changing. That warm relationship between mother and child, and hopefully with father sometimes, begins during these periods; how they handle him, how they fondle him, how they talk to him, and how they respond to his needs affects him deeply. If he cries (this is his way of saying he needs them) and they come quickly, he learns that he can depend on them. If they take time to handle him frequently and gently, he learns they are caring persons. Ashley Montagu goes so far as to suggest that the need for touching is one of the "basics" for human survival. All these positive responses are essential and reinforcing to the infant, making him feel that someone cares about him, that he has self-value, and this is the beginning of a healthy attitude toward the world. He learns to love because he is being loved.

The growth that occurs in the early years is probably greater than it will ever be again. Just as his last few months in the womb were a time for the baby to pull together his resources (laying down the fatty layer) and rest up for the hard work of birth itself, so the early years are a time for the baby to learn about his world and gird himself for the independence that comes with increasing age. As the baby's muscles strengthen, he

21

finds out that he can raise his head and shoulders by pushing on his arms, and thus get a new perspective of his world. In no time at all, he can roll from tummy to back, and then back onto tummy, another big step for him. He can turn toward the sound of a tinkling bell and see where the sound is coming from and follow objects in and out of his line of vision. Each new skill sets the stage for yet more complex ones and so growth progresses. During this time he learns primarily through his senses. He loves to see movement, especially if there are many distinct parts moving at the same time. Toy manufacturers are turning out a wide variety of brightly colored gadgets with moving parts and interesting sounds, but the one that is by far the best, costs nothing, and is the most effective, is mother's or father's face held close to the baby. The shiny, colorful eyes seem to attract baby's attention first, but eyes, eyebrows, nose, mouth, and forehead are quite close together, so he can take them all in his view. All the parts move at various times and in various ways, and, most important, there is the magic of eye contact between parent and baby. The fact that he prefers complex to simple patterns suggests that colorful, busy wallpapers, posters, and mobiles are best for decorating some areas of his room. This kind of visual stimulation is important to his developing understanding of the world around him.

As he spends less time sleeping and more time trying to participate in his world, increasingly his growth is being stimulated by physical contacts with those people closest to him. Whether his soft skin is being stroked, his tiny limbs moved rhythmically or he is just being jostled playfully over his father's head, he is getting the visual, auditory, and kinesthetic experiences he needs and indeed must have. A very quiet baby, often mistakenly labeled a "good baby," is one who may require extra stimulation to encourage him to participate more actively in his environment. Much like adults, some babies are participators and others are spectators, and it is the spectator who needs gentle prodding once in a while to help him actively participate. On the other hand, although a very active baby needs and enjoys lots of activity, he also requires special quiet times to help him relax and slow down. A quiet rock with mother singing softly and stroking him lightly will effectively calm some overactive babies, while others respond very little to the calming influence of rocking and cuddling. They simply haven't the time to waste. There is too much to do. These babies are so aware of their world and so actively involved in it that only after long periods of go-go-go will fatigue finally overtake them and give them and their frazzled parents a break.

For most infants, the mother's own tension level seems to have a great influence on the tenseness of her baby. If she is able to respond to him in an easy manner with muscles and nervous system in a relaxed state, then her baby tends to pick up this tone and he responds to her in like manner. If she is tense, then he may pick up her tenseness. The four-month-old son of one of the authors was being breast-fed in the usual manner one evening, but her husband was at the same time rushing to prepare for an unexpected business trip. Of course, the feeding was interrupted on several occasions so that the author could help with the preparations. When father had gone, and the feeding could once again proceed without interruption, the baby threw up everything, telling his mother in a dramatic way just how tense and upset he felt. He had picked up her tension that evening, and the usually quiet, positive feeding experience suffered as a result.

Most parents have some idea of the magnitude of their child's needs, especially in the first years of life, and they try to provide for him to the best of their ability those things that he requires for healthy growth. Concerned parents nourish his urge to grow and to know and they provide him with rich and varied experiences. They let him know they care. Through their efforts he is learning to feel good about himself, to feel capable and

23

wanted. He is coming to know that the world is basically safe, warm, and responsive and his needs will be met.

Touching, stroking, and cuddling are important because it is through this kind of direct contact that the baby becomes connected to the world of human warmth and can form deep emotional bonds with his parents. As he grows he is learning to feel comfortable and secure even when he isn't in actual physical contact with mother. He prefers this contact, but he can feel good just seeing and hearing her and smelling her perfume. According to some researchers, even a baby as young as one month of age will respond to comfort with a smile or the beginnings of a smile. It is not exactly as evident as the social smile more typical of the three- or four-month-old but it is a definite indication of the baby's connectedness with the parents. When he is about four months of age, his parents eagerly anticipate that smile of his, which seems to say "Hi, I know you!"

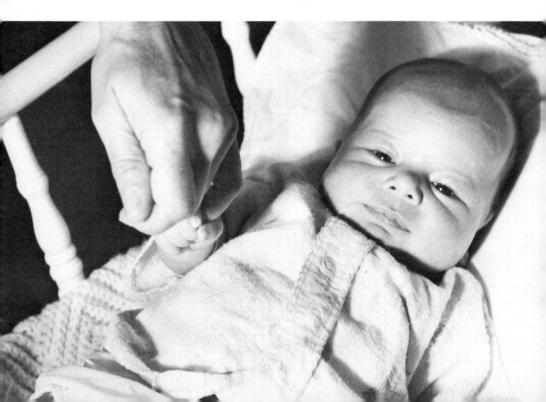

But he has been coming to know mother since the first days and weeks of his life. Babies are creatures of habit and they respond well to the regularity of routines that mother and baby have worked out to their mutual satisfaction. Mother's gentle voice, her ways of holding him, and even her footsteps soon become familiar and comforting to him and he begins to anticipate her presence. He'll quiet and arch his back as mother bends over to pick him up. This anticipatory recognition can be seen from the earliest months and it means that baby is learning how to predict what is going to happen to him next based on sound, visual, and postural cues. Hence it is important to be reliable and consistent with even the youngest baby. For instance, when he is hungry and mother holds him in the position for feeding, he tends to become quiet, as if he knows that food will come to him in that position. These are called postural (or kinesthetic) cues and baby makes extensive use of them as he grows. Babies are very responsive to their environment and this sensitivity is essential to their emotional, social, and intellectual growth.

By the third or fourth month, baby is beginning to make real social contact with people. Through his parents' loving physical handling, gentle words, and cuddling they encourage him to discover them as individuals. Mom smiles and baby smiles; she coos and he coos in return; then he crows first and she responds likewise; and he waves his arms and kicks his legs with the excitement of it all. He is reaching out to the people he loves because he wants them to respond to him. With his voice, his body, and his big smile he is beginning to get his parents actively involved. As he gets closer to six months of age, he becomes more and more spontanous in this kind of gleeful behavior. He just loves an audience!

In addition to cementing the bond of love between parent and baby, the first smile is an important indication that not only is the baby beginning to recognize people but is in fact able to remember them even when they are no longer within his sight. 25

He can follow his mother quite well with his eyes from about two or three months of age and he will keep looking at the doorway where dad was just standing a moment ago, as if expecting him to return. Babies are acute observers who can see things we cannot imagine that they see. As Maria Montessori in her book *The Child in the Family* points out, a child absorbs not only images of things but also relationships among things. She goes on to cite an example of an infant who had never been outside the house in which he was born, and had seen only two men, his father and his uncle, but always separately; then one day he saw the two of them together. The child looked at them amazed, gazing first at one and then the other for a long time. The two men stood quietly in front of the child in order to give him time to observe them. Had they left the room or said something to distract him, the child would never have made any sense out of an experience that profoundly impressed him. The two men finally left, but slowly, so that the baby would have time to see each of them and persuade himself that they were two distinct persons. This is an example of an infant's growing awareness of people around him, and also of the adults' sensitivity and awareness of the baby's needs.

Parents will be pleased to know that during the early months they are the ones who tend to hold the baby's interest the longest. He enjoys the colors, sounds, and movement of his toys but he really responds best to mom and dad. And when they have gone out of sight and the baby seems to be somewhat puzzled and is searching with his eyes, he is demonstrating a beginning awareness of a process called object permanence, which means that out of sight is not out of mind. This is an important milestone in the learning process, for it is essential in helping baby to make sense of his world and further facilitates intellectual development.

One of the ways in which babies learn is by repeating their actions. A baby loves to repeat new skills over and over again (Piaget calls this a circular reaction) until they become part of him —practice makes perfect. It almost seems as if there is a built-in drive for mastery of skills. What sometimes happens to thwart this drive later on in life is another matter, but it is indeed amazing that babies love to practice their new-found abilities. It takes a very patient parent, especially on busy days, to keep up with a baby's demands. By trying to be patient and flexible, however, in the kinds of activities they try and the expectations they have for their baby, parents will foster his growth as a unique individual by letting him develop in his own way at his own speed.

A number of activities mentioned in this chapter will give him lots of experience in developing such concepts as object permanence as well as experience with sounds, shapes and sizes, textures and colors. Don't forget that because babies are unique individuals and have had very different experiences one from another, there will be some who will be able to respond in different ways and more fully to some activities than to others. This is not only normal but expected and parents hopefully should be able to find a sufficient variety of activities to capture the interests of their baby.

Adding more fun to daily routines

The bath time can be a happy time for interaction between you and your baby, especially if he is not quite ready for his feeding. While his face is being washed, you talk about the various parts, nose, ears, eyes, cheeks, and chin or sing a little song: "This is the way we wash our face, wash our face, wash our face; This is the way we wash our face, so early in the morning." As the bathing continues you sing about each part you are washing, perhaps taking a quick minute to stroke his face softly or tickle his tiny pink toes. Tickling toes almost always recalls that old favorite, "This little piggy went to market."

While it's true that bathing takes longer with these important additions, it is well worth the time if you can manage it because it's such fun. Baby loves listening to your quiet voice even though he does not understand a word. He does hear the different sounds you make, and the tone of your voice conveys a lot of information. A quiet, softly spoken sentence says something quite different to the baby than the same sentence spoken in quick, harsh, loud tones. Your baby tells you he is enjoying this time he has with you because he smiles and watches your face intently for changes in expression. Your mouth moves in many ways, forming many different shapes. Your teeth form a contrast against your pink lips, your eyes sparkle with your own pleasure and amusement and even your eyebrows moving slightly add to the baby's fascination with your face. Is it any wonder when you pick him up that he tries to pat your face all over and poke his fingers in your mouth in an effort to explore and understand the characteristics of your face.

If your baby still does not seem hungry or sleepy after his bath, then this is a wonderful opportunity for a few gentle exercises that help to increase his muscle tone, give him different sensations and in a very elementary way help him to begin to be aware of the various parts of his body. As you do the exercises you might want to talk about what you are doing or sing little nursery songs, creating some yourself if that seems appropriate. This makes the time pleasurable and interesting for both of you.

A gentle massage represents a mild form of exercise, stimulating the surface muscles and aiding circulation. While baby powder is of little real value when applied to the genital area (since it sometimes cakes and then causes irritation) it does feel and smell lovely when applied to the main trunk of the baby. A little bit of powder on your hands can be used to facilitate a gentle body massage which starts with the baby lying on his back. Arms and hands, then chest, then the trunk, legs, and feet are massaged. With a quick turn onto his stomach and perhaps a bit more powder on your hands, the massage is repeated. In most cases the baby will enjoy the sensation of warm, soft hands gliding over his body, and, of course, the massage can be repeated several times. It is important for you to continue talking and explaining what is happening. "I'm touching your arms, now your chest, your stomach, and your legs. That feels nice, doesn't it? Let's do your back—over you go." At this age, although the baby is unaware of the various parts of his body, he is definitely interested in it and the body sensations he can experience.

Having a bottle and being held at the same time is very satisfactory for the baby. Even though it is primarily a time for nourishment, it can also be a time for those favorite nursery rhymes and songs (see Appendix for suggestions), and for special cuddling and warm conversation. It is also a time for some more of the important exploring that your baby does on his own. Your eyes and mouth move in so many different ways as you talk and smile. Indeed, your whole face may change many times during feeding, and this fascinates him. He will want to explore with his hands as well as his eyes, to touch and feel the various parts of your face, your skin, nose, hair, and perhaps a bright ribbon in your hair. To do this, his arms and hands must be free so he is not denied these pleasant discoveries.

A recent episode witnessed by one of the authors emphasizes the interest babies have in the human face. A new adoptive father with a magnificent black beard was playing with his son, holding him up so that he could see his father face to face. The baby immediately reached out, touched all parts of his father's face, particularly the bearded part, which he examined and patted extensively and with increasing excitement. Father, of course, was delighted and added to the fun by nuzzling his son under the chin. Arms and legs going in all directions expressed more than words ever could the joyous feelings this baby had about his new father. It seems obvious that babies want to be touched and need to be touched, but that they too want to reach out and touch, especially that special person who is so warm and close.

It is this kind of reaching out on the part of the infant to his parents that bonds them together in a unique pattern of responses and emotional give-and-take.

You can make the changing time equally as satisfying for your baby, facilitating in no small way this necessary task. Wiggly babies are not the easiest to change, but interested ones lie contentedly. It helps if the changing area is visually attractive. A cork board placed on the wall within easy viewing of the baby but far enough away for safe storing of the two diaper pins can provide an appropriate place for captivating pictures and, incidentally, for quick and easy replacements. Good pictures, of course, should never be discarded since they can be used over and over again in rotation. Your baby will still enjoy them the second time around. Whenever pictures are used a number of factors should be kept in mind. They should be fairly large, but not so large that he can't take them all in, with bright clear realistic features. Animals, birds, fish, food, cars, and trucks are excellent subjects, as are those pictures depicting a social role—doctor, nurse, fireman, mailman, policeman. These are usually great favorites once the baby gets a little older and they lend themselves well to a beginning language program. Aside from the fact that good pictures are fun to look at, it is a simple way of helping baby begin to understand that pictures represent real things. At this early age he hasn't yet learned this concept, nor will he for some time, but continual exposure to appropriate pictures accompanied by careful labeling will, over a period of time, help him to understand this important principle.

When it is time for a fresh diaper explain to your baby what you are going to do as you carry him to the changing table. You continue to talk to him softly, bringing to his attention the pictures, which are clearly visible to him. You must always remember to give your baby an opportunity to respond, even at this early age, with coos of his own, and acknowledge these as you go on to point out other features. "This is a dog, wuff, wuff. Here is his nose. Here is your nose and here is mommy's nose." Variations in your voice add interest. A loud voice, but not too loud, suggests a BIG dog, and a quiet voice suggests a little dog. The dog has a l-o-n-g tail and short ears. Other concepts can be mentioned in much the same way. "The dog has two eyes, and so do you," and while he does not understand a word of what is being said, or really what the pictures mean, the opportunity for listening and making the changing time pleasurable and interesting is there. Because someone is talking to him it also helps the baby to understand that language is an important part of his world.

Even more enjoyable for a baby are the little games mother can play with him at changing time. A soft light diaper is dropped on the baby's face with a quick, "Where's Johnny?" It is removed almost immediately so he won't be alarmed, especially the first time, and you answer yourself, "Here he is." If the baby looks interested, you might try a few more times, or you might cover your own head with the query, "Where's mommy? Here I am!" as the diaper is removed. "Sometimes "peek-a-boo" is in order as you hide your face behind a diaper. "Coo-coo, peek-a-boo, coo-coo, I see you." Even pat-a-cake is fun and, of course, it helps reinforce his perception of his hands. "Pat-a-cake, pat-a-cake, baker's man, bake me a cake as fast as you can. Roll it and knead it and mark it with B, and put it in the oven for baby and me!"

Simple mobiles suspended over the changing area so that they can be clearly seen by the baby and easily labeled by you are a source of interest. With babies already fascinated by the human face, a mobile made out of plain paper plates with different kinds of facial expressions is a delight as you move it gently, and what a boon for quick changing!

Bright colors invariably attract a baby's attention and it is very easy to make an appealing mobile with geometric-shaped pieces of colored cardboard or cellophane fastened together so that they whirl and turn in every imaginable way with each slight

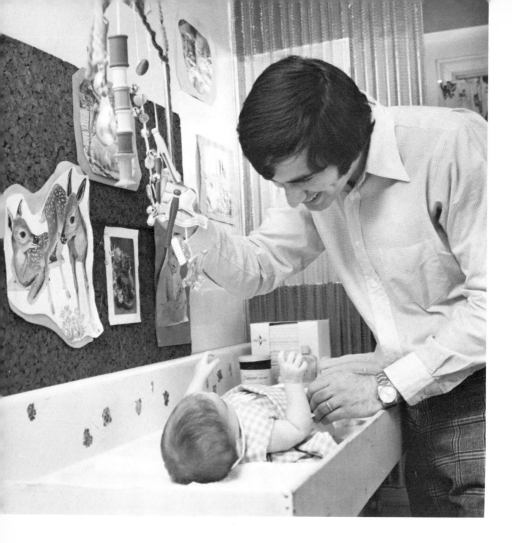

touch. The variations of movement keep him happy and busy, particularly if you point out and label colors and shapes. "This is a circle, this is a square, and they are both red. Oh, look, I'm making them move." Long pieces of colorful ribbon also make a very attractive and inexpensive mobile. Small pieces of cutlery, such as teaspoons, discarded keys, pieces of smooth wood, bells, clothes-pegs, rattles, large buttons, and empty spools of thread, when strung together and suspended on a coat hanger over the changing area, are great to look at, but, even more important, if attached to elastic they make very interesting sounds and movements when pulled and released. This kind of mobile holds a special fascination for the baby if it can be lowered so that his waving arms strike it and it makes a sound. He soon gets the idea and learns to use his arms in a purposeful way to achieve a goal —in this case, to make a sound. Even at this early age he can begin to feel "I can do it myself" and independence is a necessary tool to help us along in this complex world of ours. Like the pictures in the changing area, the mobiles can be rotated on a regular basis so that they continue to interest the baby.

Gross motor exercises

When one refers to gross motor exercises the reference is to those exercises where the large muscles of the body, principally those of the arms and legs, are being used. There are a number of simple little exercises that mothers have been doing with their babies since time immemorial. Not only have the babies relished these bodily sensations but also they have enjoyed this time with their mothers, who frequently smiled and talked, recited and sang as the exercises proceeded. In addition to these pleasant experiences, the baby is beginning to get the feeling, albeit in a very elementary way, that his body is made up of parts.

You have probably already noticed how well your baby grips your finger and with this new skill you can begin your calisthenics. Since a well-padded floor gives lots of room for both of you, it's probably the best place to be. Before you begin, make sure the room is warm enough so your baby can have as little clothing on as possible. This allows more freedom of movement for him.

To begin, let him grasp both of your index fingers and with your other fingers firmly holding on for additional safety, you gently pull his arms down to his side for just a few seconds, long enough for him to feel the mild tension. In the same gentle way move his arms over his head, then back down so that they are at right angles to his body. From this position cross each arm over his chest for a very brief period and then bring his hands together so that he can feel his own fingers. He may not have discovered them yet and this is a wonderful way to help him begin to notice them. You can reinforce this recognition in an appropriate way by tickling his hand in a slow circular movement as you recite:

> *Slowly, slowly, very slowly,*
> *Creeps the garden snail.*
> *Slowly, slowly, very slowly,*
> *Up the wooden rail.*

With a quicker tempo you can continue:

> *Quickly, quickly, very quickly,*
> *Runs the little mouse.*
> *Quickly, quickly, very quickly,*
> *Round about the house.*

This help in discovering his hands early is for his own pleasure. One only needs to observe a baby who has discovered his hands to understand what great fun it is for him. Not only does he mouth them extensively (this is a superb way to find out about fingers), he looks at them and feels them a lot too. These hands of his provide all sorts of interesting sensations. This early discovery can be further facilitated if colored knitted bands are placed on your baby's hands for very short periods during his awake times. This adds to the attraction as well as providing the additional sensory experiences of color and texture.

But legs and toes are just as interesting as arms and hands and there are a number of appropriate exercises that help your baby realize he has a truly fascinating body. Feeling his toes as you move them together gives a different feeling from that which he experiences when he feels his fingers. A soft little pat on the bottom of the foot as you recite "Shoe a little horse, shoe a little mare, but let a little colt go bare, bare, bare" adds much to the fun of these exercises with you.

If you have ever been a YWCA enthusiast then you have probably engaged in one of their physical-fitness programs. An important exercise to slim the hips is one where you lie flat on your back and cross over as far as it will go first one leg and then the other. The same exercise can be used for your baby and he will feel the same muscle sensations you did. And while you are doing it you might continue with your recitation: "Leg over leg, as the dog went to Dover. When he came to a wall, jump, he went over." Lifting your baby by his ankles from a supine position so that his buttocks are raised provides another sensation that can be accentuated if you then move his legs in a circular motion so that his hips are gently rotated.

While Yoga exercises are those which an individual does himself, there are a few you can do for your baby. The locust pose requires your baby to lie on his stomach with his arms outstretched. If he were able to continue on his own he would raise his legs up as high as possible and hold them in this position for a few minutes, but since he cannot you step in and do it for him by grasping his ankles and gently raising them for just a few seconds. This way your baby's tummy and chest muscles feel a little tension. As with all activities you talk to your baby about what you are doing and what you think he is experiencing. "I'm raising your legs up, up. Do you feel that? Now they go down slowly, slowly." Keep this exercise in mind for the time your baby is a little older and his arm muscles are stronger. You will find when you do it then he will be able to use his arms to raise the top half of his body as you raise the lower half.

The knee-chest exercise is one with your baby on his back. Since he can't bend his leg up over his chest you can do it for him, alternating first one leg up and then the other. While one

35

leg is bent up the other leg is extended down as far as is comfortable for him. In actual fact this Yoga exercise is designed to relieve gastric distress, and, who knows, your baby may find it quite helpful.

Even at this early age the baby is able to grasp, and when lying on his back and offered your fingers he reaches eagerly. Once he has a firm grip and you have one too, you pull him up so that his head is not quite raised off the floor, then he is gently lowered. He feels the tension in his arms, and while not quite ready to hold his head up, he will be able to in a very short time. When he is able to hold his head up you can continue the exercise by raising his body to a sitting position before lowering him gently down. For some more really interesting and worthwhile exercises see Bonnie Prudden's excellent book *How to Keep Your Baby Fit from Birth to Six*.

Holding him by his ankles and slowly raising his body until he is upside down gives him an unusual sensation. You may recall this was one of his first experiences after delivery as the doc-

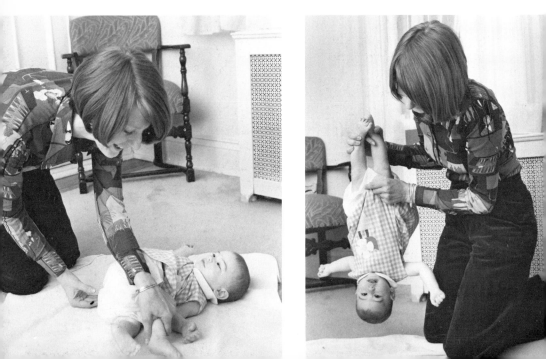

tor briefly held him that way in order to clear his throat and facilitate breathing. He probably wasn't aware of his environment then, but he certainly is now, especially when he views it upside down. That is a quite different experience.

If you happen to have a round bolster pillow which many sofas have at each end, then you have the makings for an enjoyable exercise for your baby. If you don't and are interested, see the Appendix for instructions on how to make one. It is probably a good idea to protect the bolster with an old pillowcase, but once that is done you are ready. Again, the less clothing the baby has on the more pleasant it is for him. He is placed against the bolster pillow so that his chest is resting on it and his arms are extended in front. Grasp the baby's body by his thighs and ankles and gently push him back and forth. For slightly older babies a larger pillow provides a little more excitement.

It may be that the baby has been making some preliminary attempts to roll over, and what better time for some help from you. As he lies on his back on the floor, a bright object is brought

into his line of vision. The object is then slowly moved across his line of vision and placed on the floor beside his body. While this is happening he is being slowly turned on his side and then right over onto his tummy. This way, he can continue to follow the object and eventually retrieve it. The activity can be repeated and this time the baby is turned on the opposite side. Changing the object adds new interest and new language to this experience. Sometimes he will enjoy being rolled over in a continuous roll. This is a new sensation for him. Ira Gordon and J. R. Lally in their book *Intellectual Stimulation for Infants and Toddlers* also have several interesting activities for very young babies.

Another good exercise can be initiated while baby is on his stomach. A bright-red block, a tiny brown bear, a favorite rattle, or some other object that would interest him is placed on the floor within easy reach if he stretches for it. He is encouraged to reach for the object, and here you can increase or attract his attention by banging it, hiding it momentarily under your hand, or, if it is an animal, making the appropriate sound: "Here is a brown bear, gr, gr, grr. . . . Here he comes." The first attempts should be arranged so that success is easily managed. Gradually the distance is lengthened and while still within his reach it will require considerable stretching to grasp the desired object and explore it. The object should not be positioned so that he has to move forward, as he may not be quite ready for this task, and probably won't be until some time in the second half of the first year. However, this is a good time to help him begin the process of locomotion so that he can eventually retrieve objects some distance away.

You can start the crawling process by placing your baby on his hands and knees on the floor. This is a strange sensation for him and he will probably experiment with this new feeling by rocking back and forth in one position. After a few movements he will either collapse and take a nose dive or appeal to you with a look that says, "What do I do now?" What happens next is even more interesting. You slowly move his legs forward, then his arms, making sure the distance is only an inch or so at a time in order to avoid another nose dive. Soon the baby sees he is moving forward, and what an experience this is! In no time at all he will be trying to move independently, at first with tummy on the ground, but then on all fours, crawling and ready for action. Once he has mastered the art of getting upon all fours and trying to move forward, you can encourage him by placing a favorite toy just out of reach. Can he reach it? You may have to move it within easy reach until crawling becomes better established.

Withholding a toy that is being used in an improper or destructive way is quite in order, but withholding a toy as punishment for failure to succeed in any of these activities is not appropriate, since the baby may not be quite ready for a particular kind of activity, or perhaps not interested because of hunger or fatigue. In this context it is understandable why he is not too excited about the whole situation. Another attempt at a later date may bring success, provided that he has indicated readiness for the task. The important aspect of this activity, as with all activities, is the continuing loving relationship between parent and child, enriched where possible with warm, purposeful language.

Visual and fine motor activities

By the time the baby is three months old his periods of wakefulness are longer and he is interested in spending more time with his parents learning about this exciting world of his. Several activities can be provided that encourage the baby to look, to reach, to grasp, to manipulate, and to examine. In comparison to gross motor activities, which encourage the use of the large muscles in the body, fine motor activities are concerned with the small muscles, primarily of the hands and eyes. This term also refers to eye-hand co-ordination, where the baby has to make precise visual judgments in order to reach for, manipulate, and examine objects closely. As with gross motor skills, fine motor skills become increasingly more refined and complex with age and the baby's maturation level. The opportunity to use his various muscles plays a large part in exactly when he is able to reach, grasp, and manipulate objects. This in turn gives him further control over his environment, stimulates his curiosity, and encourages his attempts to master simple problems. For example, the dangling bracelet must be reached and grasped just so before it can be brought to his mouth for further examination.

A fascinating visual activity for the baby is one in which you place him on his back on the floor and then stand or kneel above him and just slightly behind him. Let light pieces of paper, Kleenex, tissue paper, fluffy feathers of all colors, leaves, soft absorbent cotton balls, short lengths of bright ribbon, small pieces of light fabric (sheer lace, voile, silk, chiffon), and small paper airplanes sail gently near him. Each one makes its own special descent, some floating gently down, others whirling and turning, others moving straight down in a quick fall. Since some of these things are not suitable for mouthing, you need to be alert. But with a little care, it can make a safe and fascinating spectacle for him to watch as he listens to your explanations. "Here comes a fluffy yellow feather, watch it!" Gently stroking the baby's cheek with the feather gives him some idea of the properties of the object. The ribbon is smooth, the lace is rough, the cotton ball is soft.

Manipulative activities even at this early age can be initiated, provided the objects are interesting and large enough for safety yet small enough for easy handling. Tiny hands and fingers can only manage small objects, even though many objects much too large are frequently offered by well-meaning parents, and just as frequently discarded by the baby.

Through the work of researchers like Robert L. Fanz and Sonia Nevis, we have known for some time now that these clever babies of ours love to look at complex rather than simple designs from the earliest weeks of life. Thus, many things can be used to captivate the baby's interest and get him to pursue various activities. For example, colorful plastic one-inch cubes (and if they happen to have attractive stickers on them so much the better), realistic-looking animals, cars and trucks, rattles with interesting sounds and bright colors (rather than the usual bland pastel pinks and blues), shiny spoons, particularly measuring spoons, are readily available and inexpensive. Many little games can be played with the baby while he is lying on a blanket on the floor. This should happen quite often since it gives him an opportunity to view his world from a different vantage point. While he is on his back, one of the above-mentioned objects can be brought into his field of vision and then moved slowly away. He will try to continue seeing the object and will move his head to accomplish this. He is finding out that he can view an object for a longer period of time by moving his head to one side.

Positioning yourself behind your baby while he is still lying on his back on the floor, bring a bright object into his line of vision and then move it over his head (vertically) and out of sight. He will try to follow the object as long as he can and eventually will learn to arch his back in order to continue seeing it for just a little longer. If he has been trying to keep the object in sight, chances are that he would like to get his hands on it for a closer look, and he should be given it. At first his inspection will be visual, but soon a more extensive examination is desired and he will put the object into his mouth. What better way to find out how it feels? Is it hot or cold, sweet or sour, hard or soft? What a lot to discover!

With the baby well into the second quarter of his first year, he is ready for activities more in keeping with his expanding motor development. Babies like to see different things, and even the same things from different perspectives. For this reason it is important for him to have the opportunity of lying on the floor

41

on his stomach just as often as on his back. When he is on his stomach, his mother can sit behind him, just out of sight, and suspend an object in front of him so that it is in his line of vision. When his attention has been secured, the object is slowly moved over his head and out of sight. If the object is sufficiently intriguing, the baby will follow it as far as he can with his eyes, and in time (but probably not on the first few tries) will learn that he can continue to follow the object for a longer period of time if he pushes himself up on his hands and arms. During this time you can name the object and tell him what you are doing. "This is a yellow bracelet. I'm moving it up and over your head. Would you like to look at it?" If the baby does not find the activity particularly interesting, you can introduce a tinkling bell or some other sound producer and repeat the procedure. However, if he still shows no interest, it is important for you to stop and try again some other time. To persist under these conditions is to negate somewhat the very real pleasure your baby has in your company.

Another fun activity for baby can be provided by suspending several interesting objects (little plastic animals are excellent) on separate pieces of elastic, using a slipknot, with each elastic being a little wider and sturdier than the other. He will reach for the object as it is dangled in front of him, and when it is retrieved he will automatically pull. You retain the free end of the elastic and gently pull also, so that he feels the tension. As each object is offered it will provide a different degree of tension to experience. Along with each presentation you explain what is happening and the particulars of the object. "Here's a cow. She is a brown cow. Pull the cow, pull hard." You might want to play a little game with your baby, hiding the cow momentarily under your hand or behind your back. "Where is the cow? Here she is. Would you like to have her?" As the baby is examining the animal, you can mention other points of interest. "The cow says 'moo, moo.' She has a long tail. You don't have a tail, do you?" A simple little poem, especially one you have created yourself to suit the occasion, adds to the fun. One of the authors, no poet, concocted this one to demonstrate how easy it is to make up a verse to fit a particular activity or just to introduce rhythmic language:

> There was a white cow named Molly,
> Who really was quite jolly,
> She played all day
> In the grass and hay
> And mooed at her friend called Polly.

While it is important to talk to your baby, it is also important not to overdo it. He needs to have an opportunity to respond and vocalize in his own way. He also needs to have an opportunity to absorb the words and sounds you are making. One or two comments are enough at this stage; there will be plenty of opportunity for more detailed explanations when he is a bit older and indicates an interest in more information.

Now that the baby is a few months older he is ready for other fine motor tasks where he can continue to develop eye-hand co-ordination. When he's in his infant seat, rested and ready for action, is an excellent time for fine motor activities. You can begin by handing him a block of some bright primary color and then another of a different color so that he has one in each hand. Mention the colors and name the objects. Then pick up two similar blocks, one in each hand, demonstrating as you bang them together. "I'm making a sound. You can make a sound too." It may not be too clear to him just how one goes about making a sound and you may have to show him by moving his arms together so that the blocks hit against one another. It won't be long before he gets the idea about making his own sounds. To add variety to this activity, plastic blocks can be substituted for wooden ones, or a plastic one and a wooden one. Either combination will provide a unique sound. If you can stand the noise very small pot lids provide a glorious din. This is another good time for the pat-a-cake game, and as in most cases you will have to move his hands together so they clap. Again, it won't be long before the baby can respond to pat-a-cake without help and indeed will clap his hands when he sees you, indicating that he wants to play the game with you.

Another engaging activity for mother and baby can be provided with a mirror. This should not be attempted unless your baby is rested and comfortable. Enjoyment of this mirror activity is really nice if you can sit on the floor with him in your lap.

A mirror at least 14″ x 12″ is placed in front of the baby.

While he sees his face reflected in the mirror, he has no idea that it is his own face, even though he sees and feels you touching his nose, ears, and mouth. As with all other interactions language plays an important part, and each feature of the face or body is labeled as it is touched. "This is your nose, here are your two ears, and this is your mouth." If you can move your own face so that it also is reflected in the mirror, it is doubly fascinating for him because he knows it is your face. Imagine his surprise when he feels only a cool, smooth surface instead of the usual soft, warm face as he reaches out to pat the reflection in the mirror.

While sitting in your lap can be very pleasant, it can also be stimulating if another activity is introduced. This time a broad, light-weight, hard-covered book is placed on top of his lap and a small toy is placed on top of the book. At first he will try to pick it up using all fingers, but eventually, after several months, he will be able to use only his thumb and pointer finger, a much more precise and complex mode. This task takes perseverance and skill and the baby will be more likely to be motivated to persist if different and interesting objects are offered. Also, if you play little tricks, such as hiding the object briefly under a piece of Kleenex or your hand, and if, in the case of animals, you give them names and personalities—"I am a soft bunny and I hop"—the baby's attention will last longer.

Listening activities

Babies listen to every sound and even though their listening ability is not sophisticated at this age, they are certainly very conscious of sound and because of this awareness they struggle to learn what the sounds mean or represent. Parents are often amazed at how quickly their baby begins to recognize his mother's voice and even her footsteps. He cries because he is hungry. She calls to him as she moves toward him. He hears her voice and her footsteps and knows she is coming to him and he becomes quieter. He has come to recognize certain sounds as being inherently his mother's—these sounds have become meaningful to him.

There are lots of noises that fascinate a baby. The delight he shows when mother sings nursery songs, some of her own special music, or some of her favorite tunes, indicates very clearly his ability to enjoy pleasant sounds. The quick turning of the head and the alertness a baby shows when a new sound is made indicate his awareness and keen interest in sounds. Again baby must not be bombarded by a continual round of clamor but, if exposed to a few gentle sounds, familiar and unfamiliar, he will find the experience quite enjoyable and stimulating.

Small mustard and spice tins with those hard-to-open oval lids are easily handled by baby and are very suitable for this kind of activity. You start with two tins, put rice in one and some dried beans in the other. After shaking each tin in turn, let your baby handle and examine them as much as he wishes. As he gets older or seems interested a third tin can be added with buttons or stones to give a more resounding rattle. The variety is endless and you can use your imagination to provide contrasting and interesting noises by placing various small objects in the tins.

Bells have a wonderful appeal for the baby and provide a delightful way to encourage him to listen and to use his arms purposefully. This is accomplished by suspending a tinkly bell or a series of tinkly bells over him as he lies on his back. As the bell is lowered, ring it gently to gain his attention and then continue to lower it until his waving arms hit the bell and he makes it ring. On the second attempt, try capturing his attention without ringing the bell, then when he strikes it and hears the sound, he is surprised and delighted at the results and wants to try again.

If other kinds of bells, each having their own unique sound, are available they can be presented in the same way. Various objects strung together so that they produce a novel sound when struck are readily found in the average home. Pieces of wood and ordinary wooden clothespins are perfect for this, and keys, small spoons, bottle caps, empty spools are a few items that lend themselves to this kind of activity. If you normally use frozen orange juice with the tear-off plastic strip, you will find the metal lid at the top is safe to use this way. If any of these objects can be painted in bright primary colors (with nontoxic paint) so much the better. In some cases interesting stickers can be glued to the metal objects to add a new dimension to the activity as well as to add the potential for further enriching language.

It seems a little far-fetched to suggest that by learning to make a sound the baby is beginning to control his environment, but in a very elementary way this is true. When he is consciously hitting an object to produce a certain response, he is, in fact, demonstrating his ability to influence a small part of his world.

Another interesting listening activity can be provided with a variation of the "box of surprises" game, using a series of small bells each with a different sound. There are many kinds of bells on the market today that are inexpensive, large enough for safe mouthing, and which have slightly different but quite delightful sounds. The baby can be in his infant seat or on the floor. Either way is satisfactory. You reach into your surprise box and bring out a tinkly bell and gently ring it. As long as the baby is listening (and this is usually only for a short period) you ring the bell, but remember to give it to him for examination and manipulation *before* he has lost interest. After he has examined it to his satisfaction, he will discard it and you can repeat the procedure with a different-sounding bell. When all bells have been experimented with, you can ring two together for a new sound. A series of bells sewn on a piece of cloth adds a new dimension to this activity and if tied around one of his wrists for a very short period, allows him to have a whale of a time making his own music.

It should be remembered, however, that the sounds need to

47

be gentle and produced only for as long as there is interest. The attention span of the baby may be short or relatively lengthy. It all depends on him. The key is the intuitive awareness on your part that your child has had enough and you must stop. Perhaps he needs a quiet time just being close to you.

Tactile activities

We all love to touch things—paintings, *objets d'art,* and materials of all kinds. It is an irresistible impulse to know and to understand what it feels like, and so determine how it was made and of what. The baby is just as eager to touch in order to

try to understand the people and objects in his environment. He can enjoy a tactile experience when he is sitting in his infant seat or on his mother's lap. If he is in his seat, you should be sure that he has not been in it for too long. It can be tiring to be left in the same position for a long time, and if that is the case, there won't be any interest or fun. But if he is rested and ready that old box of surprises can be introduced. It can contain any object that can be easily and safely handled, including all the ones previously mentioned. Discarded spools of thread with some of the bright thread still on them, small boxes, small plastic squeeze bottles, small hair rollers (the smooth kind), small yogurt containers with lids, small aluminum tart tins are only a few of the things found in the average home that are of considerable interest to him.

The box is opened, and as each object is handed to the baby a label is given, as well as a brief description. "This is a spool of thread. The thread is blue. Would you like to look at it?" When it is presented, he will most likely grasp it firmly and look it over. He may or may not put it in his mouth, but since mouthing is an excellent way to learn about an object he will probably use this method along with his other methods of examination—feeling and seeing. When the baby is finished with his object he may discard it, or hang onto it but look around, perhaps not realizing that the object is still in his hand. Another object can be offered along with an appropriate label and description. If your baby is still attentive after all the "surprises" have been shown and examined, they can be presented again. Later, when he is older, explanations and activities with the objects can become more complex. "Hey, look, this is a spool of thread and you can roll it on the ground. Oh, that's right, the hair roller rolls in the same way and so does this little round juice can."

Another tactile activity, especially when the baby is sitting in your lap, is an interesting variation of the "box-of-surprises" game. This time the box can contain different pieces of fabric, 49 in particular those with unusual textures and colors. Fur, velvet, satin, lace, burlap, corduroy, cheesecloth, leather, felt, cotton batting, nubbly knits, and raised weaves are a few that could be used. As each piece is offered it is labeled and then gently stroked on the baby's cheek or hand. "This is a piece of brown fur. It's soft, isn't it? This piece of red burlap is quite rough. Would you like to look at it?" After examining it visually and tactually, he will probably put it in his mouth. Here he will find out all sorts of different things, especially in terms of taste, texture, and dimensionality. The pieces of cloth should not be so small that they disappear right into his mouth and are not easily retrievable. His mouth tells him a great deal and it is no wonder that he uses it so often for functions other than eating. For the mother handy with a needle, a small stuffed animal can be easily fashioned. Each part of the animal is made of different textured material so that a new sensation is provided whatever way it is handled.

Reading

Children who see parents reading frequently and who are exposed to books at an early age develop an appreciation of reading that is lifelong. The idea of reading to an infant only a few months old is, to most parents, a novel idea—one that never occurred to them perhaps. But the baby only a few months old does like to look at a book provided it is the right kind for him. A suitable book is not a story book; it is one with little or no printing, and bright realistic-looking pictures clearly defined and fairly uncluttered. Too much material on a page prevents him from taking in all the little details that are present. Animal books, especially about dogs and cats, birds and fish, are excellent since there is a fairly good chance that he will see at least one of these animals quite early in life. This kind of representation is the beginning of the reading process. At first the pictures are simply something nice to look at; eventually, however, the child begins to understand that he is looking at a picture that portrays a tangible object in his world. As time progresses over several years, this kind of reading helps to prepare him in a natural way for more abstract marks. Becuse he has learned that pictures represent real things, somewhere between four and five he is ready to grasp the idea that symbols—letters—represent real sounds.

A handy way to make inexpensive books with different pictures can be managed with a photo album that has plastic envelope-type pages. One week you might make your book all farm animals or zoo animals, or fruits or vegetables. But whatever subject you choose, the pictures can be easily changed and rotated on a regular basis. One inventive parent tells us she has three on the go and changes them about every three or four weeks in one fell swoop. This way she is able to expose her child to a wide variety of books at very little cost. Clever mother.

With the baby comfortably seated in your lap, the book is brought into his view, a page is presented and the labeling begins. For example, if it is a picture of a bird, the word "bird" is used and, wherever possible, sounds that are specific to the animal are made. "This is a bird, whistle, whistle; this is a BIG dog, bow wow; this is a yellow flower and here is a pretty blue flower." As long as he continues to listen and look, the objects in each picture are labeled, perhaps more than once, with special features pointed out.

Sounds seem to hold a baby's attention. For example, in the second half of his first year, the son of one of the authors used the sound "a-ooo" in response to "What does Gipsy say?"—Gipsy being the family beagle, who unlike other dogs does not bark but howls. Way before he learned the dog's name, he would say "a-ooo" when he saw the dog or was asked the above question. "Choo choo" came to represent train before the word "train" was used as a label. While he understood what train meant, his

51

label for it was the sound "choo choo" and he used it for quite a while before going on to use the proper name.

It may be that the baby will want to touch the page of the book while you are talking about it, scratching at the objects on the page, trying to find out whether or not they come off, and he should certainly be obliged. When he looks away or begins to squirm, that is the cue to turn the page for some more interesting pictures. In some cases he will enjoy several minutes of "reading," in other cases he may be interested for only a few short moments. But however long the "reading" goes on should depend entirely on his interest and enjoyment. He can make it clear whether or not he wants to continue.

While the baby does not understand what he is being shown, he does love sitting close to his parents, particularly if there is a little cuddling and fondling during the "reading." This warm contact helps to instill in the baby the feeling that "reading" a book is informative and pleasurable.

A variation of reading is the tour of the "art collection" hanging on the various walls of the house. Again the baby should be held so that he can see the picture on the wall, and the various parts pointed out and labeled for him. If it happens to be an abstract painting, then colors, moods, and shapes may be appropriately labeled. It's great fun for a baby to have these private tours, especially if dad is the one doing the carrying and labeling.

Summing up

Babies take a lot of mother's time; some require more than others, but for most babies the time with mother is so crucial to their well-being they will engage in many types of behavior, appealing and not so appealing, to bring her to him. If baby learns that he can count on mother's spending regular predictable times with him, he will be relatively (relatively because he would really prefer her to be with him all the time) satisfied and therefore able to share her time with her other activities and responsibilities. If, on the other hand, he is not sure when mother will have time for him because she has been somewhat erratic and irregular, he will do what he can to entice her to him. Unfortunately this usually means crying.

A relaxed, flexible routine with regular playtimes, which doesn't interfere with those spur-of-the-moment times when mother just drops everything to play with her baby, will help his equilibrium and strengthen his feelings of well-being and self-esteem. Having had close and regular contact with mom also seems to help the baby over more drastic changes, when mom cannot spend time with him. She has been predictable in the past, so a change in routine for a short while will not be too disruptive.

The activities mentioned in this chapter are suggested to give mother additional ideas (she has lots of her own) so that the time spent with baby will include not only that important cuddling and loving, but also some additional experiences that will stimulate and interest him. It should be kept in mind, however, that although baby is a remarkably sturdy and resilient human being, he cannot withstand constant activity and noise for long periods of time and parents should offer only a few of the games and exercises at any one time. Baby needs his quiet times, as well as time to be on his own, approaching the world just the way he wants to, as much as parents do.

A good many of the activities, exercises, books, pictures, toys, and sound makers will interest the baby for many months, but even more so if they are removed and reintroduced later. Your baby will be a little older, a little more competent, and he will utilize these objects in different ways. There may be less mouthing and more manipulation, for example.

The baby has been growing and developing at a rapid rate and now that he is entering the third quarter of his first year, the changes will be even more dramatic as he moves eagerly on to further his expanding horizons.

3 Expanding

Horizons

Six to Twelve Months

In this chapter we look at the baby as he grows from six to twelve months. In all books that describe child growth, there is a danger of generalizing about what a child is supposed to be like at the various ages. As we will remind parents again and again, each child is unique and so is his rate of development. Each child's environment is also unique, for no two children are exposed to exactly the same things—toys, people, places, foods—in exactly the same way. However, it seems safe to say that the order of events (sitting, standing, crawling, walking, et cetera) are pretty standard. So, take a good look at your baby and decide what stage he is at and work with him at his own level. The specified ages for various developmental levels in child-care books are to be taken as approximations and rough guidelines. By working and playing with your baby at his own level and at his own pace (some babies never seem to stay in one place for more than a moment, others are quite content to sit in a lap or on the floor for fairly long stretches of time), he will be best able to grow in all spheres of development.

This chapter is entitled "Expanding Horizons" primarily because the baby becomes mobile during the six-to-twelve-month period. Mobility is the keynote, for through his new-found ability to go *to* his world, rather than having the world brought to him, he can find out more about it on his own terms and really learn about things when he wants to. He can crawl about and see things from different angles (especially larger objects). He can now follow his mother down the hall and from room to room instead of having to wait for her to come to him. He can poke his nose into everything that catches his eye. And so, physically as well as emotionally and intellectually, his horizons are expanding. In fact, one day as he firmly grasps the edge of an armchair and pulls himself to a standing position (a feat he has become adept at) he will put one leg forward and let go one arm, the other leg makes a step and the other arm hovers uncertainly at his side. Lo and behold, he is standing alone and has taken his first big step all by himself. His look is one of triumph as he gazes around. His concentration broken, plop, he's on his bottom. Again, he'll maneuver himself into position and repeat his newly learned skill.

By nine months some babies are walking with help and by eleven or twelve months may be getting about, rather unsteadily at first, on their own two feet. L. W. Sander in *Determinants of Infant Behaviour* uses the word "initiative" to describe this period and in so many ways that is exactly what the baby is doing, taking the initiative. He is becoming independent through his newly found ability to get around under his own steam. He is demanding that mother take note of him. He wants her to do something and he won't take no for an answer. He is growing in self-assertion and is beginning to get games going by himself with mother or father as the objects of his attention. Peek-a-boo and I'll-give-you-my-toy-but-I-want-it-back-right-away are two of his favorite "self-starting" games. He wants his parents to play his game, his way. He is beginning to feed himself and often wants to help out in such routines as bathing and changing. Although he can't speak yet, his grunts and the look in his eyes seem to say, "Look, mom, I'd prefer to do this myself."

Now that the baby is more independent, mother may expect him to play on his own more than he really wants to or is able to. Babies of this age are still very people-oriented and while they take the initiative, they do want their mothers to participate in their activities. However, mother perhaps is not responding to his needs and demands as spontaneously as in the past. He senses this and complains loud and long. That is why when mother is most busily engaged with other things her baby seems determined not to play quietly by himself but demands her undivided attention. Setting aside a special time to be with him every day (even five or ten minutes) may help the baby to accept sharing her time with the necessary household tasks. Of course, she can continue to smile and talk to him as she goes about her own activities.

In the first few months the baby has flourished in the warm security of a safe, loving environment. His cries have been responded to and he has come to know that he is loved. As they respond to baby's many demands, occasionally parents ask, "Well, aren't we just spoiling him?" And we reply, "No, not at all." Under two years of age or so, parents are laying the groundwork for healthy emotional growth by demonstrating to their baby countless times that his needs are important and he can count on his parents to satisfy them. Thus he learns to feel confident and secure. When we speak of a "spoiled" child we think of a whining, demanding four- or five-year-old, one whose behavior is like a baby's still because he has not been able to let go of the total dependency of babyhood. He is scared to grow up. He is saying, "I've had to demand loud and long for my needs to be met and I still don't feel I can count on my world to provide for me. Now I'm growing up physically and mentally but I still feel like a baby." A spoiled child of three, four, or five is a frightened child. It is important for an infant as he grows into toddlerhood to know definitely that he can count on his world to come through for him, to look after him. After these security feelings are solidly built in, he should be able to weather most difficulties.

However, we do not mean to suggest that parents should

provide a completely controlled environment where nothing ever goes wrong, or one where they are kept constantly on the run meeting the demands of their baby. We are saying that during these first few years, a baby needs lots of immediate attention because his needs are often quite urgent. Babies don't cry to aggravate parents but because they have legitimate needs. In the first few months especially it is important to find out why a baby is crying—what is his need? Most mothers quickly become attuned to all the special kinds of cries their baby makes, and they can quickly reassure him. There will be many times when a mother can't get to her crying baby immediately. He cries with hunger pangs, for example, and she is not quite ready with his bottle. She calls out to him, he hears her voice and her footsteps and may even stop crying briefly in anticipation of her arrival at his side. He is learning to anticipate that his needs will be met, and he is doing so by having a mother who will come through for him when he needs her. But, by having to wait a few moments, he is learning also to handle little bits of insecurity and anxiety. The doses are small. He may not have to wait more than a minute, and he is getting used to apprehension gradually. In order for the child to be secure, he must be able to handle some insecurity. And in this early period, even under one year, he is beginning to learn this lesson.

So parents can't spoil their child by meeting his demands quickly and consistently. They can, however, teach him that he can trust his world, and even though he hates to wait, he is learning to tolerate little bits of frustration, and is finding out that a short wait really isn't that bad after all.

There is another area that some parents find confusing and often need help to see it as a positive step forward. Even then, some still view it as a mixed blessing. That is the baby's sudden shyness, or "stranger anxiety" as it is called. He no longer smiles at everyone, and may cling to mother, hide his head on her shoulder, or beat a hasty retreat to her if he is at some distance from her. This is a good sign because it means that the baby is distinguishing between the people around him and prefers the ones he knows from the ones he doesn't. However, it is often a disappointment for unhappy grandparents and even fathers, who now receive only howls for their attentions to the baby. The trick, of course, is to let the baby come to you. Give him time to take the initiative and observe for a while. A smile and hello may bring only frowns at the beginning, but given a chance most babies will approach on their own terms. Then, when they have initiated the activity and interaction, the fun and games can begin. As always, one must take his cue from the baby. Socially, emotionally, and physically he is reaching out to get actively involved in the flow of life around him.

Intellectually he is taking the initiative too. He no longer plays randomly with his toys as they happen to come to hand but more often he makes a positive choice. Now he may have a particular purpose in mind. We say that his play is becoming more goal-oriented. He can focus on activities for longer periods of time and he loves to practice over and over again his skills and games. In this way he learns through constant repetition—variations on a theme.

As in all the early periods of development, his abilities grow and mature rapidly and in complex ways. One may visualize the aspects of his development as race horses running on a track. For a time one horse takes the lead, but then he loses it to another horse as it spurts ahead; a third comes neck and neck with the second and the first lags behind for a while. This is the way it is with the baby's development. For example, he may be babbling away at a great rate. Sound games are a particular favorite and he'll spend many happy moments smiling, crowing, and squealing with delight as he plays these games with mother or practices his babbling on his own. At this time he is getting lots of practice in sound production. The "language" horse is in the lead. Then he discovers the art of getting about, crawling and later

59

walking. All of a sudden, overnight it seems to many parents, the baby couldn't care less about sound making and sound games. No matter how hard they try, they can't seem to get a peep out of him. Now all his thoughts and energies are directed toward crawling or walking, to exploring on his own. The mobility horse has taken the lead and the language horse lags behind for a while.

So it goes. There are so many new skills to be learned in such a short time that no baby can possibly give equal time and attention to all of them at once. Parents should be sensitive to this and gauge the special interests of their baby and choose activities that he will really enjoy. In the activities that follow, parents will find some which their baby just isn't interested in trying or isn't able to enjoy just yet. This is okay; one of these days he will probably want to do them.

We have stressed the importance of learning through doing, and in the preceding chapter, when the baby was under six months, we encouraged his parents to bring all kinds of experiences to the baby to arouse his interest and to stimulate his learning. Whether or not adults do "special" learning games with him, the baby will learn provided he has love and attention. In the first few months, through trial and error, he learns how to do some things all by himself. That is, when he is making lots of random movements, some of them are going to produce a pleasant sensation in his body. So, of course, he will try to duplicate this action to regain the good feeling. For instance, while waving his hand in front of his mouth, his thumb happens to go into it and he begins to suck. His pleasure is obvious. Having done this once he will go through the same behavior again. As he repeats this many times, he learns the exact movements needed to get the thumb in his mouth with just one swift movement. We see the baby learning a great deal through this kind of trial-and-error activity.

Now in the second half of his first year he is more mobile and skilled at reaching out to touch and examine objects in his world. He discovers by chance that he can do things to those objects around him that will cause him pleasure. For example, waving his arm against a suspended tinkling toy produces a pleasant sound. He quickly learns the connection between his own action and the sounds which result and he loves to practice batting at the toy to hear the tinkling sounds. He is learning about cause and effect: "I do this and that happens." It is the basic principle upon which a great deal of learning occurs throughout his life.

He has learned to repeat movements that produce a pleasant or interesting result for him and this all happens by chance. But toward the end of the first year he begins to have a specific idea or goal in mind as he manipulates an object in his environment. More and more of his activities are becoming intentional. His behaviors are a primitive means for obtaining an end. That is, he is figuring out ways to solve problems. Piaget emphasizes how important it is for him to manipulate everything in his world —everything, that is, which is safe for him. By touching, examining, mouthing, and seeing things from all different angles he learns about weight, texture, form, flexibility, and so on. And so, as he begins more and more exploring behaviors on purpose, he takes additional big steps in the learning process.

Another major milestone for him is his growing awareness that objects have an existence all their own, and not just when he happens to be looking at them, hearing them, or feeling them. If mother rolls a brightly colored ball slowly in front of him, he follows it with his eyes and also reaches out for it in anticipation of where it is going to be rolling. If it happens to go underneath a radiator he knows it is there and will probably chase and retrieve it. We call this special knowledge object permanence, or, in Piaget's term, object concept. Many of the activities in this chapter help him with the growth of this knowledge—that objects do have an existence independent of his perceiving them.

It extends far beyond finding objects in play activities. Faces are recognized and people remembered. The development of this concept means that socially and emotionally the baby is taking a giant step forward in making sense of the big complex world around him.

The period six to twelve months is a busy one for babies and changes will be many and quite often dramatic. It is essential for parents to gauge the pace of the play activities presented in this chapter to the interests and competence level of their infant. Don't be discouraged if he responds only to a limited number of suggested activities in any one period. Allow him to take the lead. Parents can often learn as much or more about their baby if they avoid too much scheduling of specific activities and sessions and simply sit back and just enjoy watching how the baby plays and learns. There are going to be numerous times, in fact, when he will actually resent his parents' intrusions into his self-initiated activities. Some babies require lots more guidance and direction than others, so parents must learn to be sensitive to the particular needs of their child.

As a general rule, remember that a child derives most benefit from the love and attention of his parents when he has not had to ask for it—that is, when it is spontaneous and natural. Let him know that he can count on his parents to be with him and that they are sensitive to his changing moods and needs. He will soon learn that he does not have to demand attention through whining and crying in order to receive it, because mother and father, while not always actively playing with him, are still showing their interest in him by a smile from across the room, a gentle pat in passing, or a few words of encouragement when he is busy playing. The special playtimes he has with his parents only add to his pleasure and interest in all that goes on around him.

As already mentioned, one of the most significant developments occurring at this age is the increasing mobility of the baby, a skill which really sets the stage for his expanding and ever delightful independence. To be able to do something on his own, whenever he wants to, without always having to call on another for help is a tremendously satisfying experience. Encouraging the baby to be mobile is important not only for his motor development but for his intellectual development as well. Now he can find out where that noise is coming from, what is making it, what is behind that chair (if it is an electrical outlet it should be safely covered), and, most important of all, he can go to his mother when he hears her moving around in another room and wants to be near her.

When he is in a room with his mother, perhaps the bedroom, where she is tidying up, he may crawl around the floor relocating objects that he has previously discovered. Just watching your baby examining the shoes in the closet is an experience in itself. With his tiny hands he tries to manipulate the shoe. Pushing, pulling, and mouthing are all part of the exploration so that he can get a complete picture. The look on his face clearly tells his reaction to that examination. Nevertheless, he does find out that there seems to be a variety of colors, textures, and sizes of shoes and, of course, that some shoes are too heavy for him to move around, especially dad's. Because his curiosity is so all-consuming, he has to get right into everything just to make sure that he hasn't missed anything, but once in a while he runs into difficulties in small closets. Getting in is not much of a problem, as he just plows in, but getting out is quite different. He hasn't refined the backing-out technique and the closet is too small for turning around in. He sends out a cry for help. But, like most mothers, you have been watching him out of the corner of your eye and you move in quickly to extricate him by backing him out gently. His fears are immediately forgotten; he wasn't really upset. He knew he could count on you, he has always been able to do so in the past and your rescuing him from his predicament confirmed your dependability. With his anxiety assuaged, he forgets his recent difficulties, looks for further adventures, and travels right out of the room. His foray is usually brief and he returns to your side, or else you go looking for your explorer if he does not return quickly after each sally.

As his feelings of security and confidence increase he becomes more venturesome and will begin to leave you more frequently and for greater lengths of time. Up to this point the supervision of your baby has been relatively easy but now the situation changes and you are about to enter one of the most demanding but satisfying periods of your life. You recognize that he needs to be independent, to satisfy his curiosity, and to experiment. You will be able to accept the challenge of providing adequate supervision with a minimum of restrictions.

During this time and until the child has reached the age of about two years, many parents have solved the problem by using a playpen. With several toys and books the baby is placed in the playpen, where he is expected to be content. If this has been the pattern since birth he may accept it, but if not, he may object vigorously. Many babies are never really content to be in the playpen for very long once they have experienced the freedom

of moving about at will. This is the dilemma of a busy mother, how to encourage independence with supervision. Many mothers have learned that their babies will accept the playpen if they know it won't be for long and if it is made interesting for them. A shiny metal mirror suspended on the playpen is a fascinating toy, and bright realistic pictures glued to both sides of a piece of cardboard and fastened in the same way are also of interest to the baby. Stringing elastic across one corner and attaching objects to it some of which make sounds provides additional interest for the confined baby. New pictures and new toys can be rotated after a few days so that the playpen can be a happy and interesting place. Of course, you should not forget to include a few unattached toys as well.

The successful use of the playpen will depend to a large extent on your not using it for very long periods of time and how quickly you read the cues from your baby and remove him before he becomes unhappy. If he is left there until he cries, he will begin to associate the playpen with unhappy experiences and each time he sees he is going to be placed there he will start to cry. To his way of thinking it is not a nice place to be. But it does have some practical value aside from the safety factor. A well-padded playpen provides a suitable place for the baby to practice pulling himself to standing position, since falls are cushioned and most playpens provide safe and sturdy handholds for the beginning "stander."

Simple gross motor activities

Until a baby becomes mobile he has some preliminary stages to master first. With some babies, crawling comes before creeping, others start right off on all fours,. some navigate by sitting up and scooting around on their buttocks, using their feet as pushers; others skip these preliminaries and start right off walking. Whatever way the baby begins to move does not seem to matter. What matters is the fact that he can now begin to be mobile and wonderfully independent. When the baby first begins to crawl or creep he is a bit unsure of himself. He needs support and encouragement and here is a place where you can be very helpful by playing a number of little games with him on the floor when he is comfortable and rested and seems ready for play.

An easy game is an extension of an earlier one where the baby retrieved a toy by extending his arm. Now he is capable of moving forward, and to encourage him to do so, a favorite or new toy is placed just out of reach. It may be he will want to try to move forward but needs a bit more incentive and this can be managed easily by covering and uncovering the toy with a small piece of cloth or Kleenex and asking, "Where is the car? Here it is. Come and get it, beep, beep." The slightest attempt should be rewarded and the toy moved into easy reach if he has not been completely successful in retrieving it. "That was a good try." While approval is necessary for all human beings, it is especially so for the baby, particularly if it comes from his mother—the person at this point in his life who is the center of his world. He loves to know his efforts, self-initiated or not, meet with her approval, and if praise is forthcoming, he beams with satisfaction. That beatific smile almost always elicits a response from mother.

Now that the idea of moving his body to achieve a goal has been at least partially understood by the baby, the activity can be made more challenging if the toy is moved away as he advances. The movement away should be slow and the distance fairly short, so that there will be no real difficulty in retrieving the toy. In this situation it is sometimes tempting for a parent to see how far a baby will move and this ends in frustration more often than not. This kind of temptation should be firmly resisted. Early success will encourage a child to try new challenges because he is already getting the feeling that he can do things —he can succeed, which lays the foundation for the growth of self-esteem. If, on the other hand, the baby is exposed to too much frustration, he begins to feel he cannot succeed at a task and will not attempt new challenges for fear of failure, and any feelings of self-esteem that had already developed start to fade.

On a number of occasions when the authors have been explaining this principle to students, the question of planning an environment so that there is maximum possibility of success has been raised. This principle has been queried on the basis that eventually the child will be entering an adult world where success is not always assured, and how will he cope with failure if he has never experienced it? One only needs to observe a baby struggling with reaching, grasping, creeping and crawling, walking and talking to realize there is no way the baby's world can be structured so that there is always success and never any frustration. The key is minimizing the built-in failures that all developing babies experience and which no one can change. The baby has to learn for himself how to creep and crawl, walk and talk; no parent can do it for him. But he will struggle with these important steps if he experiences some success and approval along the way, especially if it comes from his parents.

Thus it is important to help the baby retrieve his toy as he moves forward. The fun can be extended if you use other toys and appropriate language. " 'Beep, beep, come get me' says the red car." It should always be kept in mind that it is necessary to give your baby plenty of time after the object has been recovered, so that he can examine his "prize," the one he made all that effort to retrieve, to his satisfaction.

If he still seems interested in playing, another retrieval task, "pull the cloth and get the toy," can be introduced. A toy is placed on a cloth about 12″ x 8″, the edge within easy reach of the baby. If he seems unsure as to how he should proceed, you can demonstrate and then give him the opportunity to try his skill. "Here comes the cow," you say. "Moo, moo, pull the cloth. Here she comes. Good boy, you got the cow." As the baby examines his acquisition, you might point out one or two parts, but not so many that you interrupt his examination. "Here is her tail and here is her nose." A light touch on his nose may follow, with "And here is your nose." Varying this task by using a piece of string approximately the same length as the cloth (12″) requires a little more precision in grasping and this adds to the fun. If the string is too long, the problem becomes too difficult because a child of this age has not yet learned the technique necessary for pulling a long string in order to reach an object. The reason is quite simple: he does not understand that he has to release the string after one pull and regrasp it and pull again. He'll learn this later on.

Pulling on a string so that the object (particularly if it's a nice little red car) has to move through a cardboard tunnel is also fun. Toilet-paper rolls and paper-toweling rolls are perfect for this task. For larger cars, a shoe box with the ends cut out makes another suitable tunnel. If this game intrigues the baby a little piece of Kleenex can be taped over the opening so that the object is not seen until it is retrieved. This way there is always an element of surprise. The baby never really knows for sure what is going to be on the end of the string but he is always curious to find out. Pulling a toy through more than one roll is another variation of this game. A sort of now you see it, now you don't.

Anytime you get your groceries in a large cardboard box you have the makings of an instant tunnel. With both ends cut out, you position yourself at one end and lure the baby through the other; that is, if he needs any inducement. Since it makes a rather cozy little house, he may just decide to sit there for a while and meditate. That's all right too and you might bring him his favorite teddy bear to keep him company. Most babies travel in and out a few times just for the fun of it, and in a beginning way they are learning a little about spatial relationships. Is that opening big enough for me? How far is the other end from me? Will there be enough room for me if I sit? What will happen if I stand? What a lot to figure out and try to understand! However, the greatest enjoyment is his traveling through the tunnel. When he is a little older and more confident, longer tunnels can be made, using several cartons, but for now one is just right.

With an increasingly mobile baby, that old favorite "hide-and-seek" is just the ticket for warm interaction between you and your child, especially if you are the object to be found. Enticing him with "Where am I? Come and find me!" is always a success since the baby really wants to be with you and the joy of finding you in some out-of-the-ordinary place is very satisfying. He knows too that when he does find you—and you make sure of that by popping in and out of your hiding place—you will show him how much you love him by picking him up for a quick cuddle and letting him know how clever he was to find you. And clever he is when one realizes how complex "Where am I? Come and find me!" is to a baby. He must hear the words, try to comprehend what they mean, where they are coming from, and then set his body in motion in a certain direction. The nice thing about this activity is that it improves with age, especially when the roles are reversed and baby is the one who is hiding. What a lot of giggles when you pretend to be looking everywhere for your elusive child. "Is Johnny behind the door? No, he's not there. Is he under the table? No, he's not under the table. Oh, there he is, behind the chair. I found you, Johnny."

"Peek-a-boo" is another of those games which improve with age. You hide behind a door and pop out with a "peek-a-boo." This might be a nice time for that lovely little rhyme "coo-coo, peek-a-boo; coo-coo, I see you." Both of these games can be varied by using a favorite toy animal. You hide with a toy dog and give him a voice. "Bow wow. I'm hiding behind the chair. Find me, bow wow." At this point the toy dog is exposed briefly to encourage the baby to continue his search. Toy animals just hidden behind you, or behind a large book, can also be used for peek-a-boo. "Peek-a-boo, wuff, wuff. I see you, wuff, wuff."

Frequently it is hard for some parents to imitate their baby and to play with him on his own terms. Crawling around on the floor, hiding behind chairs, barking like a dog seem so ridiculous that the conservative parent is unable to participate without discomfort. It helps if parents can understand that almost anything that gives pleasure and joy to their small baby strengthens his relationship to them in a valuable and worthwile way. So throw out your inhibitions, get down on the floor and have fun with your baby because it is important for you to get down to his level emotionally as well as physically. Somewhere in oriental philosophy it has been written *a wise man is he who has not lost the heart of a child.*

Spontaneous play occurs at almost any time of the day when you suddenly decide to forget about the house and play with your baby. This kind of play is so satisfying to both that it should be engaged in whenever possible. But it also seems to help baby feel secure if his day is somewhat predictable and if he knows that there are several times during the day that will be his exclusive time with one or the other of his parents. He is then able to accept those other times when his parents, especially mother, are not able to give him their undivided attention. His mother may be near him, talking and smiling at him, but she is busy doing a task quite unrelated to him. No household can stand still for a baby, nor should it.

It seems practical then to choose playtimes when the baby is fed, rested, and content and when mother's other duties are not intruding. The playtime continues for as long as baby seems interested or for the length of time you have available. If the latter is the case the baby will accept the ending of his playtime because he has already learned that you will play with him again and in any event will be remaining near him and will still be responding to him. Of course if he had his way he would certainly prefer to have you spend all of your time with him but he is able to accept partial sharing of your time.

Among the gross motor activities, ball playing must be included. A small brightly colored ball is rolled as close to the baby as possible with a brief suggestion from you: "Go get the red ball." With verbal approval for his attempts, successful or not, your baby begins to get an idea of the game. If the ball is not rolled too close to him he may start off in hot pursuit, but since babies are easily distracted, he may just get diverted along the way by something else. If that new object seems more interesting, the game can be postponed for a few minutes. Of course, you have to take a quick look yourself to make sure it is not harmful. Once you are sure that there is no cause for concern you retrieve the ball and roll it back to him when he seems ready. For him to return the ball to you is something he is not quite ready for, and while he may try valiantly, he isn't too successful. By the way, this game needs a fair amount of space cleared of any objects that could be damaged if struck by the ball. Sometimes the baby is reluctant to return the ball even after he has examined it thoroughly; it's just too hard for him to give up his possession even for his beloved mother. If this seems to be the case, the use of a second ball helps to get him involved in the activity again.

A new dimension can be added by using other objects such as smooth-edged shiny disks from frozen-orange-juice cans, spools of thread, lids of jars, old bracelets, small cans (those tomato-paste ones are great for this), and even the rubber rings from preserving jars, to mention just a few. Please don't forget that after each object is retrieved there should be sufficient time for examination and manipulation and perhaps a little appropriate explanation. "This is a rubber ring; this is a spool of blue thread; this is a yellow bracelet. I'm putting the yellow bracelet on my head. What a funny place for a bracelet! It does fit on my wrist, though, doesn't it?" Perhaps without realizing it you are teaching your baby in a very elementary way that the body is made of parts and each part has a label. Of course, it will take many play opportunities such as this where parts of the body can be labeled in a natural way before he will really understand this concept. Sometimes you can't play until your baby has indicated that he is no longer interested and must end the play. If that is the case, it helps if the child is given some idea that it is almost time to stop and while he may not completely understand what you are trying to tell him, it won't be long before he will. At this age baby can't tell us how much he understands, but he does tell us through his actions that he understands a surprising amount, which will increase quite rapidly if he continues to be exposed to a rich variety of language.

At some point in this period the baby masters the difficulties of standing and is now searching for opportunities to expand this new skill. Whenever he is sitting he wants to get up, but getting up is not all that easy at first unless there are objects with which to pull himself upright. Since he has no idea of stability he will choose almost anything that seems suitable, including coffee tables, lamps, footstools, small chairs, and overhanging tablecloths, all of which may be quite hazardous. In spite of the fact that parents warn their baby of the danger, he may simply forget or be unable to control his impulse as he heads for the offending object, with unfortunate results. All too often parents get discouraged and sometimes resort to spanking to reinforce their warning. This is only minimally effective because impulse control comes only with maturity. In other words, the baby can't really help himself and punishment is inappropriate. This fact becomes clearer if one visualizes the check-out counter at the local supermarket where all kinds of goodies are attractively displayed and where adults find they are not always able to control their impulses. If adults are not always able to control themselves it is understandable why babies are not able to do so. For the time being, then, it may be practical for the parents to remove temporarily some of the more unstable pieces and to provide more than usual supervision. It also helps to remove deli-

73

cate but enticing *objets d'art*, which many parents place in areas too easily reached by their baby. Again he is simply not mature enough to control his impulses and wants to touch, to handle, and to examine captivating objects.

Some pieces of furniture are really a great help to a small baby trying to stand. Chesterfields with matching chairs are usually heavy enough for safety and very supportive. Those low kitchen drawers with their easy-to-reach handles can be used, especially if they are engineered so that they can neither come out completely nor close completely. Drawers don't always get closed by the handles and a few painfully squeezed fingers would discourage even the sturdiest experimenter. Opening and closing drawers is a fascinating pastime, particularly if there are interesting things inside. Discarded pots and pans, plastic dishes, clean plastic squeeze bottles (without tops, of course), empty tea tins, small boxes, easy-to-handle spoons, aluminum tart tins, discarded muffin tins, very large buttons, fragments of interesting fabric, pieces of crunched-up foil, and bits of gift-wrap paper are just a few of the articles that can be rotated in a regular way for surprises in this particular "discovery" drawer. This special drawer (or cupboard with appropriate box) is very practical during meal preparation time when you know you are going to be busy for a while and want your baby near you. It's easy for you to chat with him and to admire the things he shows you while you prepare the dinner. In this way the baby is happy and content and usually very, very busy.

While the kitchen is an exciting place for exploration, a word of caution might be in order regarding safety. Many products on the market today and found regularly in kitchen cupboards are very dangerous. Liquid detergent, lemon-oil furniture polish, aerosol sprays of all kinds, spot removers, shoe polish, powdered cleansers, rug shampoos, preparations for dog and cat parasites are just a few that come readily to mind and that send far too many young children to the hospital. If these preparations cannot be removed, then they must be placed in a cupboard which can be securely locked and which will be impossible for a curious baby to open.

Fine motor activities

With the infant well into the second half of his first year, the time is right for some fine motor activities, most of which involve small muscles, principally those of the hands and eyes. If mother has been able to lose some of her inhibitions, then getting right down on the floor with her baby makes for a very comfortable arrangement. It encourages close physical contact, it facilitates quick responses to difficult situations, it provides safe space for maximum freedom, and finally it helps make the adult seem less giant-size to a small baby.

A popular and easy fine motor activity can be managed with a small metal pot with the corresponding lid. The skill of fitting the lid to the pot takes patience and concentration, but it can be very satisfying if you put a small object inside for a surprise. When the pot is first offered and after the baby has finished his examination, it may be necessary to demonstrate the task. In no time at all he catches on and is eager to try.

Sitting on the sidelines watching a baby tackle this problem is a fascinating experience in itself. Some are so serious, others so persevering that it is hard for a mother not to step in and help, even though she knows intuitively that this kind of help would probably be unwelcome. The *modus operandi* for the baby is the trial-and-error method. He tries the lid every which way, upside down, right side up, hand in pot with arm in the way, at first partially covering the opening, and finally completely covering it. This is very serious business for him and he is totally absorbed in his play. Once he has mastered the task to his satisfaction or he is finished with that aspect of it, he may begin additional experimentation. If he puts the lid on slowly

75

and carefully it makes only a slight sound, but if he bangs it down quickly, he discovers a wonderfully loud noise. If you are watching at this point you will notice that he is beginning to anticipate the noise and starts to blink before the lid actually comes banging down.

If this seems to be getting out of hand, it can be quickly varied by the addition of small objects that are dropped in the pot. Each one makes its own unique sound, some easier than others on the eardrums, and your baby wants to try them all.

Small spoons, blocks, clothes-pegs, corks, plastic animals, tart tins, large buttons, lids from jars, small boxes, small empty spice tins, empty adhesive-tape rolls, hair rollers, and spools of thread are just a few items that provide a new dimension to the "pot" game. It's a good idea to give the baby two or three objects at a time rather than too many all at once. This way new additions can be added and substituted when interest seems to be waning. The objects are examined minutely and then dropped into the pot. One may get taken out or all may get taken out. Perhaps they are re-examined to see if anything has been overlooked and then dropped back into the pot. Along with this game you can introduce a little language. "This is a pig, oink, oink." Here is a place where you can really be uninhibited and imaginative. Exaggerating and drawing out the sound delights your baby and he wants to hear more and more.

Listening to different sounds always seems to fascinate babies, especially if one object appears to be responsible for the sound. At some point, when the baby indicates he is just about through with the pot, you can take a block and bang it on the lid, on the pot itself, on the floor, even on the baby's shoe, and each time you will produce a different sound. Repeated with a metal spoon or some other object a whole new range of sounds is introduced, with baby eager to make the sounds himself. From the look on his face it is apparent that he is pleased with the delightful sounds he is making. After some practice you may even find that he varies the force with which he bangs at the pot, sometimes tapping gently, other times banging hard and vigorously. He is also learning in a very elementary way that he can have an effect on his environment. This is a heady feeling, and even more so if you recognize his insight and respond accordingly. "You made that nice sound all by yourself. Gee, that's great, you're my clever baby."

Another time when you and your baby are able to be together a new variation of the "drop-an-object-into-the-pot" game can

77

be initiated. This time a piece of cardboard or a piece of thick fabric is cut to fit the bottom of the pot. One or two objects are offered, as before with appropriate language. "Here is a blue block. Drop it in the pot." The sound produced is quite different and this difference is enhanced if two pots are used, one without the cardboard or fabric insert. Why does the block make a different sound when dropped into what seems to the baby similar pots? Of course, he doesn't understand. What he does understand is the difference in the noise. He is not able to reason yet, he only knows there is a difference. If pots are not available, the one-pound coffee can is excellent for this purpose if the inside edges are either hammered in or covered with masking tape or Scotch tape so that there is no danger of cutting little fingers. One of the nice things about these coffee cans is the plastic lid which will produce a unique sound when the metal bottom is removed and replaced with another plastic lid.

Many babies find the various sounds interesting, others take a more cavalier attitude and are more interested in just putting objects in and taking them out. If he's having fun it's a good activity with you sitting close by for a quick smile, a little pat, and a few words of explanation or encouragement. This kind of situation helps him to have a cozy feeling about the world and he is content.

If you are lucky enough to find some of those almost forgotten nonspring clothes-pegs, then another "pot" game can be introduced, again using the one-pound coffee can. After several of the pegs have been placed around the edge of the can show your baby how to pull them off and then put them back on again. It's very likely he may need a little guidance getting them on but after some practice it will be an accomplished fine motor skill. Additional interest can be provided if the pegs are painted with nontoxic paint, using the primary colors: red, blue, and yellow. Green is also nice. To begin with it is helpful if only two colors, say red and blue, are used. As the baby manipulates the pegs, you can identify the color. "You put a red peg on the tin, let's find another red peg. Oh, you prefer a blue one, that's pretty isn't it?" In this way colors are introduced, and while no one expects a child of this age to learn this concept, it is an excellent way to begin. As usual, you take a positive and therefore reinforcing position. The baby has been encouraged to find the red peg. While he may have an idea what a peg is, it is highly unlikely that he knows what red is and so he chooses any peg. If by chance he picks a red one (and when only two colors are being used, he has a fifty per cent chance of succeeding), a positive response is made. "That's great, you found a red peg." If, on the other hand, he chooses a blue one, and he has a fifty per cent chance of doing just that, the response can still be positive. "Oh, you found a blue one, that's a pretty color, isn't it? Look, mummy is holding a red peg, and you are holding a blue one." A color is being identified, and the baby is getting a positive response, so does not feel he has made an error. To correct a child of this age with "No, not that one, a red one" is to tell him he has made a mistake. In this instance he had a fifty per cent chance of not choosing the correct one and with his immature reasoning ability he was simply unable to choose correctly. He doesn't need this kind of negativism and will always be more responsive to the positive approach. This is true with all stages of human endeavor and most learning, but is more crucial for the young child. This same activity but with a bit more challenge can be offered by using the spring-type clothes-pegs. He finds this type does not come off as easily as the others, but soon learns to pull hard and squeeze, and he will have it off the can. Putting it on takes a little more strength and precision and here you may have to give a little help if it seems indicated. "That's a hard one, isn't it? Push hard! That's it; you know how, don't you?" As long as you and your baby have the inclination and the time, a variation can be introduced with the long spring-type clips that are used for waving and curling hair.

Yet another exciting problem-solving task where fine motor co-ordination is necessary can be enjoyed. This task is the forerunner of what is called "form-board" tasks where geometric shapes are fitted into an opening. All problem-solving tasks confronting a baby have a built-in difficulty and it helps if the tasks are presented in order of complexity, with the easiest one the first to be tried. It seems obvious therefore that the geometric shape to begin with should be the circle, since it has no edges or corners, is the easiest to manipulate and success is usually assured. Eventually as baby matures the shapes can become more abstract. For this task several small, brightly colored rubber balls that can be handled easily and safely by the baby (these are readily available in the dime store), along with that wonderfully versatile one-pound coffee can, are all that is necessary.

A hole slightly larger than the ball is made in the plastic lid, which is then replaced on the top of the coffee can. The can and the balls are given to the baby to inspect and to do his own thing with. This usually means a quick look followed by extensive mouthing. From the visual examination the baby gets a general idea about shape, color, and size; from the mouthing he learns the ball can be squeezed, that it has a taste quite unlike anything else he is familiar with (has the reader ever tasted a rubber ball?), and that it has no corners. After he has finished his observations you demonstrate the problem. "I'm putting the red ball in the hole. Would you like to put a red ball in the hole?" He tries and succeeds, the ball falls with a thump. You respond: "Hey, that's great! You put the red ball in the hole. Here's a green one to try."

Sometimes a baby finds a small ball so nice he really doesn't want to give it up and just wants to hold onto it. In this case, you continue using the other balls, labeling them as you drop them into the can. "I'm putting a blue ball into the can. Through the hole it goes. Oh, what a nice sound it makes." Of course, in most cases your baby gets really interested and eventually tries the task himself. He is greatly reassured when you remove the lid and retrieve the balls and return them to him. After the task has lost its appeal (and hopefully just a little before that time) a quick game of ball (rolling it on the floor) may be in order if you still have a few minutes left for play and your baby is not quite ready to give up his time with you.

With a few carpentry tools and a clever dad, a few simple colorful form boards, easy for baby to handle, can be made without too much trouble. (See Appendix for directions for making the form boards.) The first one is uncomplicated, a circular insert with a corresponding opening slightly larger than the insert, and a small knob on the insert for easy handling. After the baby has looked the problem over and manipulated the materials to his satisfaction, you demonstrate how the insert fits into the opening and let him try his skill. After he has mastered this task and is looking for further challenges, the same task can be made more complex by using two different-sized but similar-shaped inserts with matching openings. A big one and a little one require not only good co-ordination, but also introduce a new concept. You should not be surprised if your baby puts the small piece in the large opening. He's pretty sure it will fit, but he sees he is running into difficulties with the large piece when it will not fit into the small opening. He then proceeds in earnest to experiment. One of the authors decided to utilize this principle by using the coffee can with a large and small hole in the lid. She handed a large ball to an interested baby and he promptly put it through the large hole. Then she handed him a small ball, which he just as promptly put through the large hole. But, of course, why would he bother about a small opening when he could see it would be so much easier if he used the large opening? Babies really are clever, aren't they? Many toyshops have inexpensive busy-board toys that are nice for children of this age. Little doors open, some slide, knobs are pressed to make a sound, and a telephone dial makes a whirring noise. Such boards are usually made of attractive, colorful plastic which most babies find appealing. There is no doubt they enhance fine motor skills in a very enjoyable way.

Another interesting activity requiring fine motor dexterity is the "ring-on-the-peg" game. There are several on the market, but a really easy one has a small peg on a stand with several round colorful rings all the same size. The task requires co-ordination between thumb and index finger and may require considerable practice before success is possible. Once the technique is mastered, the rings go on easily, and the baby is ready for something else. A more complex one made out of plastic with several rings, each a different color and each slightly larger than the next, is readily available in most large department and toy stores. Baby

needs to experiment a great deal before he learns which one goes on first in order to get all the rings on the spindle correctly. This may take some trial and error and determination on the part of the baby before the task is resolved. If one keeps in mind that the activity is provided so that the baby can have an interesting and enjoyable time, then parents should remember not to get anxious about how quickly the problem is mastered. Actually it has been the authors' experience that babies initially spend a great deal of time just putting on and taking off one or two rings (perhaps the large ones on the bottom, or the small ones on the top) before they are interested in putting the whole stack together. If the baby is not allowed to proceed at his own pace, then it will soon become a task to be avoided rather than mastered.

Other play with the rings can be demonstrated. The rings roll easily. "Here comes the yellow ring, catch it. Watch out, here comes the blue one." When your baby returns the ring to you quickly hide it behind your back. "Oh, oh! Where did it go?" And when it is discovered, "You're my clever baby, aren't you? I can't fool you." The ring is then placed on top of his head with a "Where's the red ring?" Since he feels it on his head, a little shake makes it tumble down. "There it is. That was a funny place to hide a ring, on top of your head." Or you can compare the rings for size. "See, the small purple ring fits right into the big red one." Parts of the body, colors, and prepositions are mentioned in a natural way. He has had a challenging game, enjoyed your company and encouragement, and has had a satisfying time.

Searching activities

Some time during this second half of the first year the baby begins to understand what Piaget calls the object concept (it is also called the concept of object permanence). Briefly this means that the baby knows an object is still present even though it

83

can't be seen. One knows, for example, that even though one cannot see the refrigerator in the kitchen, it is there nevertheless. Until a baby gets close to his first birthday he does not completely understand this concept. With this in mind and again when you and your baby have the time and the inclination, a new activity based on object permanence can be introduced. Almost anything that will cover a small desirable object can be used —a piece of cloth (old washcloths will do just fine), a piece of Kleenex, a plastic cup, an empty yogurt or margarine container are very suitable. The object, perhaps a nice shiny tinkly bell, is given to the baby to examine. When he is finished you ring it gently, then put it under the cloth as he watches. "Where is the bell? Can you find it?" If there is little interest, a corner of the cloth can be raised so that the bell can be seen. The bell can be given a voice. "I'm a bell, tinkle, tinkle, find me, find me." A little more incentive may be needed to whet his curiosity. After all, not everything an adult thinks should appeal to a baby is in fact appealing to him. Some games are more attractive to some children than to others, and so are some objects. Parents should not be at all discouraged if their baby does not find a particular activity or toy exciting. Something novel may provide the stimulus for action. If a piece of brightly colored string or ribbon is attached to the bell the baby's curiosity may be aroused and he will want to pull the string with a little encouragement from you. And what a pleasant surprise to find a nice bell at the end of the string! He didn't realize it was there even though he had seen it placed there. Now he is intrigued and the game can be repeated with different toys and different-colored string for as long as time or interest permits.

Once this concept of the permanence of objects seems understood, baby is ready for a slightly more complex variation of the previous task. This time two pieces of cloth, each a different color (red and blue are usually appealing to babies), are placed in front of your baby as he sits on the floor beside you.

A red car is offered and after it has been played with and re-leased, you place it under the red cloth. Given the opportunity, he will probably find the object right away, and enjoy pulling off the cloth to find the car. Again you hide the car under the red cloth, and, while the baby is still watching, remove it from under the red cloth and place it under the blue cloth. During this time tell him what you are doing. "I'm hiding your red car under the red cloth. Now I'm hiding your red car under the blue cloth." As you remove your empty hand, ask him: "Where is the red car?" In most cases the baby looks under the first cloth used. He saw it placed there, and even though he saw it removed, he still has the idea it is under the cloth where it was originally placed, and that is where he will look. Since he really expected to find it there, he is surprised when he discovers it is not there. Piaget explains this reaction by observing that the infant is unable to take into account the number and complexity of the movements of an object, and he thus attempts to find the object in the place where he was previously successful in finding the object. For example, if the red car had been placed under the blue cloth first, and that is where baby had discovered it, he would persist in looking under the blue cloth even though he had seen it being moved from blue to red. At this particular period, hiding, re-moving, and rehiding an object is just too complex a sequence for the baby to follow and thus he reverts back to previously suc-cessful behavior.

When the car is not found, you can give a clue, "Look under the blue cloth," which you indicate. He does not yet understand colors, but with your help gets the idea of what he needs to do to find his car. Again his exposure to color labeling in a natural way will help him eventually to distinguish colors accurately.

Everyone loves a surprise and babies are no exception. A game that provides much amusement is the "open-the-box-and-find-a-surprise" game. Small jewelry boxes are very practical for this activity because they are easily handled. Many of them have top sections that do not completely cover the bottom part and this makes them fairly easy for a baby to open. If the top section does completely cover the lower part, then a portion of it can be cut out so that the bottom part can be grasped without involving the top part. Large, nicely colored buttons, small but not too small plastic animals, pictures glued onto pieces of cardboard and cut to the appropriate size, bits of interesting fabric and paper, and occasionally, as a special find, a Cheerio are a few of the things that make wonderful surprises. Incidentally, parents should be on the lookout when they are shopping in the dime store, the grocery store, or the hardware store for little, safe, inexpensive objects for their child's play. When the baby is ready to play, one of the objects is placed in the box and rattled a few times to attract attention and heighten interest. How to open the box is demonstrated, and the baby is invited to try his skill. He goes at it with determination because he keeps hearing it rattle as he moves the box. It may be that he hands the box back to you to open and show him that the toy is still inside for him to find. It may take several tries and it may be that the first time he will not persevere long enough to ensure success. If he keeps trying but is not being too successful, you might step in and partially raise the top so that it is easy to remove. If it seems that his problem stems from the fact that he is still holding the top, then further trimming will help. As his expertise develops, boxes that are a little harder to open can be used. Again it is important for you to verbalize what is happening and to encourage your baby in his endeavors. "That box is hard to open, isn't it? Here it comes. Fantastic! Good boy, you got the box open. Oh, what did you find? A little brown horse."

Water play

Mothers usually shudder at the idea of water play and imagine visions of water all over the baby and all over the room. This certainly can happen, but with a little preliminary planning, it can be managed without having the house turned into a disaster area.

A little foresight needs to be utilized, as one of the authors discovered one day when her young son first began to creep and crawl. Up to this time she hadn't had to worry about her dog's dish, but one day when her child had left her and didn't return as soon as he usually did, she went looking for him. There he was, happily engaged in water play in the dog's water dish, which, fortunately (or unfortunately, from the child's viewpoint), had only a cup of water in it. Unobtrusively she watched him having a glorious time, swishing and splashing the water with his hands until he reached the point where he discovered he had no more water. He had patted it all out onto the floor. He was astounded and continued patting the dish. He touched the wet floor, then patted the dish some more when it did not bring the expected reward. From then on he had regular water play, arranged, of course, with a little preplanning.

If the kitchen is large enough, an old sheet (flannelette is nice and absorbent) is put down on the floor on top of a good padding of newspaper and the baby is put in the middle. Give him a plastic dish, circular or rectangular, approximately 12″ in diameter or 12″–14″ square and 2″–3″ high, with about 1″–2″ of water. Enough water for a bit of splashing, but not so much that the area becomes flooded if the dish gets tipped over. At first the baby will just be interested in patting, swishing, and splashing; he is learning about the properties of water. It is cool or warm, as the case may be, it can cause a splash, make a noise when hit, and it can't be held in his hand. When he puts his wet hand in his mouth he learns it doesn't have much taste. He may play with the water for some time, but when he seems finished experimenting, new dimensions can be added with a few extras. A couple of ice cubes are very interesting but must be removed when they become too small for safety. But up to that point they are fun.

Colored plastic scoops, tart tins, plastic squeeze bottles, small sieves, cups from a toy tea set, small cans with some holes in the bottom added one at a time keep baby busy for many minutes. For a little variety, a few things which float add to the fun. Corks from wine bottles, empty spools of thread, blocks, and plastic spoons are just a few of the things usually found in the home. Occasionally, for additional variety, some food coloring can be added to the water. This new aspect intrigues him because the colored water seems to have the same properties as the first clear liquid he experimented with, but he can see it is a lovely blue—just right, incidentally, for a little sailboat. A tart tin with a bit of chewed gum, dough, or Plasticine in the middle to hold a toothpick with its smart paper sail is a perfect boat. A cork with a similar toothpick sail is another kind of boat easily made. Empty walnut shells (they halve perfectly with a little care) can also be used to make lovely interesting sailboats along with small flat pieces of wood. If he seems interested in just pulling the boats apart, and this is natural at this age since he is trying to find out something about everything new he sees, then you can remove the sail and let your little sailor play with the shell of the boat as he pleases.

Creative play

All of the infant's play is creative and imaginative, but one of the many ways this creativity can be fostered and expanded is through ample exposure to various experiences appropriate to his level of development. At this age of twelve months and younger, the infant is learning primarily through his senses of taste, sight, hearing, touch, and smell. It is, in Piaget's term, the "sensorimotor" period—a time when baby learns not by abstract reasoning and thinking as much as by actually experiencing all that he is involved with. Painting, for example, is one of the most

enjoyable ways for a baby to become totally absorbed in his

work, and, as you know, his play is in fact his work. He sees bright colors, feels the texture of the paint, and sees the results of his arm and hand movements as they make designs on the paper.

One of the simplest and most enjoyable forms of painting for a young baby is finger painting. Here he is feeling the texture, trying to understand the properties of paint. It is cool, smooth, has an interesting color, can be squeezed through fingers, has a strange taste, and most important of all, permits him to "make" his own picture. This kind of experience helps him to learn once again that he does have some effect on his environment. This is a very satisfying feeling for a young fellow trying to be independent. His desire to understand the properties of objects helps to explain why a baby likes to feel his food, while mother wishes he would eat it instead of squishing it through his fingers. It is important not to be negative about his need to experiment. Some parents think that finger painting encourages excessive messing to the point where the baby is not eating properly and his health may be affected, but babies are too clever for this, especially if good eating habits have been established.

There seem to be a number of factors that have a lot do do with helping a baby establish good eating habits. His own temperament, his size, his metabolic rate, and, most important of all, his parents' attitude toward food all set the pattern. Anxious parents tend to push more food into their baby than is necessary, get very upset when he does not finish his meal, and try bribery and threats to get him to eat. This starts the pattern, with mealtimes becoming a regular daily battle. Some mothers feel a nice plump baby proves they are good mothers. "I'm a good mother; see how healthy my baby is." But frequently parents make judgments about what the child will eat and how much he will eat without regard for his appetite (adults are not always hungry at mealtimes), his state of health (he's coming down with a cold), or his preferences (not all adults like the same foods). There are times when these factors are obvious and baby understandably does not want to eat. In some cases it may not be clear why he is not interested in eating. If he has been feeling a little neglected and if you have been giving him less attention than usual, then he may resort to unacceptable methods to get you to notice him. Mealtime is one time when he can make darn sure he has your attention. He spits out his food, throws his spoon on the floor (which is clearly different from dropping it over the edge to see how it falls and where it will fall), and turns over his bowl, while you become angrier and more upset by the minute. When this happens you need to sit back for a minute and think about what has happened up to that time. Did you find time for just a few minutes of play with him? Has he been in the playpen too long? Have you been a bit too preoccupied with other tasks? Is this what your baby's negative behavior is telling you? When "I'm not getting enough attention from you" is the message, the baby is really saying, "You pay attention to me now because I'm making you. I refuse to eat and you have to spend time with me but that doesn't really satisfy me. I want you to show me you love me by paying attention to me without my having to ask for it. If I get this kind of spontaneous attention, I'll know I'm loved, I'll feel secure and won't need to misbehave." If you decide this might be at least part of the problem, there are a number of things that can help. Responding to your baby frequently without his asking, spending a bit more time playing with him, and at mealtimes serving him a variety of foods in very small attractive portions may remedy the situation.

Since babies learn from past experience, one morning of extra play is not enough, and he will probably continue to spit out his food. If this happens, quietly remove his bowl with, "Aren't you hungry today? Would you like a little dessert?" You offer him a small portion, which he may also refuse, and, of course, some milk. You might offer the food a second time, but on refusal, remove him from his highchair. Lunch is over. Hide your anxiety and talk warmly and lovingly to him as you prepare him for his nap. One cookie and some juice may be offered after his nap if that has been customary, but not several cookies to fill his tummy and make a meal on. He needs to be a little hungry for supper and this won't hurt him for the several days it may be necessary before he begins to eat again with pleasure. Helping him to feel happier and more secure will do more to help him establish good eating habits than force-feeding or punishment.

While your baby will do a little preliminary messing with his food before eating, if he is hungry, he gets on with the job. The reverse is true with finger painting. The painting mixture has to be examined thoroughly and this means tasting as well as looking and feeling. Because it is going in the baby's mouth it is very important that safe nontoxic materials be used. Many foods at home can be used for this activity, including bright-red ketchup, mayonnaise for ivory, and prepared mustard for yellow. If food coloring happens to be handy, several other colored paints can be made by using either a starch or flour base (see Appendix for recipes). Since there seems to be some reservation about a certain kind of red food coloring (see *Consumer Reports*, February, 1973) it might be advisable not to use red food coloring. Other liquids found in the kitchen can be added to the starch base for exciting colors. Beet juice makes a lovely pink color or a deep fuchsia, depending on the amount used, soya sauce makes a nice rich brown, and prepared mustard added to the starch makes a lovely canary yellow. Powdered fruit drinks added to the base provide a glorious range of colors. If blueberry pie happens to be on the menu, a little of the berry mixture added to the starch or flour base makes a lovely blue.

It might be that you decide on Monday morning you are going to arrange for painting. The starch base is made and divided into suitable portions, depending on the number of colors desired. Usually there is more than can be used in one sitting, so a portion is set aside and refrigerated in a covered container, 91 where it will keep for several days. One of the added bonuses with this kind of painting is the variety of tastes it can provide if you add different extracts. Peppermint, almond, vanilla, lemon, to mention just a few. Some taste quite nice, some not so nice, some just strange, but all interesting.

For this kind of activity a few prerequisites are necessary. Old clothes are a must. Bibs don't offer much protection and sometimes get in the way. A little extra newspaper on the floor is very helpful and a small chair and table with lots of working space is desirable (see Appendix for design). It isn't always possible to provide a special table and chair for the baby, so a highchair or a feeding table make an acceptable alternative. Almost any kind of plain paper can be used. Ordinary brown wrapping paper, paper bags free of printing, the pieces of cardboard found in shirts and in panty-hose packages are very nice. Discarded computer printouts are just the ticket, along with any size or shape of paper. There is also on the market today white paper called picnic-table paper that lends itself well to this kind of activity. It is used as a substitute for banquet tablecloths and comes in rolls rather than in individual pieces. This makes it possible to cut out pieces of the desired lengths and to cut them into geometric shapes as well. And, of course, it is a great asset when the baby becomes a toddler and wants a very large piece for painting. It's such fun to work on a picture that takes up half the floor space. One can really be expansive and imaginative. Some lucky parents have been in a position to buy large, inexpensive (inexpensive, that is, in terms of the amount of paper received) rolls of brown meat-wrapping paper which wholesale outlets provide for their grocery customers. More than one parent has saved these early pictures and made them into wonderful scrapbooks. In some cases a fortunate grandparent has been the delighted recipient of a very special gift of their grandchild's creations.

When all seems ready—paint, paper, old clothes, and baby —it helps if you do one more thing. Scotch-tape the paper down and then everything is really ready to go. At this time, after all your preparations, you may expect your baby to get right in there and make a picture. But remember this is a new experience for him and he may not know quite what to do. If left to his own devices, he will probably taste and feel the mixture carefully, poking his index finger at first tentatively into the paint, and then not so tentatively into his mouth. If he looks to you for help, you can show him, or can gently move his hands through the paint on the paper. That may end it right there and then; he is not too sure he likes the feel of that funny stuff, but another day perhaps, with two new colors, he may feel more positive about painting. It is important for you not to be discouraged after all your preparation. He has to learn, and he can only learn about the fun of creating if he is given lots of opportunity and lots of time. No one should expect a painter after just one try.

Sometimes a creative experience can happen quite spontaneously, with a little egg white left over from the lemon pie or perhaps a little batter from a cake, a pudding, muffins, or pancakes. Any of these mixtures with a little coloring added makes suitable paint for experimentation. They have color, texture, and a not-unpleasant taste. With a busy mother trying to prepare dinner and an equally busy baby wanting to be near her and to participate, a little of this kind of mixture, even just on the tray of his highchair, will help to keep him occupied for some time. As you work you continue to look at him with a smile, and to talk about what both of you are doing. Instead of the kitchen becoming a place of frustration, it remains a place where your baby feels comfortable and welcome.

Gradually, as the baby's interest and enjoyment in finger painting expands, a new dimension can be added with brushes. Almost any kind of brush can be used if it is small enough for easy manipulation. Regular paintbrushes shortened a bit, along with several brushes found in the home—children's toothbrushes, 93 nailbrushes with handles, suede shoebrushes, worn-out pastry brushes, and discarded face-powder brushes—add new zest to the experience. Other things found around the average home can also be utilized. A Q-tip is lots of fun, especially if a little more absorbent cotton is securely fastened on one end in order to make a larger mark on the paper, and two Q-tips fastened together and used as a brush make an equally interesting mark. A piece of sponge dipped in paint and then pressed on the paper is another useful idea. A creative mother can make a stencil of an animal from a piece of cardboard, which is removed after the baby has dabbed to his heart's content. Lo and behold, he has made a picture of an animal, all by himself.

A small carrot or potato cut at one end and incised with a design makes an interesting stamp. Corks and large empty spools of thread with similar cut-out designs add additional happy experiences. Sometimes small pieces of fabric or a bottle cap glued to the empty spool provide yet another special design. The small end of a cucumber or zucchini or green pepper can also be used as a stamp, as can a small lemon or lime. If your baby's tiny hands have too much difficulty handling these objects, keep this in mind and offer them to him again when he is older.

It is not too early to let your baby experiment with pasting. Flour-and-water paste, the same consistency as used for the painting medium, is quite suitable and there is nothing wrong in adding some color once in a while for a little extra dash. Nice odds and ends of fabric of all textures and colors, pretty pieces of wrapping paper, geometric-shaped pieces of colored cardboard, pictures cut out of retail catalogues, bits of colored string or wool, pieces of sponge, and even small cut-out sections from plastic egg containers can be used for pasting. All can be used singly or in various combinations to make novel collages.

Initially the baby has to be taught how to make his collage, for he has no previous knowledge or experience to draw on, and his first efforts are generally not too extensive, consisting mostly of paste on paper rather than actual collage. At first he doesn't spend much time on them either. Again with adequate opportunities and your warm acceptance of his efforts your baby will get the hang of it and find great pleasure and satisfaction in his creativity. Naturally, as he gets older he will spend longer periods painting and pasting than he is able to do now at this early age. However, it is important to start giving him lots of opportunities for these experiences.

Sand play

To understand the satisfaction of sand play one only needs to go to the beach to see children of all ages building, experimenting, designing, and redesigning their material. From an easy little hill with a make-believe flag on top to a complex castle, sand demonstrates its wondrous possibilities for truly creative and imaginative play. Dry sand has many of the properties of water: it can run downhill like a stream, it can pass through a sieve, it can be poured from one container to another, and it can take on the shape of the container. The addition of a little water turns the sand into a versatile building material with almost limitless possibilities.

Since babies put just about everything into their mouths, there are substitutes for sand, and while a little clean sand won't hurt the baby, other mixtures seem more appropriate while he is still so young. Corn meal and Cream of Wheat are two cereals that can be used for "sand" play, and are readily available winter or summer. They do not have the building properties of sand, but for enjoyment and experimentation they are fine substitutes. Some authors have suggested oatmeal as another alternative, but it is unsuitable for very small babies as it can get stuck to the roof and the back of the mouth and may cause the baby to choke.

Many babies like to get really involved, and if you happen to have a large plastic baby bath this is ideal, because your baby can sit right in it and get busy. But before "cereal play" is started, it would be wise to take a few preliminary measures. In his play the baby will undoubtedly be tossing the cereal around (that's part of the experimentation) and some at least will land on the floor. This makes for a very slippery situation and it is hazardous for both you and your child. An old double-bed-sized sheet

spread on the floor, with the plastic basin in the middle, is the answer, as it can be gathered up easily and most of the cereal recovered for future use. It is also a good idea to have the vacuum cleaner ready when baby seems finished.

What to add to the cereal to provide some interest is not too difficult. Small cars and trucks are always favorites, but sieves, scoops, plastic cups and spoons, boxes, small pots, aluminum tart tins, muffin tins, are also appropriate. Incidentally, it helps to prolong interest if objects are given to the baby one at a time, with new ones added as indicated.

Several years ago, when one of the authors was on the staff of an infant center in Syracuse, New York, she was casting around for materials other than sand for this kind of play when rather unfortunately, as it turned out, she spotted the sugar bowl in the kitchen. Without thinking the situation through, she decided this might be fun for her babies, for sugar was safe, nice to feel, and could be arranged and manipulated. Well, it certainly was fun for the babies; they loved it, especially the taste, but when the other members of the staff finally called a halt, the play area was a disaster area and the babies, although happy and cheerful, were a sticky, gooey, monstrous mess. Obviously the idea was good, but the material not so good. Needless to say, a number of rather unkind remarks were made and sugar play was removed from the repertoire, but it did lead to cereal play with happy results for all.

When the time seems appropriate, that is, when your baby is rested and eager to be doing something interesting, you can arrange the sheet, the plastic bath or basin and its cereal and place the baby in it or next to it if it is not large enough to hold him. As always, it is important to let him do his own thing—to move his feet in the cereal, to taste it, to feel it, or perhaps to let it fall between his fingers. After his examination is complete, he may not be too sure what else to do. You can show him that cars and trucks make interesting tracks in the cereal, they run into little cereal hills, or, oops, they become completely covered with cereal. "Zoom, vroom, here goes the green car. . . . Where did it go?" The sieve can be filled but empties itself almost immediately. The little scoop soon fills the plastic cup and the cereal is promptly poured out and replaced. The truck is filled with cereal, is tipped over, emptied and reloaded. Boxes are filled and refilled over and over again as your baby works with this new material, trying to understand its various properties and to utilize this understanding in different ways. Some days cereal play holds the baby's interest a long time, other times not very long. Remember always to take your cue from your baby.

Reading

Reading has already been mentioned in Chapter 2, but now that your baby is more mature, sitting easily by himself or in your lap, a new kind of reading can be provided along with the previously described "reading." He is still able to enjoy the books he read as a tiny baby and in much the same way. You point out and label objects in the pictures, make appropriate sounds but describe the objects in a little more detail, making comparisons, pointing out differences, and whenever possible in a different context and a different time. "Oh, look at the white rabbit. It has blue pants on just like your blue pants. We saw a rabbit at Mary's house. Do you remember the rabbit in the cage?"

By now your baby is ready for other kinds of books. There are a number on the market today that add a bit more zest to reading. One of our favorites for this age is *Who Lives Here?* For those readers not familiar with this little book the theme is engaging. A leafy tree has a part which, when lifted up, exposes a squirrel; an ocean scene has waves, one of which hides a fish; a lily pad in a quiet pool exposes a frog, and so on. Each page is a little surprise for baby.

Another nice book is called *Pat the Bunny*. This one is not only nice to look at but also has an interesting tactile component. The bunny has a white fluffy cotton fabric for fur, which is lovely to feel; part of dad's face is covered with sandpaper: "Oh, that's rough and scratchy"; a mirror not only reflects a face but also is smooth and cool to touch. All of these things absorb a young baby for some time.

With very little effort you can make interesting tactile books for your own child with just a little cloth or heavy cardboard and some imagination. The cloth book would have each "page" a different kind of textured material, for example, burlap, flannelette, felt, corduroy, fur, velvet, or vinyl. Each "page" would have a picture of an object made out of material quite different from the page. The velvet page could have a vinyl pig, the burlap page a fur rabbit, and perhaps the flannelette page a bird with a few feathers. The cardboard book is inexpensive and easy to make. Almost any kind of heavy cardboard will do and the book can have as many or as few pages as mother wishes. The pages can be fastened together with a metal ring, a piece of ribbon, or strong cord. This might be a good time to remind parents to examine magazines for bright, clear, realistic pictures of all kinds, particularly ones of animals. These are not only great for books but essential for the change and play areas. Pictures of cats and dogs, rabbits, birds, worms and snakes all captivate the young child, and can be displayed singly or grouped to make interesting stories. By the way, one shouldn't shudder at the thought of a worm or a snake, since this might produce a fear of these creatures in the child, which is unfortunate as many are of considerable benefit to farmers and really quite harmless. Little garter snakes are fascinating to watch.

When enough suitable pictures have been located, the book can be assembled. One picture is glued onto a cardboard page with whatever material seems appropriate. The cat and dog would have fur bodies, the bird a feathered body, the snake a vinyl body, the lady's straw hat a burlap border, the dolly a smooth cotton dress and pieces of thick knitting wool for hair. Each page of these books provides interesting feeling experiences, colorful objects to look at, rich language to hear, an opportunity for you to use your imagination, and another wonderful opportunity for your baby to be with a parent in a warm loving situation.

Fun outdoors

It's possible for you to change your baby's environment by taking him with you as you move about your home doing household duties. This does make life a little more interesting for him than having to stay in a playpen or one room for most of the day, but it would be even more fun if he could get outside each day for just a short time. Even to get out on the balcony of the apartment, provided it is safe, if that is where he lives, is an important change for him. As always he has to be in a protected area under close supervision, but the pleasure he has more than compensates for the extra demand on his busy mother.

A back yard on a summer's day contains a wealth of interesting things to examine and unfortunately sometimes to mouth. But with a vigilant parent near, no harm is done and the baby learns quickly a great deal about his own back yard. Just to savor the cool green grass, feel the sun or breeze, find a pretty yellow dandelion, watch a buzzing honeybee or a chirping robin, and perhaps see a busy ant going about his business not only intrigues him, but, with a little language from you, starts his understanding of some of the wonders of his own garden. This is the place for lots of frolicking, for water play in his own plastic pool, and for almost any of those activities already mentioned, particularly the creative ones, since it is so much easier to clean up outside (a quick swish with the hose and the patio stones are clean again).

What a wonderful place also for a special romp with dad. A galloping ride on daddy's shoulders, a brief airplane swing, peek-a-boo around the lawn chair, and even a gentle toss in the air exhilarates the baby. If dad is sitting down, then a ride astride his foot, close to the ankle, usually brings requests for more. Dad is especially good at this kind of play and the squeals of delight leave no doubt about what his offspring thinks of this little bit of shared roughhousing. He is truly growing up; he has

learned to have confidence and trust in both his parents and he is eager for new challenges and adventures.

Summing up

Expanding horizons—not only for baby but for parents as well. How their baby has changed, from his sixth to his twelfth month. In just a short time he has become a mobile little being, curious and anxious to get into everything, with no inhibitions, no fears, and little realization of the consequences of his actions. He has gained tremendous control over his body, and some precocious babies are walking well and even saying several words. It has been a time of excitement and great change, a time of phasing in and phasing out of interests and behaviors. For example, from about seven to nine months, the baby of one of the authors was fascinated by buttons. Every morning the first thing he would do when he saw mom was to touch the buttons on her dressing gown. Then when it came time to say good-bye to dad the buttons on his jacket and shirt had to be examined, and the buttons on the backs of chairs, on other people's overcoats in supermarkets, on baby-sitters' sweaters, all had to be touched and pulled with aahs and ohs. Then, all of a sudden, he couldn't care less about buttons, and the morning game became one of holding up his teddy bear for mommy to hug, and of waving bye-bye to daddy as he left—after all, he was getting to be quite a big boy, and buttons are just for babies. The "button behavior" had phased out, and although he would point to a button when asked "Where is the button?" he was no longer captivated by them. Something else was more important.

The second half of the first year has been a time when parents have been able to capitalize on the spontaneous interests and activities of their baby. A small paper bag falls on the floor and baby finds it and begins to scrunch it up, pat it on the floor, and pull at it. Mother sees his interest in the paper and she can provide him with different textured papers, tissue paper, Kleenex, cardboard for him to scrunch and tear, wave and feel. He has shown an interest in something and she has followed through on his interest. Quite often a baby indicates his interest in something in this way, but we are just too busy or too unaware to bother expanding on it or working through it with him, and a wonderful opportunity for spontaneous play is lost. As the baby grows older, there will be many an opportunity for parents to latch onto the excitement that a child generates when he finds out something new all by himself and is eager to share his discoveries with them—but we must take the time when the opportunities are there.

The next stage—"into everything"—is about to begin.

4 Into

Everything

Twelve to Eighteen Months

There soon comes a time in the baby's life when mother may begin to hear herself saying endlessly, "No, please don't do that. No, no, dear, I'm sorry, but you can't play with that. Give it to mommy, that's a good boy." But of course he won't, or, more accurately, he can't give it to mommy. So she has to take it away from him under duress and there are howls of protest. However, in a very short time all is forgotten and forgiven and he totters off into the living room while mother tries once again to finish off whatever she was doing. Silence . . . In fact, it's just too silent. "What's going on in there?" And she rushes in just in case. It is too easy for a baby of this age to get himself into real danger no matter how careful parents have tried to be. But this time mother is greeted by a big smile as he is innocently dissecting a bit of fluff from the carpet. And so the day progresses, until by evening she is beginning to wonder if she is going to last another moment. This is a hectic time for mothers and babies alike.

Parents are thrilled at baby's walking, reaching, and exploring abilities and they marvel at the insatiable curiosity he demonstrates. But even the most perfect parents come to the end of their tether once in a while. It is during this period of the baby's life, even more so than in the first few months, that father can really help by being aware of just how taxing some babies in the thirteen-month-and-on age-group can be, and give mother a break. He may come home weary after a hard day at work and prefer nothing more than his dinner and some peace and quiet. Mother, equally weary, can hardly wait to see him. For as much as she has loved the day spent with her active baby, she could really use his help as well as enjoy some stimulating adult conversation. Both of them need a little extra support from each other at this time of the day. Mother can perhaps wait just a little until father has unwound before she asks him to take charge of the baby and he can be aware of just how much easier it will be for her to prepare and serve dinner if she is uninterrupted by a small child underfoot. And most important, of course, this is a perfect time for father to play on his own with his baby. For most fathers seem to have far too little time to spend with youngsters of this age before they must be off to bed for the night.

There is a lot of work involved. For, as the baby's horizons expand, it follows only naturally that he is going to get into everything. All kinds of things capture his interest, from fluff balls to the underside of the dining-room table, from the buttons on the seat of an upholstered chair as he picks away at them to the mountain of stairs towering above him—and stairs, of course, are made for climbing, as most babies seem to know. As baby becomes more mobile, both in terms of crawling and walking, parents might take a minute some evening to get down on all fours and crawl around from room to room noting carefully, as through a baby's eyes, just what a fascinating world exists there. At the same time note and take care of all the sharp-edged ends of screws under tables, dangling lamp cords behind tables, exposed electrical sockets, and so forth. Such childproofing is a valuable safety precaution and it will most certainly save at least some of the headaches of chasing around after an active baby and trying, at the same time, to maintain some order in the house.

When he is into everything, parents must, of course, closely
supervise his activities, and the removal of as many household

hazards as possible is one good way of lessening the possibility of an accident. Locking doors to danger areas like basements and cupboards containing drugs, toxic substances, and alcohol, installing gates on the stairs, keeping handles of pots and sharp knives well away from the edges of stovetops and countertops are a few precautions. It never ceases to amaze how quickly baby grows and how high he can reach, especially standing on tiptoe. There are bound to be some things which baby can get into and these hazards are going to be a never-ending temptation to a little fellow, who is remarkably unskilled at resisting temptations. Even when he has bumped his nose, skinned his elbows, or pinched his fingers on something that parents have repeatedly warned him about, once the hurt is soothed, back he goes sooner or later. What are parents going to do?

Parents have been warned about and have read about the dangers of spanking, of yelling at their child, of thwarting his natural curiosity by taking things away from him. It is no wonder that some parents are afraid to do anything. Parenting is not a *fait accompli*; it is a process of learning to bring up a child. It is a two-way process with baby and parent learning to adjust to each other, and each new day of his growth brings new joys as well as new challenges. Perhaps the most difficult challenge for many parents is controlling their child's unacceptable behavior. Spanking is the least effective way, but occasionally parents are going to lose their cool in spite of themselves. Sometimes they are going to raise their voices a little more than they had intended, and although the baby may not comprehend the actual words being used, he does respond to the raised tone of voice and understands that something is amiss. In the experience of the authors, the technique called distraction or redirection, together with consistent limits, has proved to be an effective way of handling the unacceptable behavior of most children. While the baby is being told that his behavior is unacceptable, his attention is shifted toward acceptable behavior, toward something else he can enjoy. The focus is on the positive. Spanking and a raised voice are limited in their usefulness because the more they are used, the more the child seems to tune out and the less effective the technique becomes.

In addition, one important fact about the child of this age, a fact which needs to be kept in mind even when he is older, is that he lacks the inner control over his behavior that adults have. He can't always stop himself from doing again what mother has just finished telling him not to do. And so, to help him in the long process of developing his own inner controls, his parents need to set the limits for him. That is, they are the ones who call the shots; they act as his inner control, and in this way they show him the acceptable boundaries of behavior. Nagging at a baby and punishing him for forgetting the rules are not appropriate. If he seems to be continually doing things his parents do not want him to do, then he must have a definite reason for doing it, as mentioned in Chapter 3 with regard to possible feeding problems. He may feel that he is not getting enough attention, and he knows a sure-fire way of forcing his parents to give him that attention is to get into mischief.

For example, the usually independent son (then fourteen months old) of one of the authors illustrates the above point precisely. On one occasion, after being left with the baby-sitter all day, Michael was playing on the floor at his mother's feet. Mom, somewhat weary, was busy reading the newspaper while supper was heating on the stove. After a few minutes of play, Michael got up, put his hand on mom's knee and jabbered expressively. With a cursory tussle of his hair and an "umm, hmm" she continued reading the paper. Not satisfied with this token acknowledgment, Michael walked over to "mommy's desk" and proceeded to sweep everything off it, with his arm stretched out as far as he could reach. During this time, he was stealing looks over his shoulder and "talking" in a stern voice, since mommy had often told him that the papers on the desk were hers, and

Michael's papers were on a shelf in a bookcase close by. He usually left mommy's papers alone, with an occasional test of the validity of the rules that mom had set by pulling off one paper or taking one pencil. This time, however, it was clear. The sweeping motion of the arm and the angry tone of the jabbering made the message very meaningful. He wanted mother's full attention, and why not—after all, she hadn't been with him all day!

Another reason for a baby's testing or mischievous behavior might be because he isn't sure whether or not a particular behavior is acceptable, for it seems to him that sometimes he does it and gets a laughing reaction from his parents, and yet doing the same thing on other occasions gets him into trouble with them. This kind of inconsistency makes it very confusing for him to know how to act. He relies on consistent messages from his parents and also on their everyday behavior as models for him to copy in order to learn how to behave in socially acceptable ways. By stressing the importance of the guiding and teaching role of the parents during this period and encouraging them to see the significance of the "into-everything" kinds of activities as being his need and his curiosity to explore the exciting world around him, parents can see the next few years not just as the hectic years, but as some of the most exciting and rewarding ones they will ever experience with their child.

His growth as a person, as a distinct person, takes a big leap during this twelve-to-eighteen-month period. He is hopelessly self-centered (or egocentric, as the textbooks say). All of his experiences are seen in terms of me and mine and he is very fuzzy about where the mine leaves off and the thine begins. Even at two years it won't be perfectly clear. He needs to establish his own self first, and once this is done he can begin to focus himself more on others around him. He enjoys carrying around treasured objects hugged close to his chest. He'll relinquish them briefly for mother to hug but they must be returned almost im- 109 mediately. He loves to hear the sound of his own voice and responds well to his name. He loves to have the parts of his body named. It is all great fun for him and he is sorting out just what goes with what and what belongs to him and what to others. This sorting-out process takes a while. His fascination for objects, people, and pets is boundless, yet he may show an apparent lack of consideration for things that get in his way. He may try to walk right through the dog lying peacefully in the doorway, trip over dad's extended foot, and pile into his toys lying on the floor in a most unconcerned manner. He is seeing the world only from his point of view, and when moving from point A to point B, he is fixed on his goal and not on the objects that get in the way on the floor. Objects seem to exist only for his pleasure and he assumes that they will respond to him as he pleases.

During this age period he is busy trying to do things for himself. Or maybe he is asking himself, "Can I do it?" And so he struggles to push and pull the big living-room chair; he strains to reach the doorknob and bangs at it, knowing that when you do something like this the door opens: "I've seem mom do it a million times, but I just can't seem to get it right." Or on that big occasion when dad is carrying him about and comes to a light switch, and shows baby how to switch the light on and off. From then on the light switch is a never-ending source of pleasure for him—the thrill of being able to cause such a big result all by himself! The baby is trying out his skills, increasing his competence, and imitating the adults around him. He sees the adult doing so much more than he is able to do and it is easy to empathize with the great frustrations he has to cope with from this age until he is fairly well into the school years.

This age period also heralds the birth of the first intelligible words for most babies. They are old hands at babbling and gesture language, and the months that mother has been talking to him, describing his world to him, reading out of books and so on are now beginning to pay off in his expanding use of words. Of course, such maternal attention has also been paying off in fostering the close emotional warmth between mother and infant ever since his birth. Mother and baby have sung together and imitated each other. Now he may begin to pick up one or two particular sounds and repeat them over and over. This repetition of favorite sounds is important in the way that the repeating of motor activities of an earlier age was important. For practice makes perfect, and the more practice he gets the easier it is for him to plug into the world around him. It may be "hello" or "bye-bye," and for many babies it is "what's that?" which comes out more typically as "wazzat?" Whatever the words, he does love to hear the sound of his own voice and the responses of his parents. If he has picked up "bye-bye" he'll usually love to accompany the sound with the action. And it is amusing that at this age he'll often wave bye-bye and say the words just after the visitor has closed the door—a frustrating experience for a mother eager to show off her baby's talents. There are lots of sounds in his vocabulary now and many are wordlike and a few are actual words. They are the elements of the language spoken in the home and the baby is repeating what he hears around him. Of course, when he puts together a particular combination of sounds by chance and gets a big reaction from his parents it seems to follow that he will tend to repeat these sounds, and so language progresses.

At this age he can understand far more than he himself is able to put into words. By hearing his parents speak in a natural, uncomplicated way, he learns the rhythmic cadence of language. He will probably have his own special pronunciation of the few words he is learning, and in fact they may be understood only by mother and father. However, he is getting his message across and parents can reinforce his efforts by using the standard pronunciation of words. Baby talk is both baby's mispronunciation of words and a way that parents speak to baby, using shortened, silly labels for words. As baby grows, his ability to enunciate improves, but if parents carry on such baby talk, it means he has two languages to learn instead of one. Unfortunately, it becomes downright upsetting for his social development if he has carried baby talk on until the nursery-school age, since his special idiosyncratic labels may only be understood by himself and his parents and are likely to be incomprehensible to playmates, teachers, and other adults.

His use of language is a great help to his developing intellectual skills. Words are symbols standing for all the aspects of the big world around him. Words allow him to work with thoughts, actions, and feelings, to juggle them around easily in his mind, and, most important, to communicate with others. Words weigh nothing and can be carried around in his head by the millions, with room to spare. They are there to facilitate his thinking and understanding of abstractions like the permanence of objects, and the classification of objects into groups (such as dogs, cats, balls, trucks, et cetera). Language has been called an important mediator, the facilitator of intellectual growth and understanding.

Toward the end of the eighteenth month, his language is becoming more specific. For example, the word "num-num" used to suffice for all food and drink, but now he is able to attach a label to at least a few of his favorites, such as juice, milk, and cookie. In addition he is also beginning to get the idea that a picture of an object stands for the real object. One day he may quite unexpectedly give the word "dog" to a dog he meets on his walk with mother and later as she is reading him a story he suddenly points to a picture of a dog and calls it "dog." The connection has been made and the general concept of dog and its verbal symbol "dog" are now part of his language repertoire.

A lot is going on in his mind and body during these years of growth, and as language develops and his ability to move around increases, the kinds of concerns and stresses on parents will change. The thirteen-to-eighteen-month period takes a lot of stamina on the part of parents. For their baby makes many heavy demands on their ingenuity to protect him from physical dangers which he unwittingly exposes himself to in his mad rush to grow. He forces them to make major policy decisions as to how they are going to help him learn to behave in an acceptable way, and by the end of this period there may be toilet training to consider for a few babies. At this age and for some years to come he is dependent on the care and attention of his parents, for it is through them that he tests the tenor of the outside world.

Up to this time baby has been doing most of his getting around by crawling and certainly from his point of view learning to crawl was a great breakthrough after having to sit in one spot until someone rescued him. But baby has been an interested spectator and he has been spending a lot of time observing his world, particularly the people in it. He has noticed the ease with which parents get around. He has also noticed that their hands are wonderfully free to carry things, to reach, feel, and manipulate objects in a way he never can. He has to stop moving once he has reached his desired goal, get himself into sitting position, and only then are both hands free to manipulate his treasure. Oh, how he longs to walk by himself! He has been trying and has managed some walking with the aid of furniture and the helping hand of an accommodating parent. But this has limited his scope and thwarted to some degree the feelings of independence that had flourished when he mastered crawling. This conflict may precipitate a change in personality that parents cannot fail to notice. Where previously their child was a busy, happy baby, he now seems too easily irritated and frustrated; he is no longer interested in many of his favorite toys; he demands in no uncertain terms to be walked at every opportunity and is not really content unless he is walking. The struggle to master this monumental task is one that requires the baby's total involvement. To some degree his language may also be affected. He seems to have regressed in the production of sounds, he is not

vocalizing to the extent he was before, and parents are understandably upset at this new development. All his emotional, intellectual, and physical energies must be devoted to this new challenge and nothing else seems to be of importance to him.

Once parents understand the significance of their baby's struggle and hence his change in personality, they can accept the situation with some equilibrium, knowing their child will return to his former happy self once he is walking and his independence is regained. This is a somewhat stressful period for both mother and baby, but she can lessen his frustration and give him opportunities for walking by reorganizing his environment and planning special walking activities. These will not necessarily speed up his walking ability, but they may help him gain confidence in himself while providing, at the same time, different and interesting experiences.

Walking activities

Because your baby likes your company and your very necessary support, his favorite walking pastime is the one where you actively participate by holding his hands as he leads you in and out of each room and back again. Since you do not always have as much time as he would like, in order to give him some extra practice, which he dearly loves, you can rearrange the stable pieces of furniture so that he can travel around the room independently but holding onto something sturdy. The imaginative mother can regroup her furniture in many ways so that there is some variety in the journeys. Placing the pieces in a square, or a circle, or a bit of a zigzag are a few of the ways this can be managed without too much trouble for you. Of course, as your baby gets adept, the spaces between can be widened so that there is a real challenge. It sometimes helps him get started on this new mode of traveling if some of his favorite toys are placed on different chairs.

Any large cushion placed on the floor so that the baby has to walk over it makes a novel little jaunt, particularly if there are a series of cushions spaced about a foot apart. He has to go up, over, down, several times before he comes to the end of his roadway. Using other pillows of different sizes and thicknesses so that the ups and downs are varied adds to the complexity. It may also help the baby to begin to be a little more aware of the objects on the floor when he is walking. Many parents have been disconcerted when their child walks over the cat's tail. He is so goal-oriented that he does not really see the objects in his way as he moves toward his goal.

You can promote another task while still actively participating, if you are fortunate enough to have several large but inexpensive books that could stand a little walking on without undue damage. Three or four books placed together, end to end, until the roadway is about three feet long, make a fine walkway. Two books about the same size are placed on top, end to end, similar to a little pyramid. Sit beside your construction, which baby has been busy observing in the making, and with a few instructions and a helping hand, encourage him to try this new hurdle. If the books are not quite the same thickness the uneven surface does make it interestingly complex, and with you there, these new difficulties are easily overcome and new skills are perfected. At first it may be necessary for you to place one of his feet on the first level, and then the other foot, in order to help him understand just what is required. "Let's go up the step, Johnny. Put your foot here, now the other one here. See, you stepped up. Good boy. Move across and down the other side. That wasn't hard to do, was it?" It is quite likely baby will turn around and start back again. In fact, he may continue to do so several times until he is proficient. Another book placed on top (in the center) adds a little more variation to the activity.

Sometimes if dad has a few 2″ x 8″ planks left over from one of his own building projects, these can be cut into the appropriate lengths and used for this same task, especially if there are no books you want walked on, no matter how lightly. This same kind of plank can be used for a novel kind of obstacle course for the baby. Several blocks of different sizes, shapes, and lengths spaced about a foot apart are fastened firmly to the plank. Masking tape works quite well if dad does not want nails used. By holding onto your baby's hand he is encouraged to step onto the plank and wend his way over the course. He's pretty proud of himself when he reaches the end, and so he should be.

With these walking activities, you are teaching your baby the technique for going up and down stairs and you must remember that now the stairs will have to be barricaded securely, since they are a tantalizing challenge to a child who has just learned about going up and down. He should not be denied this experience, however, because it is excellent for his motor development, but only under the watchful eye of a parent.

"Push-and-pull" toys give the baby additional incentives to walk (it is doubtful if he really needs them), and while there are a number of good imaginative ones on the market today, many very satisfactory ones can be made from materials around the home. One half of the top of the long plastic egg cartons with a couple of pipe cleaners for antennae and a string of little bells at the end makes a beautiful caterpillar. Large empty spools of thread strung together with big buttons in between make a lovely wiggly worm, even more so if a few bells are attached to the end. The left-over cardboard of cylinders from toilet-paper rolls strung together with empty spools in between make another kind of caterpillar. Shoe boxes fastened together with a toilet-paper cylinder for a stack makes a great train, especially if a baby's shoe box is added at the end for a caboose. Any round carton with noise makers inside (buttons, bells, metal spoons, lids, or stones) and securely fastened makes an even more interesting pull toy as new sounds are produced with each movement. Shortened broom handles or short pieces of wood, like a   117 ruler, can be attached to the egg carton so that the "caterpillar" can be pushed. The cartons with sound makers can also be turned into push toys with similar pieces of wood. An eye screw is easily attached to the end of the broom handle and connected to the box or carton with a short piece of string. With all these push-and-pull toy creations the baby will get lots of walking as he travels around the house with his imaginary companions.

Some babies have more initiative than mothers really appreciate, especially when they take to pushing light kitchen chairs all over the house. Investing in a walker wagon is one way to get around this.

Simple gross motor activities

By removing the blocks, the same plank mentioned above can be used for a new game. "Walking the plank," whether on a broad fence or a railway track, has been a challenge children have enjoyed through the ages. Some babies are eager to try this game, others are a little more hesitant, but most are too curious not to have a bit of a try at it. Initially, if the plank is placed flat on the floor, even those hesitant ones are off and running, particularly if mother is there with her helping hand.

After a few excursions without help, your baby has mastered the problem and is ready for something a little more difficult. The plank is raised 1½″ off the floor by placing a couple of old magazines under each end. This does add an interesting complication and he is raring to go. After a little initial help from you, your baby may want to venture along the plank on his own, reassured, of course, by the fact that you are close by if he needs your help. The plank can be used again for an "incline" problem. As with each new experience, try to make it interesting but not frustrating. Slips can be avoided by placing strips of masking tape along the plank. Then, to begin, place a couple of magazines at one end so that there is a gentle slope, and with an encouraging hand your baby starts off. After a few times, over a period of several "walks," he discovers he can manage on his own. He is pleased with himself. Once the baby learns he can manage a good many of his daily problems successfully, he is more able as he grows older to deal with a little less success without loss of self-esteem. Because he has experienced lots of success in his early years, he knows he can succeed and that he is in no way a failure if he does not always achieve his goal. In the reverse situation, the child who has experienced little success and much failure comes to feel in later life that he is a failure when he is unable to achieve his goal.

If there still seems to be some interest in the incline task, you can raise the end more with some additional magazines. With two planks placed end to end and both resting squarely on the same pile of magazines, you have introduced an up-and-down problem that requires a little more care and dexterity. But your baby is game and eager for new experiences once he has developed some balancing skills. Rearranging the raised planks so that they form a right-angle roadway is a little more complicated, but not so complicated as to dissuade that small voyager from trying. Raising the planks just a bit higher from the floor further challenges the baby, but he will attempt it if you are there for moral, if not actual, support. You are such a satisfactory person to have around and his contented smile tells you so.

Tunneling games can be made, again utilizing the planks. The two boards are placed on chairs so that a long bridge is made, which is then covered with an old sheet and, voilà—a tunnel for your baby to crawl through. Covering the kitchen table with a large sheet makes a great instant tent and what a wonderful hideaway for you and your child when dad comes home and pretends he can't find you. It's even a cozy place for a story or two. Grocery cartons with the ends cut out make exceptional tunnels if there is sufficient space for several to be placed end to end. This kind of game may require a recreation room or a long hallway for really satisfactory results, but a back yard on a warm summer's day is even better.

Rearranging the furniture by moving a chair here or a chair there can provide a detour problem that can be stimulating and exciting for a baby. With you peeking from behind a chair he can see you, but how to reach you? It may be he will have to be shown, and if he is having too much difficulty the first time, you must help out or it won't be any fun at all. With the chairs arranged as a barricade with an opening at one end, you can instruct him how to reach you by pointing to the opening as you call to him. "Here's the opening, come and get me. Oh, you're a smart little lad." Once your baby gets the idea, the opening can be changed so that he realizes he has a problem to solve and must move along the barricade until he finds the new opening. Given the opportunity, babies will demonstrate over and over again their problem-solving abilities. One of the authors had an occasion to appreciate this ability when she noticed an eighteen-month-old child with a problem. She had a paper cup in one hand and a ball in the other. For some reason known only to herself, she wanted to put the ball in the cup, and she had the idea, correctly as it turned out, that it should fit. Unfortunately, she had grasped the cup by the rim so that several of her fingers covered a part of the opening, and each time she tried to put the ball in, it wouldn't fit. She seemed reluctant to drop the ball on the ground, so she had a problem. After some deliberation, she came to a decision. She put the cup to her mouth (in a broad sense she was using her mouth as a third hand), firmly grasped the rim with her teeth, then released her hand and reclasped the cup around the middle. The cup was removed from her mouth and the ball placed into it securely. She was pleased and satisfied —it was an impressive achievement.

Bouncing on the bed has been a favorite pastime for children of all ages and many a bed has been bounced right into the repair shop. But bouncing is an excellent gross motor activity and with the advent of trampolines an opportunity for children of all ages to enjoy this exhilarating form of exercise has been provided. The regular-sized trampolines are much too large for little ones but there is now available a smaller model. Because it has a handle for support, it is eminently suitable for babies, even those not yet able to walk but able to stand. It is amazing how quickly they get the idea and soon are bouncing with great glee. As always, the small child needs close supervision when using this kind of equipment, as it is easy for an unsuspecting baby to bounce right off the trampoline onto the floor.

Ball play has been fun for the baby for some time and a new version can easily be arranged by placing a small beach ball in one of those handy open-weave shopping bags. The end is tied with sturdy string or elastic to a beam or hook in the ceiling and the baby can be shown how to hit the ball so that it moves, or, if on an elastic, to pull it down and release it. To strike it so that the return swing doesn't hit the player takes lots of practice, but it is good fun even if there is an odd bop on the head. Parents may not be too pleased about having a ball hanging from their ceiling, and if a recreation room is not available or suitable, a hook placed in a doorway is not too conspicuous and serves the baby just as well. Attaching the ball in a similar manner to a sturdy tree limb provides many happy playtimes outside.

Fine motor activities

Since your baby has already been exposed to some simple eye-hand co-ordination tasks he is ready to begin experimenting with more complex forms and this is a place where the handy one-pound coffee container can be used again. This time you retrieve some one-inch-square wooden blocks that your baby used to bang together when he was younger and the small rubber balls used in the first "hole-in-the-pot" game. Two openings are made in the plastic lid, one square, one round, and each just a little larger than the object. The blocks and the balls have to be almost the same size so that the one object will not fit into the other shaped opening. All too often the ball will fit into the square opening and a clever baby soon figures this out and then there is no problem. Perhaps this should be stated in another way: your baby has solved the problem even if it is not exactly the way you had expected or planned. There is no doubt about it, babies keep finding the easy solution to a problem so parents have to be one jump ahead all the time.

As your baby is already familiar with the round shape and its corresponding opening, it is a good idea to start again with the ball. A little success makes for a good beginning and whets his appetite for more. After the usual preliminary manipulation, you suggest that he put the ball in the hole. He has two choices where previously he only had one, and a decision must be made. It is possible he may recognize the correct opening, but at this age it is more than likely he has not yet developed much discriminating ability and may resort to the very acceptable method of trial and error. He randomly tries the ball in the square opening and it doesn't fit, but with a few encouraging words from you, "Try it in the round hole here," he may see the other possibility, with happy results. If the task seems too complicated for your baby, and it is a bit complicated, you can demonstrate the solution a few times, labeling the objects and mentioning what you are doing. "I'm putting the ball in the round hole, and the block in the square hole. Oh, oh, where did they go?" He is pretty sure he knows where the objects went and tries to pry the lid off. Hopefully, he succeeds, retrieves the ball and block and indicates he would like another try. If this is the case, all well and good, but if not, you should keep in mind the game was offered so you and your baby could spend time with each other in an enjoyable way. If it is not fun or interesting the cues from your child tell you to offer the game some other time.

As he masters the task, a third geometric-shaped opening—a

triangle, for example—can be added. It may be that a larger-sized can is needed here. Incidentally, the triangle should be an equilateral triangle (that is, all sides the same length), otherwise the problem becomes much too difficult. Your baby may recognize the shape but he is not yet able to see the subtle differences, particularly those of the isosceles triangle, which has two sides the same length and one different, so he is frequently frustrated when the triangle won't fit in an opening he feels it should fit in. This is a problem for an older child.

Geometric-shaped puzzles are good corollaries to the "hole-in-the-can" game. If dad can make a geometric form board (see Appendix), a number of tips might be useful. Fairly small, light-weight shapes are a must for tiny hands, otherwise the baby will be too busy just holding on to give much thought to the next step. It is a great help if there is a little knob in the middle for him to hold, but unless it is securely fastened, he will work at the knob until he has it loose. The danger here, of course, is in the possibility that he may mouth it and accidentally swallow it. Dad can avoid this hazard by screwing and gluing the knob. If epoxy glue is used there is little chance a baby will be able to budge it—not that he won't give it a good try. The openings into which the inserts fit should be sufficiently large so that there is an easy fit and deep enough so that they don't fall out once they are in. The pieces should be painted bright primary colors, as babies seem to like these best, and they should be made geo-metrically accurate so that appropriate labels can be used. Any triangle should be equilateral for the reasons given above.

With your baby in a happy frame of mind and when there are a few extra minutes, hopefully one of those fairly regular times that your baby has begun to count on and look forward to, the opportunity is right for the form-board task and the round piece is offered first. He may already have the idea, in which case other pieces are offered one at a time. With the addi-tion of several pieces he may be interested in just examining and manipulating them rather than in putting each piece in its correct opening. He is playing with them, doing his own thing, and should not be pressed to do otherwise if he shows no inclina-tion. You can still interject lots of language, pointing out vari-ous concepts, noting actions, emphasizing prepositions, "Oh, the red circle rolled under the table," and with frequent fondling and warm smiles, you tell him he is a wonderful baby.

Even when very young, baby was fond of putting objects in and out of cans and is still interested in doing the same thing if there is a new twist. Stacking toys are easily obtained in most good toy stores and are excellent for a beginning, but with a little imagination you can add a new twist for a bit more relish. The kitchen cupboard contains the makings of a stacking-can game. The tomato-paste can fits inside the small frozen-orange-juice can, which in turn fits inside the larger juice can, which in turn fits inside the baked-beans can, and so on. In no time at all you have several suitable cans and with the sharp edges carefully taped (adhesive tape is very good) so that there is no danger of cut fingers, you are ready to begin improvising. If you are lucky enough to have various kinds of fabric, all the same color, you can put a piece of fabric around each can. In this way you have added a tactile component to the stacking task. Your baby has the fun of putting cans together while enjoying a unique feeling experience. You can also put various grades of sandpaper around each can so that the feeling experience emphasizes rough or not so rough. For a really novel experience, glue fur on one can, leather on another, rough burlap on another, velvet on another, and smooth satin on another. You can even glue small stones to a can if you use safe epoxy glue. What a wide variety of experiences to go along with the stacking game! When the cans are ready, you offer three to begin with, and after your baby has done his thing, you show him how they fit one into the other if he has not already discovered this for himself. As other cans are offered the problem becomes more complex and fascinating. Because no one knows your baby better than you do, you are the best judge of how difficult it should be and, as long as he is enjoying the experience, you are on the right track. Just before your baby seems finished playing, you can show him how to stack the cans in a tower. Placed side by side they make steps for a tiny doll to walk up and down. Reverse stacking has them all disappear under one big can. Where did they all go? Your baby knows and he demonstrates how he knows. He's nobody's fool, that's for sure.

Some mothers save lots of things, many of which they have no immediate use for. Nursery-school teachers do this all the time and are rewarded many times over by finding a special use for something that would normally be discarded. Boxes of all sizes fit in this category, and for the small child the little ones are the most appropriate.

We mentioned small jewelry boxes in the previous chapter, but with more maturity other more complex boxes can be introduced, still using all those treasures which captivate your baby's interest. Occasionally dad will come across the plastic containers that hold typewriter ribbons and will recognize what a prize he has. This is a little harder than the jewelry box, and if your baby is having a bit too much trouble you might try opening it partway to help give him the idea.

The Q-tip box with its drawer-type opening is much more complex, and you might want to minimize failure by demonstrating a few times and leaving the drawer partly opened. The little surprise inside encourages him to persevere and you can judge from his efforts how far open the drawer should be. On occasion, a parent finds Band-Aid containers made of metal with the lid fastened on one side. This makes another little task that can be made easy or difficult, depending on how hard you close the lid. The first attempt should, of course, be engineered so that success is assured and the baby will then be encouraged to persist with the activity.

Little rubber squeeze toys should not be overlooked. They are a delight for him, and if they are the right size he can manage them easily and make his own sound when and how often he wants to. While he is enjoying his rubber toy he is developing strength in his hands and fingers, as well as a certain amount of precision. These toys can be squeezed, bitten, mouthed, banged, and rubbed against objects or self in a number of ways to produce many squeaky sounds.

Block play is a time-honored activity that gives children great pleasure, and even greater opportunities to expand their fantasies in a very practical way. This kind of creativity, however, needs to be nurtured with lots of opportunities, lots of time, and lots of variously sized blocks. For a start, the very young child responds better to block building if he is only offered a few at a time. While he has been offered blocks before, his experience with them has been limited, and even though he is always interested in trying something new, he may need a little guidance. Providing him with a pile of blocks and a "Now build something," is not too helpful. He does not have enough experience, nor does he yet have a fully developed imagination for this type of play. He has to learn about the primary building qualities of blocks and then he can begin to participate in the imaginary world. But you are there and, along with dad, are one of his most important teachers. You show him how to build a little tower after he has had his own time to play with the blocks. First a two- or three-block tower and then, as his skills improve, taller ones. A few blocks of different sizes help a great deal, as your baby can start with the large one (hopefully you can manage to arrange this unnoticed) and begins to build as you watch quietly. If he starts with a small one and then tries to add a larger one he soon learns his tower will fall. At this point he may become discouraged, frustrated, or uninterested, and you should switch to another aspect. Blocks make roadways, tunnels, bridges, even garages for little cars and this is great fun. With a little quiet language, "Your red car is going under the bridge, on the roadway and into the blue garage," you are able to point out in a natural and purposeful way concepts, actions, prepositions, and so on, and while your baby does not understand, he will eventually if exposed to language in this way. He is learning by doing, in a warm accepting atmosphere with a loving parent as a companion.

The pressboard material that dad uses near his workbench to hold some of his tools makes a very acceptable pegboard for the baby. A small piece of 12" x 12" board is more than enough, and with a few colored pegs from the toyshop, an inexpensive but appropriate fine motor task is concocted. Because the pegs are small, there will have to be close supervision to avoid any mishaps. Unfortunately mouthing, which is such a marvelous way for him to find out about things, will have to be discouraged in this case, but with distraction this is usually no great problem. You show him how the pegs fit in and invite him to place one in a hole. The customary way a baby holds a peg—that is, by grabbing it with his whole hand—leaves only a short section free to maneuver into the hole, but he manages to put it in, even though it seems ready to fall out. If it looks unsteady, you might give an unobtrusive push to secure the peg. Unobtrusive because you do not want to seem to be interfering. You'll have to be quick, however, as one of the authors found out when she once tried to be unobtrusive. Peter, eighteen months, noticed what had occurred but didn't seem to resent the interference because he was too interested in trying to understand how it had been managed—how the peg had been pushed right in to the head. He tried another peg, and once in, flattened it in with the palm of his hand. The added force was too much, the peg fell out and Peter looked for help. The author indicated her index finger and proceeded to demonstrate. Understanding was immediate. Peter's index finger was singled out and he had another try. This new operation took even more precision, but after some persistence, his chubby little finger was hitting the peg right on. He still wasn't able to put the peg in with just his thumb and index finger, but he certainly knew what to do to keep it from falling out once it was in. Happily it wasn't too long before he mastered the task using two fingers.

As baby gets closer to eighteen months, he will be interested in refining his co-ordination this way and you can show him how it is done. Again appropriate language during the activity enriches the experience. Generally one doesn't think of a baby of this age as capable of stringing beads, but with the right material it is possible and enjoyable, and further develops fine motor skills. Safety is always a factor and the pieces used for beading have to be fairly large. Good-sized buttons with enlarged holes, milk-bottle tops, small empty spools of thread, and small plastic lids with large holes all make suitable "beads." Empty adhesive-tape rollers can also be used for this activity. The toy shop usually has a good assortment of attractive and colorful wooden beads as well. The key to successful "stringing" for baby lies with the string. It has to be somewhat rigid so that he can hold it at least one inch from the end in order to be able to push it through far enough for easy grabbing before it slips out. So often a long shoestring is offered but baby is not able to manage it because the metal end is too short for his purposes. As a rule a child holds the bead in his left hand and pushes the string through with his right. Once the cord is through the hole sufficiently, he lets go with his right hand and grasps the end. If it hasn't been pushed through far enough, misfortune is inevitable. Scotch-taping about two inches of the end should alleviate the problem. With mother there for help, approval, and language, "stringing beads" becomes a pleasant challenge.

A "stick" problem is one of those problems that has to be spontaneous to be fun. That is, you understand, those situations which are likely to be resolved with the help of some sort of a stick. This is not to suggest that such a challenge can't be arranged, it can, but it usually happens often enough in conjunction with some other activity to give the baby the opportunity to practice this skill. The stick problem, briefly, is one where the baby's arm is not long enough to retrieve something and he needs some sort of object that will act as an extension of his arm. Rulers, spatulas, and wooden spoons are just a few of the items that can be used in this way. Frequently during an activity such as ball play, the ball rolls under the radiator or heavy chair too far out of reach for the baby. You have your favorite retrieving spoon ready and show him how to use it. Once the idea is learned, he has little trouble applying this principle to other situations. Retrieving objects, especially those on the other side of his back-yard fence, is resolved easily with a handy stick. With such a clever baby, you cannot minimize your vigilance, even though he may seem quite safe in his own back yard.

You can make an excellent task for developing fine motor skills by using the tactile book principle. Each page of material has two pieces which are closed in a variety of ways—by a button, by a zipper, by a large dome fastener, or by a large hook and eye. In each instance the task should be made as easy as possible. Some dome fasteners are much too tight and some buttonholes are too small for the corresponding button: don't use them.

Cognitive activities

Everything a baby does or thinks is cognitive. In order to simplify the categories of activities, cognitive activities will be designated as those that require more intellectual problem-solving ability than motor ability.

Simple one-, two- and three-piece puzzles, of which most good toyshops have a plentiful supply, are abstract enough in shape for the baby who has been playing with geometric form boards and is now ready for more challenges. These puzzles require more concentration and manipulation as the baby tries to figure out how these funny-looking pieces fit in those funny-shaped openings. Puzzles of dogs, cats, fruits, and vegetables are favorites, and also provide good opportunities for rich language. The puzzles should be realistic-looking if children of this age are to understand the real world. And they should also be in correct proportion to each other. One common puzzle has several fruits of almost the same size, whereas, in reality, some fruits are larger than others—the watermelon is larger than the banana, the orange is larger than the strawberry. If a young child ever saw these two pairs of fruits together, and this is certainly possible, he would have some difficulty understanding that this particular fruit puzzle represented real fruit. The watermelon has another unfortunate defect. One end is slightly less round than the other, and while this may be true with real watermelons, it does require discrimination well beyond the capability of a very young child.

He does not understand why the piece won't fit, since both ends appear the same to him. The only solution lies in dad's sanding both ends so that it makes no difference which end he tries where. In addition, the pineapple piece has several pointed ends and is quite difficult to master. Rounding out the ends as well as sanding the rest of the fruit reduces the size and the angles so that it becomes more possible for your baby to achieve success. Some children enjoy the challenge of a puzzle where each insert is similar but placed at a different angle. For example, three diamond shapes exactly alike are placed so that each insert is at a different angle to the others: one is straight up and down, one leaning slightly to the right, and the third is on a horizontal plane. The baby has to do sufficient experimental manipulation before he has all the pieces in their correct places.

When the opportunity presents itself for puzzle play, you can help your baby choose one. If a two- or three-piece puzzle has been selected, you can facilitate matters by starting with one piece; for instance, in the case of an animal puzzle the head or some other part that seems least complicated. The baby is shown how it fits and after you have surreptitiously arranged the pieces so that they will fit with minimum effort you suggest that he has a try. If he is successful with the first piece then another can be introduced in the same way until the picture is complete. The first few times may not interest the baby for long, but he will get more intrigued as time goes by if he is given enough pleasant opportunities, is offered different two- and three-piece puzzles to solve, and is not pressed to finish the picture when he is not so inclined. Once he understands the concept involved, he then has the basic tools to go on to more abstract puzzles as he gets older.

Matching tasks are not usually considered suitable for babies of this age but with a simplified version they can provide a lot of enjoyment along with some learning. Hopefully, you have a reservoir of pictures you have been saving and now is the time to sort through them and find pictures of objects that are available in your home—a cup, a banana, a ball, a toothbrush, and a flower are a few examples. You glue each picture on a sturdy piece of cardboard and gather up the real objects the pictures portray. After your baby has looked this odd assortment over to his satisfaction you show him a picture and ask him to find the object the picture represents. "Look, Johnny, see the picture of the yellow banana. Where is the real banana? Oh, you know, that's really great." This game is one that can be repeated over and over again with several sets in many different combinations. It is also an excellent way to reinforce the baby's understanding that pictures represent real objects.

A slightly more complex variation of this game is a picture matching task where a picture is matched with an exact duplicate. Stickers with good pictures are available in most stationery shops and are excellent for this purpose. To start, you might glue four stickers on four pieces of sturdy cardboard, two of a dog and two of a flower. Both are quite different objects, to make discrimination and matching easier. They are mixed together, and when your baby picks one up he is encouraged to find another just like it. Whether he picks up the correct match or another one, you need not be discouraged. "Where's the flower? Oh, you picked up a picture of a dog. Can you find the flower picture?" If he doesn't seem to comprehend, and this should really be no surprise since this task is quite a challenge, you go on, "Here's the flower. I found it. It's the same kind of flower as the one you have, isn't it?" Once he gets the idea, and this may take several unpressured play sessions, over a period of time, then you can make it more intriguing by adding more pairs of pictures a few at a time.

By the time the baby is nearing eighteen months, he has been exposed through play, music, and language to the various parts of his body, particularly his face. He has pretty well sorted out all the component parts of his face as well as those of his parents. He has no trouble identifying eyes, ears, mouth, and nose and is ready for a little problem-solving task involving these parts. You can either find good pictures of eyes, ears, mouth, and nose or draw them each on a piece of strong cardboard. Then cut them to shape and attach a small piece of adhesive tape to the back. Next, find a plain, plastic-coated paper plate, draw a few strands of hair at the top and present it to baby. "We're going to make a face, Johnny. Here is his eye, here is the other eye, and here is his nose. Now he has a face. Oh, oh, that doesn't look right. What's missing?" He may not be too sure what is missing; he knows the face doesn't look right but just what is lacking is not clear. You give him the answer as you gently touch his own mouth. "I think his mouth is missing, isn't it?" The mouth is added and the picture is completed. He may not have found this idea all that great, and if so, forget it for a while and try to introduce it again some other time with a different part missing. Chances are he will soon be enjoying the problem, quickly noticing what is missing and placing the part in the correct spot. If there seems an opportunity to reverse the roles so that you are doing the guessing, it should not be ignored. Your baby loves trying to fool you.

If his parents are at all artistic, the task can easily be expanded. A picture of a dog is drawn as the baby watches. "I'm drawing a picture of a dog. Here are his eyes, his mouth, his tail, and his ears. Oh dear, something is missing. What have I forgotten, Johnny?" Johnny may or may not indicate his own nose. If he doesn't, you point out what is missing. If he does, you respond, "That's right, I didn't give him a nose, did I? Poor dog." The possibilities for variety are endless, and even more so as your baby gets older and becomes more observant.

Sorting is another task that requires matching ability. To begin, of course, you have to decide what to sort, and while there are many concepts which can be sorted, baby up to this time has been exposed to only a few, primarily color, shape, and size. He seems to enjoy working with colors, and even though he may not recognize any, if he has been exposed, along with explanatory language, he is probably beginning to get the idea. Sorting is another way to reinforce this learning. Red and blue balls or blocks are perfect for a start. The balls have the same properties—form, size, and weight—with the exception of color. The task is prepared, all the red balls go in one box and all the blue balls go in the other box. Incidentally, painting the inside of the boxes red and blue does provide another helpful clue for baby. When all is ready, the balls are produced and played with. After they have been rolled, bounced, hidden, examined, and manipulated to baby's satisfaction you bring out the boxes and ask your baby

135

to help you put the balls in. If he is not too sure he likes this (he may think the ball game is finished), you can reassure him and tell him you are just going to play with the red balls, and you should be sure you do after they have been sorted. You might also tell him it is another game and the balls are not going to be put away if he still wants to play. As with all activities you explain and demonstrate what is required and invite your baby to participate. Because he is not too sure about colors he puts a red ball in the blue box or vice versa. No matter, you respond in your usual positive way, "Hey, you decided to put a red ball in the blue box. Can you put it in the red box over here, with the other red balls? Oh, my pet, you are clever. Where's another red ball to put in?"

Clothes-pegs, plastic cutlery, large buttons, and blocks can all be used for sorting, provided each set of objects has all the same characteristics except one. The plastic spoons are red and white, the buttons are exactly the same except some are blue and some are red. As the baby begins to understand more fully the concept of color, other colors can be introduced with equal enjoyment.

In a continuous, ongoing way, your baby has been exposed in his daily life to many concepts, particularly those of feeling, tasting, and seeing, in which differences have been both apparent and subtle. The warm water looks the same as cool water but certainly feels different, sugar and salt look the same but certainly taste different, both balls are red but one is big and one is little. The baby perceives these differences but does not yet fully understand how to utilize this information. He will still try to put big things in little spaces but he is learning and can be encouraged in this learning through little discriminatory games played with you.

Because colors are still of interest, here is another color-sorting task. You need to find four containers exactly the same, except one is a different color. Plastic or paper cups in primary colors are excellent for this purpose. In addition, a small intriguing object, preferably one your baby has not seen before—a tiny plastic telephone, a gay little penguin, or even a Cheerio— suitable for hiding under one of the cups completes the preparations.

The game begins with your baby's usual examination of the cups and the object. When he is finished, you tell him you are going to hide the object. You put it under the blue cup, which you have conveniently placed close to his right hand. That is probably where he will look first, and there is nothing like a little success to whet his appetite. "I've hidden it under the blue cup, can you find your telephone?" If he has been watching, this may not be too much of a challenge, so next time drop a piece of cardboard in front of the cups so that your actions cannot be seen, remove it quickly and again invite him to play. "Look under the blue cup and find your telephone. Good boy! You found it under the blue cup." The game is repeated if he seems interested, but next time the blue cup is not left in the same position. He may look under the blue cup on your request, and he may not. Again, whichever one he chooses, respond accordingly. "Oh, you looked under the red cup. I bet your telephone is under the blue cup." A little more interest can be engendered if mother substitutes a different object each time. The baby never knows what his new surprise will be (besides, he may be reluctant to give up his surprise once he has found it). Once he has the hang of it a change can be made by using three blue cups and one red one and eventually other colors. In time your baby will develop more understanding and other more complex problem-solving discriminatory tasks can be planned for him.

Creative activities

Now that your baby is well beyond his first birthday he will be looking for new ideas to expand his creativity, and in a sense, his own individualism. Up to this time he has not been able to handle crayons or colored pencils very well but is now eager to have another try. Any kind of paper, and lots of it, and the small-size crayons are all that are necessary. In this activity, as with most creative activities, the baby has control over the situation; he determines what colors he will use and how he will use them. Sometimes he is interested in using just a plain lead pencil to "write," just as he has seen his parents writing.

It is possible that a baby may get carried away by his own exuberance and decide to do a job on the walls. They are handy and more than one baby has taken advantage of the opportunity. But baby learns the limits of what he can and cannot do because you have been near him while he has been working, labeling and responding to him, and as soon as you get a hint of what he is proposing (he heads for the wall, crayon poised for action), you steer him back to the table and let him know that paper is for coloring but not walls. (Incidentally, you should discourage eating of crayons too.) Your baby is able to co-operate willingly with this gentle handling because he loves you dearly and since you make him happy he wants to please you. If, however, he is not able to co-operate, take another look at the situation. His behavior may be an indication that all is not well with him. He may be bored or tired, or he may be feeling just a little neglected.

While finger and brush painting will always be great favorites, a little switch can add new interest. The paper for this activity needs to be fairly nonabsorbent. You take a brush and wet the paper all over with water so that it is a bit drippy. Your baby chooses a paint, and starts right in. But something strange is happening, the paint is spreading over the paper every which way as he brushes merrily on—producing in the end a soft blurry picture. Of course, other colors are offered if he indicates he wants to be truly expressive. When all is finished, he is delighted with his masterpiece and no doubt dad will be equally delighted when you proudly show him the latest creation.

Old salt shakers with enlarged holes provide yet another kind of novel painting. The same kind of paper is used and moistened as before. Dry powder paint is used and placed in the shakers, and the baby is shown how to shake it onto the paper. As the paint spreads, he may not be able to resist the temptation to get right in to feel and to spread the paint, adding to his creation. And why not, it is his picture!

Making a double picture is fun for him and simple to manage. A large piece of paper is folded in half and the baby paints the

139

half that is available. When he is finished, you fold the other half over, press it down on the picture, and lo and behold! there are two pictures exactly the same.

While one generally thinks of painting as requiring fingers or brushes, other objects can be used that help baby make even more interesting marks. Plastic spoons and forks drawn through the paint offer some surprises, as does a heavy piece of cord six inches long with a large knot on one end. The baby usually has to be shown how these are used but is quick to take the initiative and add his own actions (while mother draws the fork through the paint, baby is likely to bang the fork on the page). If this is not the case, the painting should be terminated. There are times when your baby just does not find the activity interesting even though you think it is and have spent some time planning it. Another time there may be more enthusiasm.

Colored chalk provides another medium for creative expression. Investing in some construction paper is well worth the money for the fun it gives your baby. Packages of many different colors or just one color are easily obtainable and the dark colors in particular are perfect for chalk painting. Pink chalk marks on a black piece of paper make a delightful picture, but almost any color or combination of colors produces equally bright and satisfactory pictures.

More extensive collage creations are now possible with baby's rapidly developing skills. You have been preparing for this moment by saving everything under the sun. Well, almost—attractive pieces of fabric, small lids from jars, tops from detergent bottles (well rinsed, of course), pieces of odd-shaped wood and bark, bits of Styrofoam, small empty spools of thread, shells from the beach, old plastic flowers, tiny aluminum tart tins, pieces of foil, odds and ends of wool and ribbon, interesting stones, plastic objects that used to be part of a favorite rattle or mobile, colored drinking straws, and various lengths of one-inch rings cut from the paper-towel roll are only a few of the many things that can be used for your baby's collage. With safety always an important consideration, you must be sure all objects are large enough so that there is no danger of swallowing anything. With that assured make a thick collage paste (see Appendix for recipe), prepare the paper or cardboard, and offer the baby several choices. It may be necessary to help him get started and it may be that his first effort is not too extensive, but with lots of opportunity and helpful support from you, it won't be too long before he is producing yet more masterpieces.

Shredding fancy paper for a collage is great fun for baby and he should be given this chance once in a while. This is his way of preparing his own material. Fortunately, you have been saving pretty tissue paper for just such an event. If you really want to go all out the kitchen cupboard is full of ready-to-use materials for a unique and perhaps tasty collage. A little paprika added to the paste on the paper via baby's shaking (from an old salt shaker or the tin itself) gives a rich rust color. Dried dill and chive and parsley leaves provide interesting green particles, and, best of all, cake and cookie decorations, the kind your baby can shake on, make his collage really quite special. Fine coconut, plain or colored, cereal, and even clean sand can be used in the same way. Keeping in mind that not all babies develop the same interests and talents at the same time, you should perhaps be reminded not to be the least bit concerned if your baby does not seem interested or has not yet developed adequate co-ordination for all these creative activities. If that is the case they can be kept in mind and offered a few months later when he will probably be more ready to try them.

Musical activities

Music has been an integral part of man's life since early times. Unfortunately not all adults have recognized the importance of music to the developing child. He can enjoy beautiful sounds,   141 he can make his own beautiful (at least to him) sounds even at a very tender age. You have probably already noticed how your tiny baby responded to little nursery rhymes and gentle songs, how he listened carefully to soft tinkling bells, and as he got older to other interesting sounds (airplane and car sounds being favorites. at this age). He has gradually become aware of the music on the radio and the record player and with your active participation and approval he has responded to simple finger-play activities with great glee. More sophisticated finger play, where greater understanding of what action goes with what word, along with more skill in actually carrying out the motions, are now possible for him.

Fortunately it does not seem to matter greatly to baby if you are slightly off key (many of us suffer from this same affliction); what he is interested in besides being with you is the rhythmic sound of the singing and the movements being performed. It looks like fun to him and so it is. Music is one of those activities that lends itself to spontaneity. You and your baby just feel like singing. If this is the case you can either sit on a chair with baby in your lap, or better still on the floor with baby facing you. This way he can see what you are doing and you can encourage his participation by gently moving the parts of his body in the same way as you move yours. That is one of the many ways in which he learns.

There are several favorites that seem universally enjoyable:

If you're happy and you know it clap your hands.
If you're happy and you know it clap your hands.
If you're happy and you know it and you really want to show it,
If you're happy and you know it clap your hands.

It goes on to suggest banging the feet, shaking the head, blinking the eyes, and so on. The possibilities and extensions are endless.

The wheels of the bus go round and round,
> [You make circular motions with your hands]

Round and round, round and round,
The wheels of the bus go round and round
Over the city streets.

The people in the bus go up and down,
> [You lift your baby up and down—or stand up and
> squat down yourself to show him how it's done]

Up and down, up and down,
The people in the bus go up and down
Over the city streets.

Swimming, swimming in my swimming pool
> [You do the breast stroke and then draw an imaginary
> circle or rectangle to represent the pool]

When the days are hot
> [You wipe your brow]

When the days are cool
> [You wrap your hands around your shoulders and
> hug yourself with a little shake]

In my swimming pool
> [You draw another imaginary rectangle or circle]

Breast stroke, side stroke, fancy diving too
> [You do each stroke and make a diving motion with
> your hands]

Don't you wish you never had anything else to do?

Ring-a-round-the-rosy has a different kind of action and is even more enjoyable if dad can join hands too. He'll find it not at all unpleasant and good exercise too. A number of song books with other delightful finger plays are listed in the Appendix for gradual inclusion in baby's repertoire. But music doesn't begin and end with finger-play songs, records are very useful and special favorites can be played many times while you and your baby sing along, clap along, hum along, or even dance along. He gets a big kick out of being "danced" around in your arms and an even greater pleasure just dancing about while holding onto your hands.

Special floor play

You and your baby have been playing together on the floor since he was very tiny. It has been fun for both of you and one of the big advantages of floor play has been in the equalization, to some extent, of the size differences between you. You are less giant-sized when sitting on the floor, and it does make for easier face-to-face contact. It has also permitted you to be in a position where you can see things more as your child sees them.

There are many excellent toys on the market today that lend themselves nicely to a particular kind of floor play. These toys are sets of toys rather than individual pieces, and are used as a set. One of the groupings that comes to mind is a farm, or a zoo-animal set in which the animals are fairly realistic-looking and are more proportional in size to each other than is sometimes the case with other sets. The elephant looks like an elephant with his rough gray hide and is much larger than the lion but not as tall as the giraffe. Children do learn to differentiate eventually, but it seems to help them sort out the real world if the play objects in their world are fairly true representations.

Cars and trucks always seem to be favorite toys and several models can be purchased very inexpensively for this kind of floor play. A station wagon, a taxi, an ambulance, and a school bus are quite different from the ordinary pick-up truck and dump truck, the convertible and the familiar sedan. This combination also makes a good floor-play set, especially if you use some masking tape on the kitchen floor for roadways going hither and yon. In addition to the animals and the car sets, the Fisher-Price company has produced some excellent units that are also appropriate. Their gay little dollhouse is imaginative and contains a number of pieces of furniture as well as several little figurines representing a dog, a boy, and a girl. Their garage contains a small car just right for the little dolls. The airport, the houseboat, the school, and the village are all suitable and very appealing for this age group. Happily, all these toys will continue to be popular with your child for a long time to come and are certainly worth the extra expense.

In order to maintain a high interest level in these special sets of toys, it is probably a good idea not to make them as freely available to your baby as are most of his other toys. When the time seems opportune, get one of the sets out, place it beside you on the floor and invite your baby to join with you in playing with it. If you have decided to use the farm and zoo animals, begin by using two or three animals, gradually introducing one or two more if the situation calls for them. As in the past, the baby plays with them whatever way he wishes until he seems finished. You can change the situation by having the horse engage in some action. He begins to jump and prance about and says "neigh, neigh." You make an interpretation: "I think the horse wants a playmate. Let's see if we can find a friend for the horse. Oh, here's a pretty brown cow. Let's call it Maribelle." The cow is introduced and the two animals do a little prancing together. You sing a little ditty for background music:

> *This is the way we dance today,*
> *Dance today, dance today,*
> *This is the way we dance today*
> *So early in the morning.*

Both animals fall down. "Oh dear, I'm afraid they are all tired out. Shall we put them in their barns?" The barn is a large box with a flap for a door. It is not at all unusual for your baby to take a hand and begin to co-operate in playing with you. Your horse decides to hide and your baby, catching on to the game, has Maribelle searching everywhere. He may then hide both animals, or he himself may hide and you and the animals go looking for him behind chairs, behind doors, under cushions, and finally find him tucked away in a corner. He thinks he is hidden because he has placed himself in an area where he believes he cannot be seen. Sometimes children place themselves in such a way that they can't see the seeker and so they assume the seeker can't see them. One of the authors had a delightful example of this kind of reasoning. She was playing hide-and-seek around a big tree trunk with a young child. At first she hid behind the tree so that Susie, seventeen months, would be able to get the idea. When this became clear, Susie decided it was her turn to hide and ran to the same tree. Instead of hiding behind the tree out of sight, she turned her face toward the tree and closed her eyes. She was hidden. After much searching around bushes, and after a suitable effort, the author discovered the "hiding" place. Susie seemed pleased with herself; after all, she had not been easily discovered. Children do not reason as adults do, as Piaget has extensively demonstrated during his many years of studying and observing children. Because they reason so differently, parents should not be surprised when their offspring does something which seems quite illogical to them. No doubt the baby has a very satisfactory explanation—at least, satisfactory to him.

Your baby's special way of thinking may manifest itself during floor play, and many other times. You find that your baby has given you a little challenge. Impulsively he tugs at your sleeve and jabbers away; what is he telling you? He takes you by the hand and with expressive jargon tells you he wants something. You offer him juice, cookies, and so on, but nothing seems to please him; this is not what he is trying to say. He will make strange sounds and movements with his toys that you are sure you have never used, or he may take off across the room on an errand of extreme importance (or so it seems to you) and return to you empty-handed, with a big smile and hug. What baby is thinking you may never find out. Without extensive language to communicate his thoughts and feelings, your baby uses his special jargon and gestures and you often have to second-guess his wants and needs of the moment.

Floor play is one of those great activities that can give rein to your imagination. If you happen to have some sewing skills, you can make a few simple dress-ups for the toy animals: caps, scarves, and even little boots are not much trouble to make and give your 147 baby a whole new area to explore. At this age he is just beginning to experiment with fantasy and as he gets older his fantasies will become increasingly more imaginative and complex. Along with this development will be the ability to differentiate, to some extent at least, the real world from the world of fantasy. Your baby is growing up, developing many skills both verbal and intellectual, and with his fairly sophisticated walking he is now truly a toddler—he is no longer a baby.

Summing up

This has been a marvelous age for the baby, who has gained yet more independence through walking and the beginnings of comprehensible language. His eager "into everything" explorations have at times worn out the most energetic parents. But his confidence and independence may bring problems and frustrations he has never encountered before. While the large armchair and the couch can be clambered onto with ease, the bed is too high, and the swiveling kitchen chairs just won't stay still long enough. As he sits teetering on the arm of the chair, he can't quite understand your concern and efforts to get him to sit on the chair, rather than on its arm. And why shouldn't he sit and stand on the end table? He sees the world from a new vantage point, and he did exert a lot of effort to clamber onto its slippery surface. He may find himself in spots that were easy to get into but not so easy to get out of. While crawling under the crib to get his treasured toy, once it's retrieved he finds himself stuck or tries to sit up to examine his trophy and whacks his head. He runs after the cat or you and in his eagerness trips over his feet or the edge of the carpet—boom, there goes another bump or bruise. A hug from you or dad is all that is needed and off he runs again to some new adventure. Triumphs, conquests, a few setbacks and tantrums—but this is all part of growing up and learning.

The more precocious baby has probably been trying out his new motor skills on the stairs. Up is a breeze, down a little more tricky, but, like Mount Everest, they are there and must be conquered. The more timid baby has probably been exploring every nook and cranny of the kitchen cupboards and bedroom drawers and using tentative negations to test out his limits with you. You say no; do you mean it? He says no and probably doesn't mean it at all. It is a powerful word though and can bring about all sorts of interesting reactions. Whatever kind of baby you have, by now he is probably a little charmer and thoroughly enjoying his world. You have been enjoying him too in all the things you do together. And, who knows, while experimenting with your baby in creative activities, you may find out that you have hidden talents you never suspected you had.

While he has been getting into everything the baby has grown from a physical and mental standpoint—he is no longer a baby, but is now firm on his feet and is truly a toddler. He is still impulsive and filled with whims and fancies, love and eagerness to learn, tenderness and tears. As his language skills develop he will undoubtedly start to unlock some of the mysteries about what is going on in his mind. He will be able to express himself in words as well as physically acting out his feelings. As his speech develops, so will his charm and his antics, and the next period of his life will be filled with lots of language and laughter.

5 Language

and Laughter

Eighteen to Twenty-four Months

A toddler is a wonderful combination of candor, naïveté, and spontaneity. He has a direct approach to life that is so refreshing that at times it may be a little disarming and even embarrassing to some adults. Left to his own devices, especially when he is in the right mood, he can find a game in almost anything and become absorbed in it for an amazing length of time. Simplicity is a keynote. He sees and understands life in simple terms. If the cat eats out of a dish on the floor, why is mother so upset when she discovers her toddler sitting with obvious delight next to the cat sharing a delicious repast? Dog biscuits are delightfully crunchy and are enjoyed with special relish if they have been attained after a lot of effort and hard work (after all, he had to stand on tiptoe to reach the box, wiggle and pull it off the shelf, and, if the contents did not spill on the floor, open the box to retrieve the prize). Such rules as separate bowls of food for cats and dogs and toddlers must seem strange to a twenty-month-old. He still has so much to learn about the adult world and its ways.

The toddler lives primarily in the freedom of the here and now, building on past experiences and processing the wealth of information to be found through his many senses without fully understanding the how, why, and wherefore of what goes on. He stands at the window absorbed as the raindrops strike the glass, and as they slither down the pane he traces their route with his pudgy finger. Imagine the marvel of seeing a ladybug wending its way across the window sill or the robins that congregate on the lawn after the summer shower in search of worms. We do not know what the child is thinking when he is silently observing an event that has attracted his attention, for we cannot get into his head. But we do know that something wonderful is going on by his absorbed and rapt observation, his concentrated efforts, and his silent wonder, which may be punctuated by grunts and sighs, or by sudden handclapping and laughter, signaling the pleasure he has had during his contemplation. He is eager to know the what and how of life, and in his own way, in his own time, he seeks the help of his parents.

Labeling is essential to the growing intellect of the child, but it need not accompany every activity the child is engaged in. At times "silence is golden" and many a time adult explanations will not really be heard or indeed welcomed as the toddler is deeply absorbed in a sensory experience. He is trying to make sense of his world in his own way, and should be given the opportunity to do so. He loves to hear the sound of the rain, to look at the crazy pattern of the raindrops on the window, and to feel the cool, smooth surface of the glass. There are also times when he is not seeking information or absorbed in a task, when language will be comforting to him. When he is feeling unhappy, or has hurt himself and is crying hard, mother's or father's words comfort him, together with the warm feeling of being held close as they reassure him. However, this is a time when language is extremely important to the toddler. While parents have many opportunities to label and talk, now is the time when the toddler himself will apply labels and often "chatter" in long, complicated vocalizations with such sincerity and earnestness that mother can be sure he is trying to tell her something very interesting. Often the sound of a barking dog, lawn mower, car, or airplane catches his attention and he insists on giving it a label. Excitedly he looks and points upward and says "ai-pla, ai-pla" over and over again. If he is outside, he will probably be lucky enough to see the airplane and know that his label has been correctly applied, reinforcing the three-way connection between object-sound-word (or label).

He is a charming mixture of infant and child, observer and doer, sensualist and intellectual, and at times an enigma to parents as he grows toward maturity. His own name is a great teaching tool to help him to develop a sense of self. By now he knows the sound of his own name and loves to hear it being called, sung, rhymed with other words, sounded softly and loudly, high and low. By the time he gets closer to two years he may like to see what his name looks like. Some of his toys, his closet, and his toy chest could perhaps sport his name punched out on the plastic strip labels that are readily available in stationery stores. And how about a big name sign in colorful construction paper on his bedroom door. The words "These are Johnny's shoes" spoken by mother as she dresses him in the morning almost always seem to evoke an extra special reaction from Johnny. He is coming quickly to an awareness of himself as an individual and language forms an integral part of this self-discovery process. He takes great pride in himself and his accomplishments. In fact, at this age toddlers have been known to proclaim grandly, "These are Johnny's shoes," while trying to hold up both feet at once for the admiring adult to see.

His growing sense of pride in his accomplishments may make this a good time to introduce him to the potty, preferably his own potty chair, enabling him to get used to being on it by having his feet planted firmly on the floor. This will help him have a relaxed, secure feeling about sitting on the pot. At about this age he will probably be starting to develop some control over his elimination and so there is some possibility of success on the toilet. Keeping a chart to get an idea of his elimination patterns will give mother a pretty good idea of when she should put him on the potty. With her praise and patience and his own physical

maturing he begins to connect up in his mind his physical feelings of elimination with sitting on the pot. By staying with him
for the brief time he is on it and explaining in simple terms that,
"Here is where you go to the toilet just like mom and dad,"
mother helps him to get the idea. Copying something that he
sees his parents do may be a big selling feature and so if they feel
comfortable about it, it may be helpful for him to see them in
the bathroom as well. He may take to pottying quite readily, responding with pride when he accomplishes the desired goal and
with pleasure to the warm parental praise he receives. Such early
success, however, may be short-lived and it would not be at all
unusual for him to begin to balk at the potty and prefer to return
to his old diaper days for a while. If mother is viewing potty
training with eager anticipation as a time and mess saver for her
primarily and not as a learning experience which depends on his
psychological and physical maturing, then she may find his progress somewhat discouraging. At the tender age of nineteen to
twenty-four months the main concern is for him to be introduced
to the potty as a positive and pleasant experience and not as a
do-or-die situation in which he feels compelled to perform. It
will be a long time yet before he can be expected to be fully
potty trained. In fact, toilet accidents are part of being a three- or
even a four-year-old. So if he is resistant, it's perhaps best to dis-
continue the training for a while and try again later. Eventually
the time will be right for him and he'll have little or no trouble
at all. As it is, in all areas of growth, with his parents' love and
consistent guidance he will accomplish what he is able to when
he is able to, according to what seems to be his own natural time-
table of development.

As a baby, the toddler used to play around with sounds by
cooing and making vowel sounds, experimenting with new sounds
as his vocal muscles and tongue dexterity increased. Now he is
playing around with words and wordlike sounds. He will pick on
particular words—"eyes," for example—which for a few days will

be the password for all games. He will insist on poking mommy's eyes, the dog's eyes, teddy's eyes, and eyes in books as he applies the label over and over again. It will probably be the first thing he says to daddy when he comes home, accompanied by a deliberate poke in the object that has fascinated him since birth. It is a little confusing to him since nobody seems to object when he touches their nose in his labeling, but eyes are a different story and this only seems to increase his need to explore them. He has many such favorite words during these early years and they make great spontaneous games between parent and child. It is not unusual to hear a young child playing with syllables, repeating over and over again some favorite sound as he lies in his bed in the early morning before getting up. Not only does he love to hear the sounds he is producing, he seems to enjoy the silliness as well. A child may take the sounds "da" and "dee" and repeat them in many, many ways, while laughing and chuckling over his game. In fact, the son of one of the authors has a wonderful game going with his daddy which he starts off by calling "Daddy" in a soft, drawn-out tone. Daddy answers in a similar way, using his son's name, "Michael," and the game progresses, with Michael calling out "Daddy" in various tones of voice, slowly and rapidly, and in combinations of two or three repetitions. Daddy responds likewise with Michael's name and both laugh and have a jolly good time of it. The game is usually terminated when Michael thinks daddy is getting a little bit too silly with an emphatic "Oh, Da-dee!" and a big hug. Another fun game is the "Hi" game, where he looks up at mother or dad out of the corner of his eye and with a big grin whispers "Hi," really emphasizing the "h" sound. Again he gets a whispered response and continues with variations of "hi-hi," "hi, mommy" or "hi, daddy," and so on. It is interesting to observe that very often as children play these word games, special gestures will accompany special games. The more rambunctious "Daddy" game calls for much waving of arms, bouncing up and down, and outright laughter, while

155

the whispering game is accompanied with coy looks, or a gentle leaning forward of the upper body as the word is whispered.

Spontaneous sound games where mother and her toddler play with a sound, repeating and varying it in all kinds of ways, is a great activity and will likely evoke hearty laughter from both parent and child. Laughing is a universal way of expressing and sharing good feelings inside, and when a youngster has not yet mastered more than a few expressive words, what better way than laughing to express his joy and love? Typically, a baby will laugh outright somewhere around his third or fourth month, and he often does so in response to tickling or nuzzling of his tummy. By six months or so he seems to laugh in imitation of the adult laugh; although he hasn't a clue what he is laughing about he does love to respond to his parents. By the time he gets close to two years of age, he is beginning to understand and see the funny side of all kinds of daily situations, like his shoes being put on the wrong feet or his pants on backward. Mothers have great fun doing something wrong purposely and then sharing the joke as the toddler laughs. Sometimes he gets the joke and sometimes he is simply responding to mother's mirth as she clowns with him.

Language has opened up many new areas to the young toddler and with his increased use of language comes an increased self-awareness coupled with an increased awareness of those around him. While he is still very self-involved and egocentric, it is fascinating to watch how he orients and responds to other little ones. While being wheeled around in the supermarket on a shopping expedition, he looks at everything with great interest, applying labels to things he knows and maybe kicking up a fuss as mother whizzes past the cookie isle; however, it is with obvious glee and interest that he clearly enunciates "baby" as he sees an infant or a toddler being pushed around as he is. He looks intently at this other being and hangs over the edge of the cart to catch yet another glimpse of this creature who is his size as he is wheeled away. It has been assumed by some people that children of this age are neither capable nor interested in playing with other toddlers. This belief seems to come about because many do not have any regular contact with children of their own age. It has also been assumed that young children engage primarily in solitary play because that is all they want to do. Observations of children in infant day-care centers and informal play groups indicate that this solitary play is not an exclusive pattern for most toddlers, and many mothers can attest to this fact. If Johnny had his way he would rather have someone to play with, even though the playmates might go their separate ways periodically. For at least some of the time they do get together and engage in an activity which has a common goal. Teachers working with young children have been surprised at how early toddlers discover each other and attempt to play a co-operative game.

One of the authors noticed with amazement two crawlers, just under a year old, crawling in a line on a sort of follow-the-leader game with the first one stopping often to see if his companion was still behind him, and then going on, aware of each other and enjoying their game. It is not always possible for a parent to arrange for a playmate every day but even once a week makes a big difference for a toddler. He has already been engaging in co-operative activities of all kinds with his mother and father and yet becoming accustomed to other youngsters his age is a new and exciting experience for him. However, for many years to come he will need supervision and direction from an adult as he plays with others. The toddler has a great deal to learn about sharing, being fair and patient and self-controlled. He also has to learn what is hurtful and what is not (banging the table with a hammer may dent the table, but banging another being with a hammer definitely leaves bruises). He has to learn not to clobber his friend with whatever he has in his hand at the moment to get attention when something is annoying him. Close supervision and fast diversionary tactics by mother when trouble is brewing between two little friends will help the toddler to develop his social skills and give him good positive feelings about playing with his peers.

Finally, after a busy day, he comes to the point where, collapsing limply against mother's leg or flopping himself across her knees if she is sitting down, he whimpers a bit and wants to be held and cuddled. Growing up is great—but the old security of being in mother's arms is sometimes hard to give up. It takes time for him to grow.

It has become quite apparent to mother that her little toddler prefers to be with her, even if she can't always play with him.

He has come to accept this sharing of her time because she has arranged frequent regular playtimes with him and he has been able to accept this as a reasonably satisfactory alternative. But now that he can really get around, has improved his fine motor skills and has more language comprehension, he has discovered he can participate with mother in many household tasks. This not only gives him more of mother's companionship but also the opportunity to learn about the intricacies necessary to keep a home running smoothly. He learns the specific ways he can "help" mother with her tasks, and while mother frequently wishes he would not "help," she has come to recognize his need to learn as much as he can about his environment and responds to that need.

Household activities

The kitchen is one of the toddler's favorite places. There are so many interesting smells when mother is cooking and so many interesting foods to cook that he would like to get right in there and cook. This is only possible if the mother is able to allow more time for cooking than usual. Lunchtime, perhaps, when only she and her toddler are home, may be one of those times when he can participate. Scrambled eggs are a whiz-bang favorite and provide an excellent learning experience. When the table is set, the bread in the toaster, and the frying pan near at hand, but not too near, you begin by explaining what you are going to make. Show him an egg, explain that it must be handled gently because it will break easily, and hand it carefully to him. The first few times you are well advised to have a wet washcloth handy and a bowl under the egg as it is examined. Many toddlers already know the meaning of "careful" and no mishaps occur, but there are others who do not realize their own strength (or perhaps the egg has an extra weak shell) and soon learn its meaning. It is safe to say that should an accident occur the meaning   159 is eminently clear. After the egg has been examined and you have mentioned some characteristics—the shell is smooth, white or brown, more rounded at one end than the other, and easy to hold—it is returned to you. Break the shell and allow the inside part to fall in the bowl as you point out the fact that there are two parts, the yellow is called the yolk and the clear part is called the white. A cautious touch by your toddler rounds out his observations. He may also be interested in examining the empty eggshell with its slippery interior and thin shell, giving quite different visual and tactile experiences than the whole egg. You beat the egg and then allow him to finish beating while you hold the bowl. In the meantime, the butter has been melting in the frying pan and emitting a pleasant aroma which both cooks have not failed to notice. Salt and pepper is added (your toddler can manage a few shakes of pepper without too much damage), and the mixture is poured into the hot pan and allowed to cook. Explanations are still in order as the mixture changes in form: "When the scrambled eggs are all cooked, they will be firm and easy to eat with a spoon." When all is ready, toast and eggs, each diner helps himself to a portion. It might be wise at this point for you to remind your child the eggs are hot and perhaps demonstrate this concept by gingerly touching your food. A similar touch by your toddler will help him to understand what hot means and the sooner he learns this for himself the safer for him. With all this co-operative effort no one should be surprised if the scrambled eggs get eaten as though there were no tomorrow.

Applesauce can be made in the same way. You get your equipment and supplies ready and with your cohort seated close by begin the preparations. While apples are a familiar sight to most toddlers there is a lot to know about them besides the fact that they are a fruit and grow on trees. Some are big, some are small, some are red, some green, and some yellow. They are not quite round, are usually hard, are not always easy for a toddler to handle, and are delicious to eat. But cooked apples are also very good to eat, as you are about to demonstrate. Begin to peel and core the fruit, mentioning the various points of interest as you proceed. "This is called the core and it holds all the seeds. Can you see the brown seeds?" When all the apples are ready and a piece has been saved for the toddler to munch on while waiting, they are placed in a suitable pot. The correct amount of water and sugar is added by the "helper" under your watchful eye. He adds a dash of cinnamon and begins to feel that he has been making the applesauce practically by himself. Turn on the heat and take over the job of stirring, this time under the watchful eye of your child. In no time at all the apples have changed in form and color, are cooked, and after a short cooling time are ready for tasting. The supreme moment has arrived for the junior cook—just how good is his applesauce? He finds it very tasty and much to his liking. You may have to be careful here or else you may find yourself being urged to make applesauce every day! But cooking other things can be just as much fun; instant puddings, fried eggs, French toast, pancakes, bacon, and sausages are just a few of the foods that can be prepared with the active participation of a willing "helper."

Any time you have to be in the kitchen doing your necessary chores you can keep your toddler busy by giving him some interesting tasting and feeling experiences. Your spice shelf contains a number of clear extracts which you use regularly in your cooking. Peppermint and almond are two of the more common ones. Find five small plastic dishes and put diluted peppermint (full strength is not exactly pleasant) in one, diluted almond in another, sugar water in another, plain water in another, and slightly salted water in the last one. To the toddler they all look alike and all feel the same, but as you present him with one or two at a time for examination and tasting, he finds that they are not the same after all. After tasting and feeling the mixtures extensively, your toddler is a bit puzzled. They should taste the same since they all look and feel the same. "Tasting tells one what they are flavored with. This one is flavored with sugar, this with salt, this with peppermint, this with almond, and this with nothing." All this may not be completely understood but the toddler is relieved to know his mother has an explanation for this complex situation. An elaboration of this puzzle can be provided by using small amounts of flour, cornstarch, baking powder, baking soda, and icing sugar in a similar way. They look and feel alike but on tasting differences become very noticeable. How does your toddler resolve this apparent absurdity? You label each one and explain that they are all different things which can be used in different ways. Other spices with similar characteristics can be utilized to give him a wide variety of experiences. It won't be long before he begins to realize that all things seemingly the same may not be the same at all. He is finding out that looks may be deceiving.

Other household responsibilities can be shared in much the same way and while they always take longer the learning experience will pay big dividends in terms of the toddler's development. Washing dishes can be a horror when a toddler is involved, but with a little care it can be managed without your becoming a nervous wreck determined not to do "that" again. If you have a double sink, you can have your toddler stand beside you and wash as you wash. If not, you will have to wash separately. This is not half as much fun but it is still worth trying. The first prerequisite for successful washing is a small amount of soapy water, then, with a few pots and pans, one or two spoons, or a couple of plastic cups, all is ready for a great session. Of course your "helper" needs to be protected, and so does the floor. A shortened green garbage bag with appropriately cut holes makes a suitable apron. Lots of newspaper on the floor allows for spills, and disaster is surely avoided. You wash your dishes, your toddler washes his, and both carry on a lively conversation about the relative merits

of this mutual task.

Tidying up the house together is another worthwhile venture. Mother and child enjoy each other's company, and the child learns to follow simple instructions and to carry out simple tasks. He can help carry things, he can assist with the cleaning chores such as dusting, bedmaking, picking up his own toys and putting them in the toy box, and he learns generally what needs to be done and why. Not only that, he also learns something about the importance of order. It seems to please his parents to have things orderly, but, more important, he is discovering for himself the value of order: things can always be found in a regular place. His toys can always be located in his toy box if they are returned there after each use.

Gross motor activities

Most toddlers, if they are normal, healthy children, seem to have an unlimited store of energy that may get them into difficulties if it is not directed in acceptable ways. One of the best solutions, as most parents are fully aware, can be found in the back yard. Playing outside with a few pieces of equipment—a ball, a sandbox, a small slide, a large cardboard-box tunnel or house—helps a great deal to satisfy the energy requirements of most toddlers. Hanging old tin pie plates, long pieces of wood, discarded pots, and odd pieces of metal on a cord on the fence or from a sturdy branch adds another dimension to the interest in the back yard. If this banging activity is likely to disturb the neighbors, then it may have to be curtailed somewhat or eliminated altogether.

If one is not too far away, the park is another great place where running and jumping can be given full rein. Frequent visits and walks around the neighborhood not only give a much needed change in environment for both mother and child, but also allow for additional "blowing off of steam." Unfortunately, some streets are very busy and a harness may have to be used for safety's sake. But this still permits some running and jumping along with the walking, visiting, and observing.

As these excursions are not always possible, other outlets must be found to satisfy the busy toddler. A kiddie car is a good beginning because even at this age he can push it around with his feet until he learns how to use the pedals. There are, of course, very attractive kiddie cars without pedals and these are excellent as well. Since a kiddie car can be a dangerous vehicle in the hands of a daring driver, it may be a good idea to arrange for this kind of activity in the basement when you have to be there anyway doing some washing or ironing. If your toddler is not the vigorous type, certain other areas of the house might be made available for kiddie-car fun.

Rolling and tumbling are suitable outlets for your toddler and with a few old blankets on the floor for padding the gymnast can start his exercises. You show your toddler how to roll over and over on the floor. No doubt this is not new to him, but watching you roll over and over probably is new to him. Of course, any little hill outside is also a great place for rolling. Teaching your toddler how to somersault is a little trickier but he is always a willing participant, even though he is usually a little surprised at the end result as he is turned over by a parent. This does not deter him for long and he wants to try it again and again.

A sort of "follow the leader over an obstacle course" is a great hit with your toddler. Begin as the leader and after you have arranged the course away you both crawl. A line of books placed end to end to go over, a table to go under, a chair to go around, and a big cardboard box to go through are very little trouble to organize. This is an excellent place where the roles can be reversed and you follow the leader through and around the course. Incidentally, dad ought to be pretty good at all these activities.

"Steppingstones" is another game that can incorporate the concept of color in the activity. You cut out large red and blue squares from construction paper and place them randomly over the floor. If there is carpeting there is no problem, but a vinyl floor can be slippery and it may be necessary to put some masking tape on the back of the papers to avoid any accidents. When all is ready explain the object of the game, mentioning the colors at the same time as a little reminder. After listening to your instructions your toddler is eager to start. "Johnny, you find a red square and stand on it. Okay, find another square that is just the same . . . another red square. Good boy, that was clever. Can you find a blue square now? Oh, I tried to fool you but you are too clever for me." This remark as he successfully finds the blue square. For a change of pace the roles are reversed and Johnny directs you. You "accidentally" make a mistake, which he promptly points out. If this game is mastered easily by your toddler you might introduce another concept, big and little. A few of the squares are made very large and the instructions now contain two concepts. "Johnny, please stand on a big red square. Now a little blue square. That's right, you've got the idea, haven't you?" For some young toddlers just getting to a square, any square, is the extent of their understanding, as they have not yet grasped these concepts. No matter, he tried to carry out the directions

and certainly partially succeeded. Your response as always is positive as you point out the color he did stand on. "Hey, you found a blue square, didn't you? That's good."

Skipping per se is too advanced for the toddler but he can be given opportunities to learn and enjoy some of the preliminary steps. A long piece of sturdy cord (it shouldn't be too light) or a plastic skipping rope tied to the leg of one chair and you holding the other end is all that is needed. At first, the cord is rested on the floor and the toddler asked to jump over it. If he is not too clear about what is required, you can tie your end to the leg of another chair and demonstrate for him. The first few times will be a sort of walk over but you can show him how to jump over keeping his feet together. This may take a fair amount of practice and your toddler may lose interest. If that is the case, the game should be terminated and tried another time. If all is going well and the toddler is eager to carry on, you can complicate the situation by raising the cord slightly off the floor, keeping control of the other end to lower it quickly if he seems to be having difficulties. Various complications geared to the child's interest and skill can be easily provided.

Ball play up to now has been elementary as the young child has not been able to do much more than throw the ball. But with rapidly developing motor co-ordination he is able now to engage in more demanding ball play. Outside, of course, is the best place, but with a little care it can be managed indoors as well. A broad plastic bat or a light flat piece of wood with one end shaped so that it can be held easily are great for hitting the ball, provided that the ball is not too small. It can't be too large either, as that may require too much strength to make it move. With this game you need to be prepared to be the left fielder but you can take your turn "at bat" occasionally and let the other ball player do some chasing. At first the ball is stationary (on the floor), but as your toddler becomes more proficient you can start rolling the ball toward him. This takes more judgment, 167 but with a slow roll he may be able to hit it successfully. He certainly wants to try.

Bowling, surprisingly, is another game that a child of this age can manage if it is properly prepared for him. The two-quart milk cartons with a few blocks inside for additional stability and Scotch-taped at the top make acceptable "bowling pins." If several are placed close together in a line horizontal to the bowler, he will have little trouble knocking down at least one. He is, as usual, shown the aim of the game and invited to participate. You have the fun of being the "pin boy."

Rolling a ball in a hole takes the same kind of skill. A large cardboard carton, the kind found in the grocery store, with a large hole about 18″ x 12″ is all that is needed besides the ball. Your toddler is instructed as to how to proceed and, standing only a few feet from the box, begins his rolling. As he develops expertise, the distance can be lengthened or the opening made smaller (another side of the box can be used for the new hole).

Large cardboard boxes also have the makings for a good basketball game. The trick is harder than it looks, but after a quick demonstration your toddler has his turn. This game is a real challenge, and a beach ball starting to deteriorate has less bounce and makes it more possible to achieve success, as it stays put a little better. The box is placed on the floor, open end up, and the toddler makes a basket by tossing the ball into the open box. Another kind of basketball for outdoors can be managed by taking a coat hanger and spreading it into a circle. The handle is bent so that it is at a right angle to the hoop. This in turn is fastened to the fence at the appropriate level. All is ready for the game.

If the basketball game has been a bit tough, another kind can be introduced which guarantees success. An old sheet is cut so that it is about five feet square with a good-sized hole in the middle. Each corner is tied to the leg of a chair (it may be necessary to sew on some cord) about eighteen inches from the floor.

There will be a bit of a sag in the center, so that if the ball lands anywhere on the sheet it will roll to the hole and, presto, through the hole into the waiting box below.

Sometimes toddlers just have fun throwing newspaper balls. They are simple to make with crumpled newspaper and a bit of adhesive tape to hold them together. Make several and offer them to your child. In no time at all they all have been thrown to the other side of the room. You can either toss them back or encourage him to retrieve them and throw them again, this time to the opposite side of the room, or onto an armchair or sofa. For quieter times, you and your toddler can sit on the floor, some distance apart, and roll a rubber ball back and forth. Adding a second ball makes for a bit more interest, as you and your toddler simultaneously roll the balls to each other.

Chalkboards often escape the notice of parents as being of any interest to the toddler, but they do allow him to make wonderful freehand drawings. A good-sized board attached to a wall makes it possible for a mother to work alongside her little artist, he in the lower section and she in the upper section. You are careful to refrain from asking what he is drawing or making any suggestions as to what he might try to draw. He really can't follow your suggestions anyway and why should he? The work would not really be his under these circumstances. Making sure there is a good mixture of colored chalk always expands the artistic possibilities. Some toddlers will have great fun making broad, expansive, sweeping marks with the chalk, others may tap gently at the board, and still others may want to create by using their fingers and palms to meld the chalk marks into one swirling creation.

The cobbler's bench by Playskool should not be forgotten as another good way to allow the toddler to let off excess steam. Once he learns how to turn it over to repeat the process, he may spend a fair length of time at this activity, perfecting his skills. It has one slight disadvantage: it is usually a pretty noisy affair, 169

much too noisy for you to tolerate very often or very long. But choosing the time and the place for your toddler can make a difference. Certainly on a warm day the back yard might be just the place.

Cognitive activities

There are a number of activities that stimulate the language and problem-solving ability of the enterprising toddler. One of these activities is called a tactile box task and is based on the child's ability to determine an object only by feeling it. Normally he can utilize all his senses, but in this case he can only rely on his sense of touch and his memory. Happily his language is at the stage where he can tell his parent what he thinks the object is before he has a chance to look at it.

A good sturdy box—one in which small appliances are shipped is quite acceptable—has a small flap cut into one side, large enough for a little hand to enter but not so large that the objects inside can be seen. There isn't much of a problem if that is the case. Gather a few common articles, each with a distinct shape and familiar to your toddler—a ball, a car, a spoon, a bracelet, a crayon. Let him examine them closely, encouraging him at the same time to label them. Naturally you provide the labels if he is not sure. After he has finished looking over these treasures you tell him you are going to play a game. Put a few, perhaps only three, of the objects in the box, remove the others out of sight so there will be no distractions, ask him to put his hand in and tell you what he has found before he shows it to you. Eagerly he puts his hand in, feels around, and proudly announces that he has found a ball. And, lo and behold, that is exactly what he has found. (It may be necessary to start the game off by putting just one object in the box for easy identification and practice.) No doubt about it, he has got the hang of the game. After a few more successes a more complicated problem seems indicated. Fortunately this is not hard to do. A few plastic knives, forks, and spoons, the kind used in the picnic basket, can provide just the problem since they are the same weight and made of the same material. They have similar properties and your toddler can make a correct judgment only on the basis of form. In the previous tasks there were few similar properties among the objects. He tries his hand, declares he has found a fork and produces a knife instead. You wonder, "Doesn't that look more like a knife?" and encourage him to have another try. Fabrics can be used in the same way, starting with a few pieces, each with distinct textures. Fur, burlap, and vinyl are excellent for a start. After the customary exploration and labeling, ask him, "What does it feel like, is it rough, smooth, or soft and furry?" With that query answered, the three pieces are placed in the box and the problem solver is enticed to choose one and say what kind it is. If this task seems a bit too difficult you can backtrack and start off with six pieces, two of each kind of material: two of fur, two of burlap, two of vinyl. You put one of each kind in the box and ask your toddler to choose one "which feels like this one." He touches it, and you may gently stroke his face with it to reinforce his understanding of how it feels. Once the solution is clear, you can go back to the more complicated task if it seems desirable.

Sorting on the basis of color where all the other properties of the objects being sorted are the same (small red wooden blocks in one pile and small blue wooden blocks in another pile) is still fun for the toddler but not too much of a problem for him. You decide to make it more challenging by using a number of objects, all the same color but dissimilar in other ways. First a couple of red blocks, a red bracelet, one or two red balls (hopefully not the same size), a red car, a red box, and perhaps a piece of red cloth. You add an assortment of objects of various other colors and mix them all together. After playing with this mound of interesting objects and having them all labeled with some emphasis on the red ones, ask your playmate to help you put all the red things into one pile. Of course, it is quite likely he may add one or two things that are not red, but you handle this in your usual positive way: "Oh, you decided to add a blue car to the pile of red things, didn't you? Let's see if we can find some more red things to go in the pile." If several of the remaining objects happen to be of another color, these can be put into a second pile.

Sorting on the basis of shape is another possibility you might want to consider. You locate several objects, some of them round and some of them square or rectangular. A couple of balls, a few wooden stringing beads, and an orange mixed in with one or two blocks, a square box, and perhaps a cracker or two for a little spice are all that are needed. During the usual play you point out the concept you want sorted. "I have a square block, what do you have? Yes, that's right, you do have a round ball." This kind of labeling, especially where the toddler can participate, helps to reinforce his understanding of the concept. With all the preliminaries taken care of the invitation to help put all the

round things in one pile and the square things in another pile is extended to your toddler. An interesting complication to this task can be provided by using several pairs of objects, one big and one little (a big block and a little block, a big ball and a little ball, a big spoon and a little spoon, a big car and a little car, and so on). Again during the play and labeling, mention the concepts you are interested in having sorted. "Where did that little ball go? Oh, you have the little ball and the big ball." When the toddler has indicated he is through with his examination, ask him to help you put all the big things in one pile and all the little things in another, keeping in mind that whatever he does it can be a good learning situation if you always comment positively on his attempts.

Matching tasks that require the same kind of discriminatory skills are excellent for further expanding the child's problem-solving ability. By now the simple picture-to-picture matching has been pretty well mastered by the child getting close to his second birthday if he has been exposed to it frequently. If so, he is ready for more puzzlers. Pictures of the same species but with different characteristics make a match: a collie dog to a French poodle; an Angora cat to a Siamese cat; a blue jay to a cardinal; an angel fish to a zebra fish; a monarch butterfly to a cabbage butterfly; a bumblebee to a honeybee. In this situation the toddler has to recognize the species and find the correct match. Other combinations using plants and foods can add much interest to the task.

Puzzles, of course, have intrigued the toddler from the time he was very young and will continue to do so for a while to come. But now that he has learned to be a bit more careful about things and does less mouthing, you can make other puzzles, as easy or as hard as seems warranted, and without having to spend a penny. Just make them out of cardboard. A good clear picture is pasted on a piece of sturdy cardboard and then cut into however many pieces seem indicated. If by chance the first effort is too easy for the now experienced puzzle solver, you can easily remedy the situation with a pair of scissors. A four-piece puzzle quickly becomes a six- or eight-piece puzzle and a new challenge for the toddler. Geometric puzzles made this way are even more intriguing. The square can be cut in many ways—into triangles, rectangles, squares, and even combinations of these three shapes. Similarly the triangle, the rectangle, and the circle make equally fascinating puzzles. The careful mother can point out the fact that several parts make a whole, and while there is no reason why she cannot mention halves and quarters when appropriate, she does not allow herself to get hung up on trying to teach her child fractions. Introducing this concept of "part-whole" in a natural way and whenever possible—for example, an apple is cut into halves—will do more toward helping the child understand this principle than if she tries teaching. This is not the time.

Another interesting part-whole task that Ira Gordon mentions in his book *Child Learning Through Child Play*, is one where an attractive picture of an object, perhaps a lovely fluffy kitten, is attached to a sturdy piece of cardboard 8″ x 10″. A plain piece of paper the same size is cut into strips from right to left leaving one inch uncut at one end. This uncut strip is then glued to the picture so that the strips completely cover the picture but can be easily turned back to expose it when desired. You show your toddler three or four pictures, including an exact duplicate of the covered one, label and explain the various properties of each object, making sure he is looking at the picture while you are doing this. Then ask him to tell you what is hidden under the strips as you peel them back one at a time. It may be that you will have to completely expose the picture the first time before your toddler will realize he can tell what is underneath even when only a part is exposed. But given time he will soon catch on and enjoy the challenge of identifying the mystery picture when it's only partially exposed.

Dramatic play

Most adults are more than a little surprised at the idea of the under-two being capable of and interested in make-believe games. As a matter of course the young child, who is by his very nature an extremely keen observer of the life around him, has already tried to engage in this kind of play. The role of the adult is assumed by him when he helps his mother tidy the house, wash the dishes, do some cooking, and shove his sticky little spoon into her mouth in an attempt to feed her rather than the reverse. And it is fascinating for him because he is so curious about the world of grownups. How does it feel to be an adult? How does it feel to play a certain role in that world? Play acting is a great way for him to act out his hidden wishes. "I'd like to be a fireman and ride a big red fire truck." It helps him to express his feelings—dolly gets put to bed whether she likes it or not and it gives him an opportunity to utilize his environment in a new way. The big cardboard box becomes his very own house where he is the lord and master.

Because this kind of play has so many benefits besides sheer enjoyment, you might want to try to plan for this kind of fun periodically. Just dressing up in old clothes is a good beginning. Discarded hats, gloves, shoes, purses, dresses, and skirts are just a few of the things that delight the toddler. A five-pound paper bag with the edge turned up and the top squashed down at one side makes a pretty good chef's hat, and a paper hat for a brave soldier or a pretty nurse are also simple to make. The magic marker makes an easy black band for the nurse's cap. If parents want to provide an even greater variety of materials for playacting the toyshop usually has a good assortment of inexpensive hats that designate a specific role. The construction hard hat, the fireman's hat, the football helmet, the baseball cap, and the cowboy hat are often good reproductions well worth the extra cost.

When the opportune time for dramatic play arrives, a companion, usually yourself or a small friend, completes the preparations and the fun can begin. Once he is a little older, your toddler can enjoy himself without always having a partner, but at this age he needs another playmate. Because he is so intimately involved with you, his observations of the adult world have centered primarily on the mother or "lady" role and he frequently chooses this one to portray, at least in the beginning, his dramatic experimentations of the adult world. He decides therefore to dress up as a lady and is enchanted when he sees himself in the mirror. Once dressed he is at a loss as to what to do next and you might suggest a visit to Mrs. Whatshername (that's dolly) to have some tea with her. That seems like a sensible idea and dolly is seated at a table with a few tea dishes. Incidentally, a little juice and a few cookies are always excellent for a little realism. Another alternative for the "lady" is shopping. A small table or a sturdy cardboard box can be the store. A few boxes, cans, and packages from the kitchen cupboard along with a few pieces of cardboard for money can be used and all is ready for business. The "lady" can shop first and then reverse roles with the grocery clerk. One nice thing about store playing is the wide variety of products besides food that can be "sold." Sewing thread, large buttons, ribbons, wool, toys, books, and small articles of clothing can all be purchased at the "store," and what a vehicle for language, as questions, explanations, and discussions are all an important part of "shopping."

Doctor and nurse roles always seem to be of considerable interest to the young toddler, as he frequently has had some first-hand experience, hopefully not unpleasant, with this kind of situation. With your old black purse as the doctor's bag, a tongue depressor for a thermometer, a few strips from an old sheet for a bandage, and one or two Band-Aids, the doctor is ready for the "patient"; and guess who is the patient—you, of course, if no playmate is visiting. The doctor role has another implication, as you can reinforce the idea of a helping friend who makes sick children well again. This often does soothe the anxious child when he is really sick and needs the doctor. As he gets older your toddler's playacting will become more elaborate and imaginative. A series of cardboard boxes or chairs become his train and he is the engineer; a sheet over a table becomes his castle, from which he sallies forth as a brave knight to do battle with the elements.

One large carton becomes his fire truck, his airplane, his boat, or his car. It is whatever he wishes it to be and that is the fun of dramatic play. And it sure is fun if the squeals and exuberant chuckles are any indication.

Listening activities

Sounds of every description have captivated the young child since birth. His curiosity about sound, what produces it and how it is produced by him, make it easy for a mother to provide a number of unique sounds different from those he hears in his daily life. Sound shakers are not much of a problem for the mother who has been saving everything and who now discovers among her treasures several small cans or boxes. Ideally the cans with removable lids and easy for the young child to handle are best. Boxes can be used but do not make quite such good "sounders" since they are made of cardboard. Baking-powder cans, some spice cans, and small cocoa cans are good, but in a pinch the one-pound coffee can be used even though it is more awkward for small hands to manipulate. In order to heighten the sound differences start with just two cans, put rice in one and in the other a few medium-sized stones. A quick shake of each can and interest is immediate. The two shakers are turned over to your toddler for his inspection and are opened, if this seems indicated, so that he may see and handle the objects making the different sounds. His queries about the sound makers may or may not be extensive and you answer them accordingly. If possible encourage him to answer his own questions. In any event, he will probably enjoy shaking them one at a time and perhaps both at the same time, now fast, now slow, producing different rhythms and sounds.

If interest is high a third can containing dried beans can be added so that there are three distinct sounds. A fourth can with a small piece of wood or with larger stones can give yet another 179 disinctive sound. However, when rice or beans or other similar foods are being used for play experience, your child must be closely supervised because of safety factors. Unfortunately, unattended children have put beans in noses and in ears with most unhappy results. Parents have to be on the alert all the time with children of this age, but luckily mothers often develop a sixth sense which sends them flying to their little one when some inexplicable feeling tells them their child is in danger. But under supervision, the sounders are safe to handle and examine.

An interesting kind of "guess-what" game for your toddler is one that involves animal sounds. It helps if you are clever at making the "oink, oink" and the "moo, moo" noises, but if not most toddlers are willing to accept a reasonable facsimile so you don't have too much to worry about. For some children mother needs only to make the animal sound and the child can tell her which animal it represents, but if she has some good animal pictures, this makes it easier. They can be spread out on the floor and looked at all at once. After the pictures have been viewed, discussed, and labeled, tell him you are going to make an animal sound and you want him to find the picture of that animal. Starting with a sure-fire one, say a cow, gets the game off to a good start. If he wants the roles reversed so that he makes the sound that is just great too.

Musical instruments through the ages have given man many beautiful moments. Children also have appreciated the sounds that special instruments make and for this reason have enjoyed making their own music as well as listening to the music of others. Adult instruments are rarely appropriate for use by small people so it becomes apparent that another kind of instrument must be provided for these budding young musicians. Again the toyshop has a good selection of miniature musical instruments that are excellent for toddlers. The xylophone, the drum, the cymbals, the tambourine, and the triangle are fairly inexpensive and good quality ones can be found with careful shopping. Happily a number of these instruments can be made from odds and ends around the house. The drum can be made out of that handy one-pound coffee can. Both ends need the plastic lid but this is a minor detail. Two pot lids about the same size are a natural for cymbals, and the tambourine can be made by using two aluminum pie plates sewn or stapled together. Actually only one pie plate needs to be used but this makes a rather fragile tambourine. Several holes are punched around the rim and small bells are tied to the rims in such a way as to be free hanging. A "guitar" can be made with a sturdy box. Elastic bands of different widths are looped around the box. If dad is a

cigar smoker he might consider just this once buying in quantity and getting a sturdy wooden cigar box. These are excellent for guitars. Bells strung on heavy string make pleasant sounds and can be attached to ankles and wrists if dancing is contemplated. Shakers are always appropriate and easy to make. The simplest kind is one where two smooth-edged frozen-orange-juice lids are fastened not too securely onto a flat piece of wood. Light wooden paint stirrers are just right for this. Another kind utilizes the

large-sized tart tins and a flat piece of wood about ½″ wide and 8″ to 10″ long. The stick is inserted between the two tart tins, which face each other, with the end of the stick protruding slightly from the other side. The tins are sewn together with heavy thread or wool. Just before the final stitch is made, rice or beans are placed inside and the sewing completed. With so many inexpensive musical instruments, all easy for the toddler to handle, the house should reverberate with the sound of happy music. For other musical instruments, see Appendix.

Puppets provide excellent listening experiences and are equally easy to make. Paper-bag puppets are the simplest. Draw a funny face on a paper bag, make a hole for a nose (your finger) and, presto, a puppet. You slip your hand in the bag and fasten it at the wrist with a rubber band. The stage can be made using one of the big armchairs or, with the help of a low stool or pile of magazines behind the chesterfield, another "stage" is easily arranged. A large cardboard box with front and back parts removed can also be used. The "stage" is placed on a table with a chair for the puppeteer, and when the audience is ready the play begins. Any story, not too complicated, where some actions such as jumping up and down, bowing, or hiding behind something can be imitated is bound to captivate your toddler, especially if the puppet talks directly to him and involves him in a conversation. Snake puppets made out of old socks are a great crowd pleaser. The toe is cut around the edge and a piece of cloth sewn in so that the "mouth" can open. Large buttons make beautiful eyes and if you want to go all out you can add a bit of curtain fringe for eyelashes. What a wonderfully silly-looking snake, just right for a silly little story. Oven mits with ears, eyes, and noses sewn onto them also make fast hand puppets and are a great outlet for your creativity. Another easy puppet can be made by using a large plain paper plate. Again you draw on a funny face and perhaps even add some yellow wool for hair. A Popsicle stick is glued on for a handle and another puppet 183 playmate is ready to share a story. Incidentally, with eyes, nose, and mouth cut out it makes a very suitable mask for a little fellow who wants to be someone else.

Reading

Reading has had an important place in helping to develop a child's relationship with his parents, his language, and his understanding that pictures represent real objects in his world. This is all managed while providing a stimulating yet quiet experience. In the early months the emphasis was more on looking at interesting pictures than on the actual story the pictures represented. Usually a mother would point out and label the objects and their features and turn the page without much more elaboration unless the baby expressed interest by his obvious rapt attention and continued observation. With the child nearing his second birthday this kind of reading has gradually been changing in focus, and while the toddler is still interested in the pictures, he is now equally interested in the story that the pictures help to embellish.

Choosing a book for this age-group is not always the easiest thing to do, but generally parents tend to choose one first of all with attractive pictures, and secondly with a story line they have found particularly appealing. This is a good rule to follow. A dull storybook for an adult to read will be a dull one to listen to. Fortunately there are many excellent books available for children, some of which become quite special and must be read over and over again. So familiar is the story, your toddler soon is doing the "reading," telling you the story as each page is turned. Sometimes for a little diversion you might try to change the story, but your alert companion corrects you in no uncertain terms. He knows what his special book says. Favorite books can sometimes disintegrate into dog-eared oblivion if you don't do a little extra protective work. This can be avoided somewhat by covering the pages with a handy plastic covering that can be cut to size and pressed firmly in place. A little book tape on the spine adds further life to it. It is well worth the extra trouble for you will find that favorite books get carted around, perhaps tasted, banged against objects, and read with loving care as your toddler sits on the floor or perhaps on his potty.

Felt boards offer a new kind of reading and for imaginative parents an avenue for their own creative talents. It helps if the story line is well worked out, especially if you are using your own story. There is certainly nothing wrong with using a story from a favorite book if that is preferable. A sturdy piece of heavy cardboard about 18″ x 18″ (a grocery carton is good for this) is covered with a piece of brightly colored felt. Small felt figures are cut from appropriately colored pieces of felt and the story can begin. Goldilocks and the three bears is easily adapted to a felt-board presentation. Three bears, large, medium, and small, are cut out of brown felt. Goldilocks is cut out of pink felt with a blue felt dress and yellow wool hair. Three chairs, bowls, beds, and table can be cut from almost any color available. A felt outline of a house or even a chalk line complete all the necessary accouterments. If you wish to elaborate further you can add flowers and trees for a garden and more furniture inside. On the other hand the story can be simplified so that only a few pieces are needed. After all, Goldilocks can just pay a friendly visit to the three bears if she wishes.

The floor is the best place for this kind of reading and you begin with the house, adding the pieces of furniture as you go on with the story. If this has interested your toddler he will soon want to participate in the felt-board story. Favorite stories that have been especially appealing to him can sometimes be presented in this way without too much trouble for you and with eager anticipation and participation from your toddler.

Since dad has altogether too little time with his child, reading bedtime stories is often his special opportunity to really get to know and enjoy his toddler. He has a bigger voice than mummy and because he too is an individual he can read the stories in his own inimitable way. He may even find he has hidden talents and special "sound-making" abilities as his child enjoys not only daddy's reading, but also daddy's own made-up stories. In this kind of a situation father and child each are able to appreciate and love one another. The bond deepens.

Summing up

While Eliza Doolittle in the popular musical *My Fair Lady* may have been "sick of words" and Professor Higgins sick of drilling Eliza to enunciate, the toddler delights in them as he repeats over and over again some weird and wonderful word for mother to decipher. His insistence that she understand his message together with his patient repetitions echo his mother's own repetitious labeling of objects and conversations with her toddler. Language has indeed become a meaningful vehicle of communication, as yet a little lopsided, for the toddler understands far more than he can actually articulate, which he feels he must use and practice. Along with idiosyncratic labels and special sounds, the toddler by now probably has many clear words in his vocabulary. His communicative skills have increased tremendously in this period, both physically and linguistically. As he gets thirsty, he may go to his mother wherever she may be and lead her to the kitchen while repeating "juice, juice" over and over again. His skills will continue to develop as he experiments with various language sounds and ways of getting people to interact with him.

Language and laughter go hand in hand with the toddler's growing independence. He seems to develop a very special sense of humor with which he delights not only himself but his parents as well. His *joie de vivre*, spontaneous gestures, and swiftly changing moods make mom's day both wonderful and frustrating. As her toddler experiments with acceptable ways of behaving he throws his juice cup forcefully on the floor with a knowing smile. Then coyly he looks at mom as if to say "just testing," and before she can say a word he becomes very serious and declares "no-o." In an instant he picks up the cup, hands it to mom with a big smile and a "di du," meaning "thank you," and all is well. . . . How can mom get angry at that innocent smiling face? He knows he shouldn't throw the juice cup on the floor, but it always gets a reaction from mom, sometimes negative, sometimes positive, as she just can't resist her little charmer. Besides, if he's really quick and there's some juice left in the cup, he can play in the spilled juice before it gets mopped up.

The toddler's language reflects his interests and his current concerns. As he learns single words and practices them, pretty soon he will be putting two words together, such as "more juice." Often they become a sad commentary on the fact that daddy has to go to work every day and the toddler won't get to see him for a while, thus "daddy bye-bye" or "bye-bye daddy" are also well-worn phrases. The first three-word sentence that the sixteen-month-old son of one of the authors used was "daddy car bye-bye," since his daddy went to work in the car.

The toddler has made so many gains during the past six months that parents have had a hard time keeping up. Is that really their "little baby" who is telling the dog off in no uncertain terms for eating a biscuit that he so generously offered? Yes, indeed, full of fun and boisterous, or quietly studious as he ponders a problem, he is growing physically and mentally by leaps and bounds, and during the next period will go on to consolidate the many new gains he has made to date.

6 Consolidating

the Gains

Twenty-four to Thirty Months

By this age the toddler is beginning to look more like a little child and less like a baby. His body proportions are rapidly changing and by the age of two and a half or so, he may actually reach half his adult height. There has been so much obvious growth and maturation in the last two years. In his social, emotional, intellectual, and language development he has already passed some important milestones and now, at this age, it seems to be a time for consolidating these gains, a time to unify and make sense out of the countless fragments of life that he has been picking up around him.

In his play activities he is experimenting with and practicing what he sees in a more sophisticated way than ever before. There are more pretend activities of cooking, washing dishes, talking on the telephone, and interactive social play such as tea partying and playing doctor or shopkeeper with mother or a playmate. He has engaged in these kinds of activities for some time now, but by this age he is able to pay more attention to the finer details of his pretend activities. He is aware that the telephone must be dialed first, and he has the idea of saying "hello" and "good-bye." He may carry on a conversation which is quite understandable. And, of course, there are the young ones who love to race to the real telephone when it rings and quite appropriately say "hello" when they pick it up, but often their skill ends there and the unfortunate caller has the task of persuading the youngster to get his mummy to the phone. Should the child get the idea, it is still uncertain whether he will hang up the telephone before he runs his errand or drop the receiver with a painful crunch to the caller's ear.

He has been watching his parents and learning so much detail as he refines his social behavior and expands his knowledge of many of those everyday activities that adults take for granted. He naturally wants to know more detailed and specific information and demonstrates this need by asking for more and more labels and explanations for things in his environment. In keeping with his increased awareness he is more sensitive to changes that occur in his home. For example, he notices when furniture has been shifted around or when there is a new and unfamiliar car in the driveway. He may react with great curiosity to new furniture and perhaps even with indignation to the familiar living-room furniture being changed around. If a piece of furniture is moved to another room without his seeing this being done, he will probably react with puzzlement when he sees the changed position but then recognizes the piece, and having mother's acknowledgement that, yes, something is different, he accepts the change and goes on his way. Perhaps by this age he will take pleasure in pointing out to dad when he comes home at the end of the day that there is something different or new in the house.

Gradually he is coming to be much more aware of the passing of time and also beginning to understand what time means. Words referring to time like "soon," "later," and "in a minute" are becoming more meaningful but he will still continue to mix up today, yesterday, and tomorrow. If parents have been in the habit of using these words as part of their everyday, natural conversation with him, then they do have a vague meaning for him. At least he knows that yesterday and tomorrow are not right now and this is a start. Although he is beginning to understand time, and the words "not right now" and "later" have some meaning for him, this does not mean that he can be expected to wait very long for something he wants to do right now. Waiting is hard, even for some adults, and a child this age will need help to master this skill for some time yet. One of the authors was treated to an example of this time phenomenon when a young child who had transferred to another day-care center came back to Mothercraft for a visit (after about six weeks) and in a very self-satisfied manner announced for all who cared to listen, "I was here yesterday!"

Although this is an age characterized by consolidation in the various spheres of development, there are some who refer to it as the unavoidable and difficult age of the "terrible twos." This is unfortunate, as it tends to overemphasize the natural growing pains of the child and may even lead parents to anticipate trouble. Such expectations could bring about additional difficulties, and, in fact, this kind of expectation is frequently referred to as a "self-fulfilling prophecy." The toddler is still very young, testing his boundaries and the limits his parents have set for him. There are lots of times when he is going to be his good-natured self, so perhaps it is wiser to forget the "terrible twos" and focus on these good times as well as on other areas of his behavior that may need special attention.

The child is beginning to learn that he can control his behavior, or at least that his parents prefer certain kinds of behavior to others, and they expect him to begin to be able to control himself. For example, the two-year-old does not necessarily view physical violence the way adults do. Whacking another child with a toy shovel is not necessarily done with anger or malice. It may be experimentation or imitation of similar actions he has seen around him—maybe on TV or when the dog has been disciplined. This kind of physical violence should be handled in a different way from when a child hits out in anger. A child of this age, when angry, often crumples up and cries rather than strikes out, or throws an object in sheer frustration. So when he does hit out, one has to discern whether or not it was in anger or as part of his natural experimentation. A large part of the whole learning process regarding hitting is his realization that hitting hurts. He has to learn that people and pets feel physical pain, just as he does.

Of course, he has a long way to go yet before there will be any measure of success in such inner control, but he is becoming aware of it. However, this does not mean that he has to control his *feelings* about his behavior. He is learning that it is all right to be mad at mummy, but not to hit mummy. By the same token it is acceptable for mother be angry at her child, but it is no more acceptable for her to strike out at him than it is for him to strike her. If she has the confused notion that it is all right for her to strike her child then what she is teaching him is: "When I get to be big like mommy, I can hit too." However, parents should keep in mind that sometimes they do lose their cool, and should they hit their child on impulse after a particularly frustrating time, all is not lost. This is a human reaction and parents feel just as badly about it as their child does. Intellectually he can begin to understand that he should not hit, but if he is hit by another child, a brother or sister, it will often be hard, if not impossible, for him not to retaliate. Nevertheless, by being encouraged not to hit and then being redirected or separated, as mentioned in Chapter 4, he is learning more acceptable ways to behave. Parents are not always going to be there and ready to step in quickly. Knowing what should be done and then being able to act appropriately is a challenge for most people no matter what age. He needs to know that while his parents don't approve of his lashing out in anger, they do understand his inability to always control this impulse. For the two-year-old in particular, the ability to reason about feelings and emotions in an abstract way is only just beginning to develop.

This age is also difficult for him because he is striving to do so many things that he sees others around him are able to do. The situation becomes especially touchy if he has older brothers and sisters. They can stay up later, they can go in and out of the house as they please, they can go off the front lawn, they can cross the street, play ball, and do a whole list of things that he is just not able to do on his own. But he wants to do them so much, and parents can applaud him for his eagerness, for this wish for independence shows his interest in the world and, very important, his willingness to get involved in it. But mom and dad must often check his enthusiasm and spoil his fun. As mentioned earlier, the best remedy seems to be to have ready a number of alternative activities that he really enjoys. He may complain loud and hard at first when this "trick" is pulled on him, but as mom and dad make the effort to engage him in another activity he can't resist for long and soon he is happily at work or play. To forgive and forget seems to come naturally to children this age if they know that they can basically depend on their world and the people in it.

Fine motor activities

The two-year-old, after being exposed to a wealth of opportunities for less complicated manipulative play, is now at the stage where his understanding of how to handle more complicated manipulative tasks may be ahead of his motor ability. He knows what to do but cannot always do it. He needs to refine his fine motor skills, and while this is a maturation process, practice with a few interesting tasks may help.

Plastic jars and bottles with all the various sizes of lids make an acceptable fine motor problem for an interested two-year-old. And, of course, there is nothing wrong with increasing the motivation to open the jar if that seems necessary by putting a little something in each container. For a beginning, two or three bottles, all exactly the same, will intrigue an inquisitive toddler 193 after a quick shake indicates that each one houses a different object. For the tall, narrow detergent bottles (don't forget to clean them well first) a small chain, an old bracelet, a string of beads on a very secure string, a pencil, or a crayon are just a few objects that will fit in easily and make a nice sound. Incidentally, empty tubes of lipstick and mascara, as well as eyebrow-pencil containers all make exciting detergent-bottle "finds." They also furnish a problem within a problem, since they in turn can be opened by clever little hands. The lipstick container can provide

even more dash if you tuck a roll of interesting material into the space that held the lipstick. You probably will have to do some digging first to remove any residual lipstick. A little picture rolled around a drinking straw which has been cut to the correct length is another surprise which can be found in a lipstick tube. For added enjoyment the picture and the material can be changed many times. The mascara brush on being retrieved is great for a new kind of painting, and the eyebrow pencil, hopefully with a little bit of the marking material still left, can be used for drawing.

For the wide-neck plastic jars, the possibilities for surprises are more extensive. Certainly large buttons, good-sized nuts and bolts, empty spools of thread, small compacts (the kind used for eye shadow), small balls, plastic animals and toys as well as clusters of bells all make fantastic "finds" and provide interesting sounds as well.

It is not likely that you will need to do much explaining or demonstrating to establish what is to be done, but a little encouragement may be necessary to get the "bottle opener" started. A quick shake and a "Hey, what's in here?" usually does the trick and the activity soon has your child's undivided attention. Frequently just unscrewing and rescrewing the lids keeps him happy and busy as he repeats the operation over and over again. In fact, parents are sometimes surprised at the extent of the repetition. He is trying to perfect a new skill. This same kind of perseverance has already been noted in the younger child—the lid was placed on the pot over and over again. No one understands the axiom, "practice makes perfect" better than a child.

There are some tasks at which dad outshines everyone else and one that comes to mind is a "threading board." An easy threading board can be made using the necks and corresponding tops of several plastic detergent bottles (see appendix for illustration). Screwing and unscrewing the tops takes good coordination and provides a wonderful feeling of accomplishment. 195

In order to make a more complicated board, in this case, dad, who knows all about the various kinds of things that are threaded together, especially in the plumbing and construction industries, goes to his local hardware shop and looks around. He is looking for large nuts and bolts (safety is a factor that has still to be considered), large wing nuts with corresponding bolts and different-sized metal and plastic adapters. A piece of smooth plywood, perhaps with ¼″ round edges and about 12″ square is the next item required. Painting the plywood board a bright color makes it very appealing but is not really necessary for full enjoyment. Assembling the threading board is quite easy. For additional safety the *smaller* pieces (the nuts) are glued to the board with epoxy glue. It is a good idea as well to do the same with the two pieces that make up the adapter task. It is also a good idea to start the board with only three problems, since this number is more likely to ensure initial success. More pieces can be added at a later date if this seems indicated.

If dad is a bit of a perfectionist he may want to cut out a few inserts so that some of the adapters can be firmly embedded and not stand out too much. For a little complexity some of the new additions can be set at an angle, or right on their sides so that the toddler has more manipulation to do in order to have the parts fit correctly.

When the board is first presented, time for the usual preliminary examination is made available. Since the size differences of the nuts and bolts are quite fine, the "carpenter" will try by the trial-and-error method to fit the pieces together in various combinations, some of which will fit and some not. At the conclusion of his examination, your toddler is shown how each bolt fits into its corresponding nut, that is, of course, if he has not already figured this out. Once the task is mastered, that will not be the end of it, as he will still want to spend time unscrewing and rescrewing the pieces. He is again trying to perfect his skill and consolidate his learning.

Another kind of "open-and-close-the-door" board is a natural for dad. Back to the hardware store, or, if he is a sailing enthusiast, to his special supply store. This board is a little more complex because it requires two sheets of plywood, one on top of the other. The top piece has a number of little hinged doors, each opened with a different kind of catch. Ordinary cupboard catches, cupboard turns, cupboard bolts, elbow catches, hooks, and safety hasps are just a few of the more conventional types used in the home or boat.

It is not hard to add extra zest to this activity by making the board in the shape of a house with pictures of people and objects   197 behind the various doors and windows. With regular picture changes this board could really become a favorite.

The many kinds of colorful self-locking building blocks readily available in most toyshops should not be overlooked for fine motor experiences. Aside from their building properties, their bright color, small size, and light weight usually make them captivating for the young toddler. There are several excellent types on the market—Lego, Minibrix, Tinkertoy to name a few. Since these blocks come in large sets, when they are first offered don't overwhelm your child by giving him all of them at once. Rather, start with half a dozen or so and let him examine and manipulate them to his heart's content. When he seems finished, and only then, step in and show him how they fit together if that seems necessary. At first two or three are joined, then, as interest increases, you can go on to more complex structures—a tall tower, a bridge, a garage for a favorite car, or a house for a favorite doll. As you continue, your companion may begin to construct his own buildings. He wants to do what you are doing, it looks so interesting.

While one does not ordinarily think of hair rollers and clips as having building properties, they can nevertheless be utilized in this way. Clipping the rollers together so that they are side by side is a good start, but they can also be piled one on top of another in all sorts of strange conglomerations. Once your toddler gets the idea he needs a fairly good supply of rollers and clips so that he can build whatever he wants. But oh, what fun, what creativity, and maybe what a mistake as you find all your rollers have been purloined and now seem to belong most definitely to someone else.

The toddler is not quite ready for sewing as such but a kind of sewing can be provided that is both safe and inexpensive. Pegboard is needed for the "fabric" and a piece of sturdy cord with one end reinforced with Scotch tape is needed for the "thread." The pegboard need not be much more than 10″ x 10″

and the cord about 18" long. A safety pin attached to one end of the "thread" will keep it from slipping through. When all is ready, show your "tailor" how to sew. In and out and in and out. With so many openings the sewing can go on for as long or as short a time as interest prevails. A long shoelace with the end blocked either with a large knot or with a safety pin can sometimes be used equally successfully. Shoelaces have the added advantage of coming in different kinds of material and in different colors. Such a mixture can make a very attractive mosaic.

Science activities

The term "science," for our purpose at least, will be used primarily in reference to the plant and animal world as well as to certain other scientific phenomena that seem relevant to this age-group. Animals, of course, are a source of great interest to children as well as to adults and there are many species which can become an enjoyable part of a household. Dogs and cats are usually considered first, but while these make lovely pets it may not be possible to consider them because of space or other restrictions. If this is the case, the smaller animals may be just the thing.

Gerbils are particularly good, as they are quite small, do not require a large cage, and are easily cared for. They will sometimes bite when frightened or if they have not been handled frequently when they were young. The caretaking part is of interest to you since you will likely get this job more often than other members of the family. Food for gerbils is not much of a problem. Scraps of lettuce, celery, and carrot, and sunflower, watermelon, and pumpkin seeds form a large part of their diet. Shredded newspaper for the bottom of the cage facilitates cleaning and can be easily replaced when necessary. This isn't too often as this animal needs very little water, most of which comes from the lettuce and other vegetables, and because he needs so little water he excretes almost no urine. As a matter of fact, gerbils only produce about three drops a day. But his cage does need changing occasionally, and if cedar shavings are available (they are fairly inexpensive), then replacement of this material is required even less frequently. The gerbils need to be handled often and in a gentle way from the time they are purchased. In no time at all they will become used to handling and will not be frightened when they are taken out of the cage. This is the part which is so enjoyable for the toddler. To fondle and stroke this tiny furry animal is an experience that should not be missed if at all possible.

Hamsters, rats, mice, and guinea pigs also make satisfactory pets for small children and do not require very much more care than the gerbils. But the care needed is well worth the time and effort because of the enjoyment provided by these tiny pets. Since children learn by observing how these animals are handled and fondled by adults, they will imitate the adult and handle them in the same way. If, for example, you really do not like a certain animal but purchased it because you thought it would be nice for your child to have, then you probably will pass on your aversion to your child in spite of your best efforts. Better to have an animal both parents can enjoy right from the beginning, and then your toddler will be able to learn to love it, to enjoy it, and eventually to take good care of it.

For those situations where these four-legged animals are not suitable, an aquarium makes an acceptable alternative. A small one is not too expensive, is easy to maintain, and costs little for fish food. If you aren't too sure about the value of fish and do not want to spend money unnecessarily, you might consider a couple of goldfish in a bowl for a start. But once having made the decision to have an aquarium, there are many kinds of beautiful and exotic tropical fish that provide a fascinating picture whatever the time of day. Some of the fish are quick moving, darting hither and yon, others sail slowly by, still others glide by with long trailing fins. Snails should be added to keep the aquarium clean and they are also interesting to watch as they climb up the side or crawl over the bottom. Adding a salamander makes the scene even more interesting, as this little lizard moves around the water in his own special way. When he runs out of oxygen, he comes to the surface and rests on a platform that is attached to the side of the aquarium for just this purpose.

Turtles have always delighted children, but in recent years

it has been discovered that these little animals can transmit salmonella, a disease that can be quite serious for both children and adults. Unfortunately a turtle can be a carrier. Even if it is apparently healthy, it is able, nevertheless, to pass on this infection all too easily. This is sad news for turtle lovers, but when there is a serious health hazard it cannot be ignored. In most cases, the value of the turtle, delightful though it may be, is far outweighed by the risk.

For those families lucky enough to have easy access to the countryside, an inexpensive but fascinating aquarium can be provided by utilizing the animals found in many of the still unspoiled ponds and streams of North America. Margaret Waring Buck has written an excellent little book called *Pets from the Pond* in which she describes how to make and stock various kinds of aquariums using the water plants found at the edges of lakes, ponds, and streams, as well as the snails, clams, fish, tadpoles, frogs, newts, salamanders, and crayfish also found there. Included in her book is the food necessary for each species and the method of feeding. What a wonderful experience for a young child to plan, stock, and care for his own aquarium. All this does require considerable effort on the part of parents, but they might be surprised at how enjoyable they find this science adventure, learning and exploring with their child.

The terrarium is another source of keen interest to the budding biologist. Several kinds of animals make very suitable and exciting inhabitants if the terrarium is planned as far as possible so that it resembles their natural habitat. It should be large: a five-to-ten-gallon container is ideal. Fine-mesh screening, which lets in light and air, is necessary to cover the opening so that the little creatures will not escape. It should also have moist and dry areas, small plants and rocks (snakes need rocks to help them shed their skins), and a large flat pan with enough water so that the animals can submerge themselves when necessary. Frogs, chameleons, salamanders, newts, and snakes can find life in a terrarium quite comfortable under these circumstances. The salamanders and newts eat worms, raw fish, meat, fish eggs, and insects. The chameleons eat flies and mealworms and are not as suitable as the other animals since they eat only live food. The frogs eat earthworms, insects, bits of raw meat, and fish. Garter snakes (one of the most common and harmless in North America) eat worms, small fish, and frogs. The idea of having a snake in the house is unfortunately abhorrent to some adults, and if this is true in your case, this creature would not be suitable for your terrarium. The aversion to the snake, as to the mouse, would most certainly be transmitted to your youngster. In spite of this, parents can help their child be unafraid and able to value these beneficial animals (snakes are beneficial because they eat crop-destroying rats and mice) by trying not to exhibit their own fear, by not attempting to destroy them whenever they are stumbled upon, and by pointing out the many beautiful characteristics of these reptiles. In this way they will help their young naturalist to have a positive and healthy attitude toward snakes.

Tadpoles by themselves make an interesting spectacle. After finding the frog eggs among plants in shallow water, they can be placed in a regular fishbowl, a large gallon jar, a plastic dishpan, or a regular aquarium with enough water from the pond or stream in which they were located to keep the eggs well suspended. A few water plants make an attractive setting. When the tadpoles begin to hatch, only a few should be kept and the remaining unhatched eggs should be removed. If they are not removed they begin to decompose and all the tadpoles will die. There is simply not enough oxygen for very many tadpoles. One of the authors had such an experience when her youngsters found a mass of eggs in a little stream close to their home. They weren't quite sure what they had discovered but their father had a good idea and accompanied them back to the stream. They all returned with several clusters of eggs that were put into 203 an unused aquarium and closely watched. Some eggs hatch in a few days, others take longer. These particular eggs seemed to be the slower kind and were not watched as closely or carefully as they should have been after the initial excitement of discovery had died down. They hatched eventually and the inevitable happened. Not only did they all die, but their decomposition produced a powerful, nauseating odor. What a disappointment to the children, but it was now too late to get more eggs. The lesson was hard, but both adults and children learned from it. Tadpoles will eat the algae that form on the plants, but raw lettuce, spinach, and sometimes bits of hard-boiled egg yolk are quite tempting. Larger tadpoles will eat bits of raw meat and fish as well as prepared fish food. Once the tadpoles are hatched their progressive changes into frogs make a fascinating study bound to entrance adult and child.

For the child really interested in the natural sciences, a Formicarium is well worth the effort. A Formicarium is an observation ant home. It can be made from two panes of glass, 18" x 18", with a tight-fitting wooden frame that holds the glass panes no farther apart than two or three inches. This allows for easy viewing of the ants. There are two openings in the frame for eyedroppers, one of which is used to provide honey and water, the other to moisten the soil at weekly intervals. Too frequent watering often causes molding. Small scraps of food from the table can be added, but again only in minute quantities. These scraps should be removed if not eaten in a few days. When all is ready, dad and toddler scout around for an ant hill, dig it up, and place it in the Formicarium. It helps if the glass is covered with red cellophane on the outside, as this permits observation without too much disturbance to the inhabitants, who are used to working in the dark. Better still, keeping it covered until viewing is desired encourages the ants to function in a more normal atmosphere. After all, the underground is a dark place. What excitement as the cover is removed and the ants are observed going about their business, constructing their nest, feeding their queen, and caring for their young. A truly fascinating scene with endless activity and variety. There is, as well, endless questioning and information processing for the young observer.

While the ant home involves a fair amount of work, an insect cage capable of housing a caterpillar or a praying mantis, a spider or a cricket on a short-term basis (just a few days) is quite easy to make. A gallon jar with soil in the bottom, a branch for climbing, and a wire screen for the top are all that is necessary. Caterpillars need leaves for food, spiders and praying mantises need insects of all kinds, and crickets eat soft leaves if they are the outdoor kind. Crickets that live in cellars and other dark damp places eat meat. In China and Japan, crickets are kept as musical pets and dine on lettuce, cucumber, masticated chestnuts, bits of fish, and a drop of honey every now and again. The chirp of the cricket varies with the season and according to the species of the cricket. In the home, in addition to soft leaves, little bits of bean, lettuce, and moistened bread from time to time make a varied diet. A little bit of bonemeal added to an insect's diet will lessen cannibalism among them.

Birds should not be overlooked as pets for a young child. The two most popular kinds are the canary and the budgerigar, usually called a "budgie." Since both species have many colorful varieties and produce lovely singers, the question of which bird is better suited as a pet needs to be answered. Budgies appear to have a little edge over the canaries since they are easier and quicker to tame, can be taught little tricks, and, more important, can be taught to speak. Male canaries make beautiful singers and can be trained to a certain extent. They can be trained to sit on an adult's finger without becoming frightened but are probably too delicate for a child to handle. Canaries do not seem quite as versatile, entertaining, or interesting as the budgie and for these reasons one would probably choose the latter.

205

Once having made the decision, wise parents, unless they are already familiar with birds, need to consult the public library for basic information on the care, feeding, and handling of the pet. As soon as the basics are understood, their child can then begin to get involved by handling his budgie very gently and always under adult supervision. He can also begin teaching it to talk, and what a wonderful learning experience that is for both of them.

If it is not possible to have a bird indoors, bird feeders to attract wild birds are a very satisfactory substitute. Of course, if the parents are living in a high-rise apartment this may not be practical. But for those families able to have a wild-bird feeder in their yard, an exceptional experience for both child and adult is at hand. Naturally the feeder has to be arranged so that neither squirrels nor cats can reach it, and yet it must be easily reachable for replenishment when necessary. Pieces of suet are a great favorite in the winter, and, along with wild-bird seed, suet is available in most supermarkets. Bird-watching under these circumstances is great fun, especially when a new arrival appears and becomes one of the "regulars." And what joy when the first robin appears; that always makes everyone pleased for it means that spring is near at hand. With each new visitor make a point of looking up the species in the bird book (this is a must) and show the picture to your child, who may begin to surprise you with his interest and growing knowledge. Along with this understanding is a greater awareness of the many living creatures in his world that are beautiful and fascinating to observe.

Sometimes it is just not possible to have any of these animals as pets and, if so, parents can turn to the plant world to give their child a knowledge of living and growing things. However, to have to wait is very hard for a young child and delaying gratification is not really one of his strong points. When he wants something to happen, he wants it to happen right away and finds it

difficult to understand why it takes so long for a seedling to sprout or a new leaf to appear. Many plants take time to sprout and grow, but some do grow quite quickly and it helps a lot to introduce the child to the world of plants with the fast-growing kind. Radishes, oats, and grass will start sprouting about a week after they have been planted in soil or vermiculite. Beans also grow very quickly and if placed between a moist piece of blotting paper and the glass of a jar, progress is easily observed. After starting the quick-growing seeds, you might want to consider introducing other plants that take longer. The sweet potato, partially suspended in water (toothpicks inserted will keep it from being totally immersed) will produce a lavish green vine that grows and grows and grows. Potatoes and carrots can also be started in this way and transferred to pots when the roots are well developed. With this method of growth, the lengthening of roots and the unfolding of the leaves can be closely observed by the young gardener. The top part of the carrot can be placed in a shallow pan of water and if kept moist (this is critical for all seeds) will grow just as well this way. All you need to do is to remember to save the top of one of the carrots you served for dinner. Parsnip, beet, and pineapple tops also grow in this way, but the pineapple grows much more slowly. Nasturtiums, pansies, zinnias, and marigolds, planted in egg cartons containing soil (nurseries usually have suitable mixtures for all plants), are great fun, especially if the carton is the kind that can be painted by the young gardener-artist first. This makes a very attractive gift for the garden of a favorite aunt or that very special grandfather.

If the young gardener has been interested in the whole process of planting, watering, and observing plants, it might be worthwhile to introduce him to bulbs. Narcissus, tulips, hyacinths, and daffodils produce lovely flowers. Unfortunately, the flower is a long time coming so far as the child is concerned, but frequent checks for progress, along with the business of planting faster-growing seeds, will help minimize the wait. The narcissus can be placed on stones in water and left in a dark cool place until roots develop. It can also be potted and kept in the same place, with water added sparingly. After two months it should gradually be brought into the light and watered more frequently. Not so often, however, that it becomes saturated. Tulips, crocuses, hyacinths, and daffodils are treated in the same way, and will produce lovely flowers. If they are started in late fall, what a gay spring garden they will make in the middle of winter!

If there is space in the back yard for a small vegetable garden, then both parent and child will have a lot of fun growing things. The toddler is a natural digger and loves getting the soil ready for planting. He is also a very helpful waterer and general all-round handyman. In fact, you might have to let him know that too much care will prevent the plants from developing. Drowning plants don't need any more water. Besides the sheer joy of working with earth, the value of this kind of garden is in your child's growing understanding of where some of the food he eats comes from. And what a wonderful feeling of achievement when finally his first very own home-grown tomato is served at dinner with mom and dad suitably impressed. Grapefruit, orange, and lemon seeds can also be planted. They seem to get a good start if they are wrapped in small pieces of newsprint that are moistened, put in a plastic bag, and placed in a warm area. A check each week for moisture and for assessing progress is all that is necessary. Once the roots are developed at least one inch they can then be potted and will continue to give pleasure to both mother and child with their deep, rich, shiny-green foliage.

For a busy mother, however, gardening may not be possible or even enjoyable and, if so, she should not be too concerned. Your walks with your child, especially in the park, or a trip to a greenhouse or a botanical garden can certainly be utilized to bring the plant world to him in a quite delightful and worthwhile way.

The child who has been allowed to explore, solve simple age-related problems, and encouraged to ask questions is the child who is going to continue to develop an inquiring mind about the world around him. As he moves into the first half of his third year, he becomes more aware of basic scientific phenomena and looks for understandable answers. Here is a place where parents can provide interesting little experiments with fairly simple explanations.

The toddler has been playing in and enjoying water from the time he was a tiny baby. He is already aware of some of its properties. It can be poured from one container to another and takes the shape of the new container, it has no taste, cannot be held in the hand for very long, and is clear in color. Now is the time to introduce new properties. The ice-cube tray is brought out and one or two cubes are put in a bowl. Naturally, it must be thoroughly examined by the budding scientist. When he is finished, you suggest one ice cube be put in a pot and heated in order to see if anything happens. Something certainly does happen: an object which just a short while ago could be held in his hand, was very cold and hard, is now only slightly warm water. You explain that the ice cube is frozen water, and to further demonstrate put the same water from the melted ice cube back into the ice tray and refreeze it to its previous form. One of the nice things about winter is the profusion of icicles that provide additional understanding when your toddler notices them dripping water and then disappearing completely into water when brought inside. A snowball brought inside disappears into water in the same way but more quickly. How come? he asks, and the same explanation, "It is frozen water," is sufficient. A lengthy discourse on frozen vapor producing snow is much too complicated for now.

During his water play, your toddler may have already noticed that some things sink to the bottom and some float on top of the water. If this has escaped his observation, he would probably be interested in having it brought to his attention. 209

You do not need a lot of water but you do need a number of objects to demonstrate this principle. Fortunately, it is not too difficult to find things that float. A quick look around the house and a wooden spoon, a bar of Ivory soap, a cork from last night's dinner wine, a teething ring, a wooden block, a rubber ball, and a wooden toothpick are located. Along the way you have also retrieved a number of objects that sink—metal measuring spoons, a hair clip, a house key, a large stone, a paper clip, and a metal button. Water play can make a bit of a mess but you can save yourself some grief by using lots of newspaper on the floor with

a large piece of plastic underneath for an added precaution. If the house is warm, the least amount of clothing, and that well protected with a plastic apron or the already-mentioned plastic garbage bag with the large holes for head and arm saves some extra work. Incidentally, parents do not need to worry about accidental smothering. With so many openings in the bag it is highly unlikely that this will happen. The unused plastic bags are kept well out of his reach, and during the water play the child will always be under your careful supervision. This careful supervision is necessary because this activity can quickly get out of hand if the enthusiastic toddler does not have his energies directed in a positive way.

When you have made adequate preparations (this really doesn't take too much time), your toddler is given the various objects to examine and manipulate in the water. During this play utilize whatever opportunities present themselves to point out the phenomenon that some of his playthings float and some sink. "Oh, look, your key has sunk to the bottom of the water but your wooden block is floating on top." At this age he may not ask why this is so, but if he does he is simply told that the block is made of wood and wooden things float, the key is made of metal and most metal things sink. While engaged in water play you might demonstrate how some paper absorbs water and some does not. Paper towels and Kleenex quickly take in water and when squeezed release the water. On the other hand, smooth glossy paper or good-quality stationery does not take in water and so does not release any when squeezed. Again, if an explanation is required, you respond, "The Kleenex is made up of a lot of tiny pieces not as close together as the other paper and this helps it to hold water."

Children do not give the air around them much thought, primarily because they are not really aware of its existence. It cannot be seen and is seldom felt. But it is all around, of course, and children can be made aware of this by a number of simple   211 activities that usually delight them. The well-protected summer fan allows your toddler to "feel" the air when you turn it on. A large mirror placed so that he can see himself will allow him to observe what the air does to his hair and will undoubtedly intrigue him. "That's air, and the fan pushes it so that you can feel it," is an explanation that you can make. To reinforce this understanding tie several pieces of colorful ribbon to the fan and again turn it on. Something is moving the ribbons in the same

way his hair was moved. Inexpensive windmills found in most dime and variety stores add a great deal of fun to this experiment. Once again the fan is turned on and away the windmill goes. A little cork boat with a toothpick and paper sail can also be used to demonstrate the presence of air. The fan is turned on the small boat floating on top of the water in a shallow pie plate. The water itself indicates the presence of air when the softly flowing breeze produces a little ripple and the tiny boat sails gently along.

A parachute doll is another way to emphasize the presence of air. A piece of cloth at least twelve inches square (one of dad's handkerchiefs is just the thing) is fastened on each corner with a string and all four strings are then fastened to a tiny, light-weight doll, which floats gently down when tossed in the air. If you are lucky enough to have two dolls exactly the same and both are tossed in the air at the same time, your toddler can clearly see the difference in the rate of fall. Why is that? is sure to be a question. You explain: "There is air under the parachute (he has already been told dad's handkerchief is now a parachute) and this keeps dolly from falling too quickly. The other dolly had no parachute and so he fell much more quickly. Here, let's do it again, and you toss them up this time." Dad's paper gliders should not be bypassed as another way of emphasizing this fact and as dad and toddler toss their gliders to see whose goes the farthest a simple explanation should be made. Balloons are even more exciting in helping to teach the toddler about air, but only if you are able to blow them up—no mean feat. Releasing the air near your toddler's face again allows him to feel that "something" that he cannot see but is beginning to understand is present everywhere nevertheless.

Whenever your toddler is out for a walk you can point out that the clouds being blown across the sky (if they are dark you can also explain that the clouds are holding water, and it will rain soon), the leaves fluttering on the trees, and the flag waving

213

from the top of the building are being moved by air, and while he still cannot see that air, these moving objects confirm its existence.

It is not too early to introduce the magnifying glass and it probably pays in the long run to buy a large one. A small one is too hard for the toddler to focus on and he soon loses interest. With the right size, the magnifying glass can provide lots of interesting scenes. There is one excellent magnifying glass on the market which is on a tripod, and, because it is stationary, makes viewing much simpler and less complicated. Both hands are free if necessary and there is no movement. Your toddler will at first be interested in his own body, and when he sees his hand and fingers enlarged he is surprised. The explanation, if necessary, is simple. "This is called a magnifying glass and it makes your hand and all sorts of things seem bigger than they really are." A small salamander placed in a box so that it can't travel far and then viewed under the magnifying glass looks like a dinosaur and walks as one imagines a dinosaur would walk if it were alive today. Small wiggly worms, creepy caterpillars, and busy ants are equally fascinating to watch. Bugs, leaves, flowers, pretty stones, blades of grass, and twigs found on walks and observed in this way provide a great deal of intensive viewing. There is no doubt that the magnifying glass makes the toddler's world even more impressive than it was before. He is beginning to realize what a truly exciting world this is.

At first glance magnets seem way out as a source of interest to the toddler. This is simply not so because he is intrigued with everything he hears, sees, smells, tastes, and touches. He may not understand—much of his world is not understandable to him yet —but this is not to suggest that he does not find it absorbing. Fortunately there are a number of magnets in all shapes and sizes—bugs, flowers, bars, and horseshoes—that can be used in a play session. For really effective magnet play it helps if parents purchase at least one good one. This usually means an outlay of two or three dollars but is well worth the extra money because a strong magnet can hold many more objects. Parents shouldn't be surprised if they find the magnets just as much fun as their toddler. Most adults do. For a start, a square Pyrex baking dish raised on two sturdy books so that you can put your hand under it when you want to, and a few safety pins or paper clips or metal clips you use to set your hair are adequate for the experiments. The objects are placed in the dish and the magnet is moved slowly toward them until they jump and cling to it. "Hey, what's happening?" you wonder as you see the look on your toddler's face. It is a puzzle to him, so you explain, "This is a magnet and it pulls metal things. Isn't that something?" Once again the clips and pins are placed in the dish but this time you place the magnet underneath the dish and slowly move it around. "The magnet is pulling the pins around. Would you like to try?" Another experiment can be performed. A paper clip is dropped into a glass of water and your toddler, with your help in guiding his hand, slowly draws the paper clip out of the water and over the top of the glass. If dad is lucky enough to be able to find some iron filings, he can make them stand up when he places the magnet under the dish they have been placed in. He can also make them follow the magnet as he moves it over the bottom in the same way the clips were moved. Your toddler is eager to try his hand and, as usual, he should be obliged—participation enhances the relationship as well as the learning.

Another great activity can be played with a little sailboat similar to the one used in the wind experiment. This time the cork has a screw or nail placed inside it and the toothpick mast with its paper sail is pressed into the cork. The boat is ready for action. Just enough water is put in the dish so that the boat is free floating and the magnet is placed against the bottom of the dish close to the boat and then moved slowly away. The sailboat seems to be sailing by itself. A half walnut shell with a thin band of metal wire, not aluminum of course, around the bottom pro-

vides another kind of boat with the mast easily fastened with some well-chewed gum.

A dartboard using magnets can give the toddler lots of enjoyment. The dartboard design is made on a piece of paper at least twelve inches in diameter and is fastened with Scotch tape to a cookie sheet (not the aluminum kind; this does not work). Next you need to find several of those magnetized hooks that are used to hold up hand towels or hot pads in the kitchen, and remove the round magnet in the bottom. They usually have a little round hole in them and feathers can be pushed through until they are firmly embedded and the protruding ends clipped off. The dart is ready and the game can proceed. If making the equipment is too much trouble, and it is a bit of trouble, then you might canvass the toy stores for a commercial model. In the beginning it helps if you place the dartboard on the floor and show your toddler how to let the darts fall, hopefully near the center. If he tries to throw, he may not be too successful, as this takes the skill of an older child. Don't be surprised if you have the urge to toss a few yourself; it is fun and will give you a good idea as to how well co-ordinated you are. This is another one of those games that improve with age (the toddler's age, of course) especially when he can really throw the darts and the board is hung on the wall.

Fishing has been one of man's greatest pleasures and a small fisherman can begin enjoying this experience with his very own fish pond. That handy magnetized kitchen hook suspended on a string about two feet long and fastened to a fishing pole (your long wooden spoon is perfect for this) completes the first requirement. Next you need to find interesting but small objects made of metal that can be used for exciting "finds." They have to be fairly light so the magnet will hold them, but if there is difficulty here, the stronger magnet, which has a more powerful pull, can be used just as well. If dad feels really creative he might consider making some fish out of picture wire shaped in various exotic forms. An aluminum-foil fish with a paper clip for a tail works very well, as the clip can be magnetized where the aluminum cannot. But in actual fact your toddler will have fun retrieving anything from his "fish pond." A little bit of water colored with green food coloring placed in his old plastic baby bath or a small plastic dishpan will make a fine pond. In order to ensure success, the bottom of the "pond" has to be fairly well   217 covered with "fish." Once he gets the hang of it, the fisherman will be able to develop a little more skill in directing his fishing line to a specific spot.

Since magnets will work through wood, dad can make a game that will provide fun for both, but only if your toddler has been managing the magnet fairly well. A thin piece of plywood 18" x 12" standing on four legs about 4" high is the first pre-requisite. A roadway is painted on the top, a garage made from a small box is placed in one area, a couple of cars are added, and the fun can begin. The toddler is shown how to move a car around, holding the magnet under the wood. This is a place where a good magnet comes in handy because it is hard for the child of this age to figure out exactly where to place the magnet in order to move the car. If he is fairly close, a strong magnet will do the rest. It should be remembered that this game is only enjoyable if it can be mastered. With too little success and much frustration it is no fun and should be put away and offered again when the toddler is older.

Visits

Most parents understand the value of taking their child with them when they go places. In some cases there is not much choice, particularly when it is the weekly trip to the grocery store. It is just not practical and a bit too expensive to leave the inquisitive toddler home each week with a baby-sitter and deprive him of a fascinating experience. He never seems to get tired of looking at people and things, all of which seem to change from week to week, so that there is constant variety and stimulation. This is a golden opportunity for language as you label the various foods, explain where they come from or how they are used. "This is a bag of flour and I make your cookies out of flour. Here are some green peas in their pods. Let's buy a few so you can see the peas inside." Sometimes a clerk is offering samples of some

new food. This must be tasted as well. No wonder grocery shopping is so enjoyable.

While it is a little harder to transport a small child around by a bus or train, once in a while it is worth the trouble and inconvenience, especially if the parent can manage to get in the front car of a subway train. This is an excellent Saturday excursion for dad, who will probably find the trip more fun than he expected because his small child is so entranced going in and out of long dark tunnels. Explanations are always required, of course. "The train is called a subway train because it goes underground. This way there is more room on top for houses and other buildings and we can also go faster because there are no cars or trucks to get in the way." For those who travel by bus, the front seat near the driver is the place to be and naturally our young commuter puts the ticket in the box just like the grownups do. The streetcar or trolly bus is worth another special trip, again with the eager passenger right near the driver. One important fact needs to be noted. Trips of fairly short duration are in order. Long trips tend to tire and bore a small fellow and then the glow of a great time is suddenly lost.

Early exposure to the local library with its long shelves of books and magazines and its children's story time all help your child appreciate the library service and the books it provides. He begins also to understand that there are a large number of adults, including his own parents, who love reading and who have come to the library, as he has come, to choose a book. Regular visits can only enhance this appreciation.

It is not too early to consider visits to more exotic places, for example, the museum, where the time spent need only be geared to the level of the child's interest and energy, or perhaps your level of energy. Most museums are so large and contain so many fascinating exhibits that only a small section can be examined at any one time, but that just means there will be lots of opportunities for return visits. The same holds true for the zoo, where the explorers may wish to spend a couple of hours concentrating on the reptile house or the aviary or the jungle beasts or whatever.

The firehouse is an appropriate place to visit—that is, if visitors are allowed. If it is permitted then it is eminently suitable, as a recent experience of one of the authors demonstrated. A group of young children from her day-care center went for such a visit and it was discovered that although the children had read stories and seen pictures of fire engines, perhaps had small ones themselves or had even seen one from a distance, they were unprepared for the spectacle they faced when they first entered the firehouse. The sheer size of the engines amazed them. This was quite clear to the teachers present when they saw the look of amazement on the small faces. Fire engines viewed up close are enormous, and it took a few minutes before the children were interested in approaching these huge red monsters. But with a small hand safely tucked into an adult's hand, they finally ventured forth and began a protracted and excited examination. The *pièce de résistance* occurred when several of the delightful firemen slid down the pole. They seemed to come out of nowhere. The trip was a great success and the next day parents reported hearing lengthy stories about it, parts of which they had trouble deciphering because of their offspring's excited chatter.

Sometimes a suitable play or puppet show designed for children is presented and should not be missed if there is any opportunity to attend. Parents usually find this form of entertainment enjoyable and when they look at the enraptured face of their child they know it was a good idea and they decide to repeat going to the theater as often as they can manage. Not all these various kinds of excursions will have a happy impact on each child, but chances are that a good many will provide them with enjoyment and will prove worthwhile in terms of the child's interests. Exposure to variety will help parents determine which ones are most appropriate for their child.

Summing up

While the toddler has been consolidating his gains during this period, life has not come to a standstill as many new events have been added to his busy schedule and growing repertoire of exciting experiences. He has developed his gross motor as well as fine motor skills and has added many new words to his rapidly expanding vocabulary. As he vacillates between his earlier dependence and babyhood and his feelings of independence and confidence he is often confused by the demands that his newly found sophistication places on him. He becomes easily frustrated when he tries to express himself verbally and is just not understood—he knows what he wants, but how can he get his point across? Understanding parents realize his dilemma and draw upon their strength and patience to help him through those awkward times.

While his attention span has probably increased tremendously, especially when he is doing something that intrigues him, his patience and ability to delay gratification are still limited. He wants what he wants now. In the case of an object he often resorts to grabbing, pushing, and pulling to get it. This angry outburst is short-lived if a suitable substitute is found and he is told he can have a turn with the object or toy later. For example, one of the authors arbitrated in an argument over a toy that two toddlers just had to have at the same time. Since one of them had located it first, the other toddler was told that she could have a turn after a little while. A substitute was offered and grudgingly accepted. After five or ten minutes the disputed toy was discarded by the first toddler and the author took it over to the other toddler, who was now quite happily engaged in another activity. When presented with the toy she had just had to have a few minutes ago, the toddler gave it the merest glance and continued in her activity. This is typical when disputes occur over a treasured object provided a satisfactory substitute can be found. The gesture, however, must be made by the adult because a promise was made and the child should have the option of having a turn with the toy when it becomes available. This helps to reinforce the idea that when mom or someone else says "later," or "in a few minutes," they really mean it, and can be depended upon to deliver.

With his ability to walk for greater distances, the pleasures of the outside world become more a part of the toddler's life. How exciting it is to walk in a shopping mall, along the street, or in a park rather than being pushed in a stroller all the time. How much fun it is to go on visits to special places in special vehicles such as buses, trains, trolleys, and subways. And, oh, what joy to splash through puddles on a rainy day and make tracks in freshly fallen snow. All this may be somewhat exhausting for busy parents but the joys of having a healthy, curious toddler bring a warm glow as the family grows and learns together. While nothing startlingly new has happened during these past six months, it has been fun as well as frustrating, and has also served as a preparation time for the toddler as he now shifts into high gear to meet the excitement, challenge, and broadening scope of the preschool years.

7 Shifting

into High Gear

Thirty to Thirty-six Months

The three-year-old has come a long way from his early bassinet days. During these first few years of life his growth has been steadily and rapidly accelerating—so much to see, hear, feel, and taste; so much to attempt, to achieve, and to feel good about! By this age he has mastered the basics. He walks, talks, runs, and climbs to quite a degree of proficiency. Now his language is becoming clearer and more sophisticated while his physical coordination permits him to perform all kinds of antics and derring-do. Socially he has been developing the basic skills and now he is becoming more poised and is increasingly extending his interest beyond the family. Such essentials as toilet training and bladder control are also well on their way to becoming an accomplished fact. He'll still have his emotional ups and downs and can be expected to lose his cool in a sudden blast of temper occasionally, but it is usually over as suddenly as it began and he is happy again. He is able to handle his feelings better and appears to be somewhat more open to accepting with grace the adult direction that is still very necessary.

His infancy and toddlerhood have flown by and now, shifting into high gear, he enters his preschool years, a time that brings a further honing and refining of all his skills, helping him to blossom into the independence of childhood. Everything he has learned to do is being done better everyday as he practices his many talents. Nothing succeeds like success, it is said, and this is certainly true of the young child. The more he accomplishes the more he will try new ventures when given lots of praise and encouragement from those he loves.

He likes to "chat" with his parents and his language skills enable him to carry on quite an adultlike conversation which is not the least bit one-sided. He is very quick to express his views and relate the many items of great importance that have occurred in and around the house and neighborhood in his busy day. And in the evening it may be he, rather than mother, who gets the first opportunity to share time with dad. Adult rules of conversational etiquette are little known to a three-year-old, and as mom and dad try to greet each other his method of getting a word in edgewise is to outdo them both with his excited chatter. He'll insist on making his contribution at the family dinnertable discussion, demanding at least his fair share or more. Parents of preschoolers resign themselves quickly to holding off any really serious discussions until their bubbling offspring has been gently tucked into bed for the night.

His language skills are only one indication of his growing independence. He is quickly passing the age when he will expect mom to guide all his daily activities. Before this time she has been the one who has had to come up with many of the ideas for his play activities and direct his effort in the daily routines. More and more now he prefers to tackle all kinds of tasks on his own. A mother's spontaneously offered help may not even be welcomed at times by her preschooler. He knows what he wants to do and he is the one who is going to do it. In dressing, for instance, as long as he knows his underpants go on first, what matter if everything else is somewhat askew? However, more than one hurried mother has had to bite her tongue in impatience waiting for her independent preschooler to finish dressing himself. But the wait is worth it as finally he emerges, his clothing for the most part done up in the proper manner.

226   His independence comes through in his play activity as well,

where he may be inclined to view his mother more as a resource rather than as his helper and playmate of an earlier age. He may prefer her to remain unobtrusively in the background and yet available to him when he wants to be with her or when he seeks her out for assistance for some activity in which he has momentarily become stuck, or when he is looking for some new ideas, or he needs a person to show things to. And, of course, she comes up with the misplaced glue or more odds and ends for a collage or she will do some cutting with scissors when needed. Although most children of this age are beginning to display such growing-up behavior, there are no doubt some who will still remain dependent on mother. They are not quite ready to strike out on their own, but by gently being encouraged to think up fun ideas before mom actually suggests one, they will soon be able to be more self-directed in their play activities.

The preschooler is probably becoming increasingly interested in playtimes with a friend of his own age. Spirited giggles as well as vigorous disagreements are part of the fun of this joint play. He is developing an understanding and acceptance of sharing that help him to explore such activities as social-role play, joint block building of forts and roadways, and housekeeping and doll play. He and his playmate see and comprehend the world in their own way, occasionally leaving mother quite puzzled as to what the two friends could possibly be talking about and enjoying so thoroughly. But, of course, they understand each other perfectly well. Mother may even see an amusing and yet quite astutely acted-out interpretation of her own housekeeping and child-rearing techniques as seen through the eyes of her child. Frequent play periods with young friends, where learning and sharing fosters his growing independence, are fruitful preparation for his later school adjustment.

Gross motor activities

The walking board was mentioned in an earlier section for some simple gross motor exercises. Now that the child is fast approaching his third birthday, he may be interested in more complicated walking-board tasks. The same 2" x 8" plank is used for these "walk-the-plank" operations. The board is raised two inches off the floor with the aid of a few old magazines, and the preschooler is invited to try his balancing skills whatever way he wishes. Once he has run through his own repertoire mother might suggest he try walking sideways across the board, then heel-toe, that is, with his heel placed next to his toe so that there is no space between. In effect, he has to balance on one foot for a few seconds while he positions his other foot. Of course, you demonstrate if he is not completely clear about your instructions. If this seems too tame you can suggest he try a crossover walk, where he again stands at right angles to the plank, crossing one leg over the other and then crossing one leg behind the other as he travels the length of the board. Walking forward on the plank, toe out, makes a silly sort of gait, but no sillier-looking than the toe-in walk. These two are bound to provide a lot of giggles, especially if you have a plank of your own and have been doing all the tasks simultaneously with your child, once you were sure that your toddler was proficient enough so that he did not need your support and steadying hand.

Once the above tasks have been mastered, you can propose he try walking backward on the plank, and then heel-toe while traveling backward. The latter is no mean feat, and what a challenge! Whenever an activity seems enjoyable and there appears to be interest, you can usually find ways to make it just a little more difficult. In the case of the "walk-the-plank" tasks, you can really complicate the situation by suggesting your "tightrope walker" try these with a narrower board (2" x 4") or while blindfolded. Naturally, you are close by in your role as accident preventer and let him start off with the board flat on the floor. It can be raised when necessary. Doing anything blindfolded takes real skill and care, as the preschooler soon finds out, but his satisfaction at succeeding makes it well worth the effort. Some of these "walk-the-plank" tasks can be done on tiptoe and that really takes skill and not a little practice. It is best to use the wider plank and, of course, to start with the easiest, the simple walking forward. The crossover front and back can be suggested next, and if there have been few difficulties (falling off the plank is one that gives a mother the feeling her child is not quite ready for "tippy toe") then more complex assignments such as moving backward on tiptoe or using a narrower board can be proposed.

Most little people have been doing some jumping ever since they learned how to travel on two legs. Jumping down that last step of the stairs with a hand firmly tucked into mother's has almost become a ritual. Sometimes, of course, the whole series of steps is navigated one jump at a time. Jumping down from the walking board, keeping both feet together, is an easy jump, but jumping back on takes more practice and more than just a little support as you make sure the board will not slip when he lands.

Responding to specific commands is more difficult because the preschooler has to comprehend first and then decide how he must move his body in order to carry out the request. For a start tell him you are going to play a jumping game and that you will give him some instructions as to what to do, then he will have a turn and tell you what he wants you to do. You ask him to jump up and down twice. The junior jumper has a pretty good idea about the first part but may not understand exactly what "twice" means. Tell him it means he jumps two times and proceed to demonstrate: one jump, two jumps. "I did it twice, now you jump twice. That's great, now you have the idea. What do you want me to do?" This is a new kind of game and most likely he will repeat your command. On each successive round ask him to jump over an object, forward, backward, sideways, or any series of these. Again the instructions may have to be clarified by demonstration, but what a peculiar sight (at least you feel a bit peculiar) as you hop around in various directions, hoping that no visitor will suddenly pop in and see you in this comical situation.

Hopping can be fun when managed in the same way. You make various requests and demonstrate. "Please hop twice. Now try hopping on one foot, then the other, like this." (You do a little jig.) "Hop forward. Now try going backward. Let's hold hands and we'll both hop forward as far as the kitchen. Oh, you're getting really good at this." As the hopper gets more agile, complications can be introduced. "Hop twice and then jump up and down twice. That's the idea. I thought that one would get you. How about a really hard one: jump backward and then hop forward." The ingenious parent can think of many variations of walking the plank, including hopping and jumping on the plank, but only pursues them if there seems to be interest, success, and enjoyment. An enthusiastic response is worth waiting for.

Because children are keen observers of all life around them, their imitative behavior has always included an array of animal characteristics. In very young children it was the sounds that various animals make, while for the older child it expands to include the various ways in which animals move. Children become butterflies or birds by flapping their arms, they become animals by crawling on the ground in certain patterns. The "bunny hop" is a special favorite. Here the child bends down so that his back is arched and then he jumps forward so that his feet are next to his hands, which he then moves forward in preparation for his next hop. The "duck walk" is fun because it makes a comical picture. You are sure to be delighted to demonstrate this one. Bending down as before the child grasps each ankle and then proceeds to move forward step by step in what can only be described as a waddle. The inchworm moves in small steps and so does the imitator. Again he bends down, back arched and hands some distance from his feet, then slowly he moves his feet forward in small steps until his feet are up to his hands, which he moves forward for the next series of tiny steps. The "monkey walk" is similar to the inchworm, at least in the beginning. As the child moves his feet forward he moves his hands forward as well, but still keeps his back arched. The "penguin walk" is a sort of Charlie Chaplin walk. The feet are turned out as far as possible and the knees are kept as straight as possible. With arms held close to the sides of the body and hands turned to the back, the waddle begins.

Imitating an elephant is a real snap and easy for you to dem-   231 onstrate. Your hands are clasped in front of you with your arms extended, your body is bent at the waist so that the clasped hands make a "trunk." Then with trunk swinging from side to side and with heavily stomping feet, an elephant is produced. A kangaroo hop is just as easy. You fold your arms upward against the chest with hands extended out so that they are at right angles to your body. A really big hop with feet together and you have your kangaroo.

The donkey kick is a little harder to do, but if you think your child would be interested then by all means show him how it is done. Place your hands flat on the floor with your back arched. Give your body a push upward almost as though you were going

to do a handstand, and when your trunk is airborne, kick your feet outward. If your lower extremities are slightly heavier than is desirable you may find this one easier said than done, but for the agile preschooler it is lots of fun.

The "crocodile crawl" is done on hands and knees and takes a little more practice and skill. For this reason some youngsters may find it too complicated and if this is so it should be postponed for another time when he is older. If he wants to have a go at it you can show him how a crocodile moves one side and then the other. The right leg and the right hand move forward simultaneously and then the left hand and left leg and so on. The "horse walk" is even more difficult, but this too can be saved for another time if it presents too many problems for the child. If it is not appreciated by the child then it is not a learning experience and has little value as an activity. The reader is urged not to lose sight of this goal. In the "horse walk" the right hand and left leg move in unison, then the left hand and right leg move. With back arched, it is complicated and does require good co-ordination for a young child. Another one which takes some doing is the "crab walk." Sturdy muscles are needed for this one. The child sits down and then by putting his hands on the floor raises his bottom off the ground so that he is on all fours. Once in this position he moves backward in imitation of a crab, in spite of his having only four "legs." The "crab walk" is one which may require a demonstration in order to get the idea across, but no doubt you are again delighted to oblige. After all, it's not every day one gets a chance to do a "crab walk."

Inanimate objects have also provided children with a source for imitation as well. They love to pretend to be a log rolling down a hill, a train chugging down a track, or a wheelbarrow carrying some "let's pretend" sand. The "wheelbarrow" particularly seems to give lots of pleasure, probably because two people have to participate. For the child in the house this means his beloved parents and what a time they have traveling around   233 the house. For extra variation the "wheelbarrow" can go up and down a wide plank, or up and down the first few steps of the stairs. If the "wheelbarrow" isn't too hardy, with lots of practice he will develop plenty of fine sturdy muscles, an important part of building a fine sturdy body. For other helpful exercises the reader is referred to Bonnie Prudden's excellent book, *How to Keep Your Child Fit from Birth to Six*.

Walking stilts seem to be a thing of the past, but with a couple of low, wide tins about 4″ in diameter and 2″ high, they can be introduced into the child's life for a little zest. A hole is made on each side of the can close to the unopened bottom (the opened part now becomes the bottom) and a tough piece of cord is looped so that the child can grip it. This allows him to keep his feet firmly on the can while providing some support. Getting organized with both feet placed correctly on the cans takes real talent and lots of help, but once on, the fun can begin. With increased mastery taller tins can be used for heightened excitement. Incidentally, this is definitely an outdoor activity where the grassy surface cushions falls and minimizes slips. Tile and hardwood floors are much too slippery and stilts are also very hard on these types of floor surfaces.

Fine motor activities

Fine motor co-ordination is something that has been developing along with many other skills. The soon-to-be three-year-old can draw, paint, paste, use a pencil, and manipulate puzzles and small toys with ease. He is not quite ready for scissors, however; that comes just a bit later.

With this increased skill more advanced pegboard tasks can be initiated. For this, you will need two pegboards about 12″ x 12″, and pegs, one set for yourself and one set for your companion. When the time seems appropriate present the two boards and invite your child to put in a few pegs and then try to duplicate what he has done. It is your turn next and you can start the ball rolling with a simple design, perhaps a peg in each of the four corners. At each try make the designs just a little more complex, always keeping in mind that you should end the activity if interest seems to be waning. This game is very good for a little number counting, provided it is done naturally. "Let's see, I have to count, one, two, three pegs over and one, two, three pegs down. There, that is where it goes. Now it is in the same place as yours, isn't it?" The complexity of the designs can easily be geared to the child's level of interest and skill, but making his own patterns for you to copy and then figuring out yours is an excellent problem-solving task involving good fine motor co-ordination.

Stringing large beads and buttons was suggested for a younger child, but stringing small beads, buttons, short pieces of colored straws, or bits of macaroni are now fairly easy for this older creator to manage. And what lovely bracelets, necklaces, and Christmas-tree decorations they make! In spite of growing maturity mother still needs to be close by for assistance and supervision. Children of this age as a general rule do not put things in their mouths, but some still do occasionally and some even put small objects in noses and ears. Careful vigilance must continue until the child terminates the activity himself. This way no accidents can occur.

Sewing cards are lots of fun and even the most unartistic parent can make a drawing that can form the basis for such an activity. The card should be quite sturdy and about 10" x 10". This makes for easy handling. A face, a house, a ball, or a geometric figure can be drawn with small holes punched intermittently in the outline. A blunt but good-sized needle with brightly colored wool about 14" long and knotted at one end completes the requirements. You can demonstrate and then allow your sewer to take over. Remembering not to sew always from the top is tricky, but, even so, if the child is having fun it doesn't   235 really matter how he sews his card. It's still excellent for further developing his fine motor co-ordination.

Weaving is a possibility for some children nearing their third birthday. The kitchen chair turned upside down provides the outline. For the frame string colorful wool or strips of fabric from leg to leg so that it is fairly tight. Then string strips of fabric from one side to the other, firmly fastening each end, keeping the strings about 1½" apart. You may have to Scotch-tape the corners where the wool has been fastened so that the frame does not slip during the procedure. The weaver is shown how to start and then allowed to go to it as he wishes. Again it does not matter if he weaves in and out exactly. Having the opportunity to have some enjoyment, to try something new, and to refine his skills is the important factor, not the end product, which is bound to be interesting whatever way it is woven.

One generally does not think of embroidery as being of interest to a child of this age, but with the right preparation it can be offered for additional pleasure and challenge. If you do not have an embroidery frame, you can make one from a plastic cottage-cheese carton. The inside circle of the lid is cut out so that there is a quarter-inch edge. The top half of the carton is cut out so that there are two rings, one of which fits inside the other. A single piece of cheesecloth is placed in the frame. (Anything thicker will prevent the rings from fitting properly.) A blunt needle with a knotted length of embroidery thread completes the necessary equipment. As usual, you may have to demonstrate and then let your child have a whirl at this new task. If he is sewing at all, if he seems to be finding it interesting, if he is not experiencing too much frustration, then it is worth the effort on your part. If you do not have a real embroidery frame and your child has enjoyed the work then you might consider purchasing a small one for your charge. The cottage-cheese frame will not stand up to too much wear and tear and probably will become a permanent part of each embroidered picture.

The reader has probably noted that the sex of the child has not determined the suitability of a toy or an activity, but rather his interest, his development, and his unique skills should determine this factor. We believe that it is healthy, more fun, and very stimulating to expose both male and female children to all sorts of experiences. Girls like to try their hand at what some adults traditionally believed to be "boys only" games and boys do like to play some of those "girls only" games. In particular, boys as well as girls are often interested in doll play. They like to role play, they like to pretend to be mother, and if permitted to do so they will not grow up to be the kind of father who feels that he should not have anything to do with a baby. This kind of father never played with dolls, and so now may miss one of life's greatest experiences—caring for and loving a tiny baby.

Creative activities

With the toddler well into his preschool years his increasing co-ordination along with his full-blown imagination allows him to engage in more complicated creative activities. He will still enjoy all the various kinds of painting he has been doing in the past, but now with more maturity he is eager for different kinds of experiences where he can continue to grow, to experiment, and to learn. If he has not had the opportunity to use an easel there is no time like the present to give him that chance. With the help of a cardboard-box easel (see Appendix for instructions) and the usual equipment he is ready to paint. Taping some old sheeting to the easel instead of paper makes for a different kind of painting which is equally satisfying. The nice thing about this painting is the fact that the cloth can be washed and used again after the original has been viewed for a sufficient time.

Have the toddler lie on the floor on a large sheet of paper. You then draw his outline, which makes it possible for him to

237

see his own image as he is at that moment. He may then want to work on a large outline of either of his parents. Since you are more available you get chosen, and in most cases have to draw your own outline freehand. Certainly if your companion decides he wants to do it himself, the end result will no doubt be very interesting. If a little collage work seems desirable, bits of wool for hair, large buttons for eyes, and pieces of fabric for clothing can add some interest. It is important for you to keep in mind it is your child's picture and he should be able to make it as he wishes. Who knows, the results may show him to be a junior Picasso! In any case, the important thing is the painter's enjoyment in creating, rather than the end product. (If there is still a

tendency for the child to put things in his mouth, you need to be careful that only safe objects are available, or that potentially unsafe ones are used only in your presence and under your watchful eye.)

With more strength and dexterity the small squeeze bottle comes into its own. For this activity the paint needs to be a bit on the runny side in order to make it easy to use. Thick paint would be just too hard to squeeze through, as the hands and fingers of the child are still small and cannot exert very much pressure on a larger object. The procedure is simple. The bottle is filled with a moderate amount of paint and then the paint is just squirted onto smooth paper in whatever way the painter wishes. For a little variety several bottles, each containing a different color, can be used, and what extraordinary designs are produced! If the painter has not already discovered that two paints when mixed together frequently produce a third color (red.and blue make purple; blue and yellow make green; red and yellow make orange), then this is an excellent time for you to point this out. "Look, you made a purple color when you mixed red and blue together. Let's see what happens when you mix blue and yellow together. Hey, how about that, they made a green color." The same squeeze painting can be used with a discarded medicine dropper. A blot of runny paint is placed on a smooth piece of paper and air is blown on by squeezing the dropper. Blowing through a straw produces the same effect, though the air blown through the straw can be more forceful and the paint scattered much more widely. Empty plastic Windex bottles with spouts and runny paint provide another mode of painting.

While collage has been part of your child's creative experience for some time he is now really able to be more expressive and imaginative with this medium, especially if you are there to help plan some specific projects. "Would you like to make a pencil holder for dad's desk, or perhaps a purse to carry some of your treasures, or a poncho for yourself?" Before the collage begins, delve into that drawer where you have been saving things for just such an eventuality: large buttons, small lids from pickle jars, pieces of fabric, bits of wool, colorful feathers, and gay strips of ribbon. The cottage-cheese carton makes a good base for the pencil holder and after being covered with a thick paste of flour and water, by the young artist, of course, the rest of the work can proceed. And what a masterpiece is produced after everything has been pasted on and a new design created by the young designer! Dad can be sure no one else has such a unique *objet d'art* as this wonderful pencil holder made with such joy and pleasure especially for him. The purse is made in a similar way with a long narrow box as the base. A piece of bright ribbon makes an acceptable shoulder strap. The poncho is equally easy to make. Take last night's newspaper, select a double page, and fold it at the crease. Cut a hole in the middle of the crease large enough for your toddler's head. You then cut the bottom two corners until you have shaped the poncho just so. All is ready for the decorator—he can paint or add collage; the choice is his. If you happen to have some old sheeting or fabric, a sturdier poncho can be fashioned, one that will stand up to a bit more wear and tear, because the poncho once made will certainly be worn by the creator. How else can one admire his handicraft?

While a good part of the time the painter may only want to make pictures using lots of different kinds of materials, given the opportunity for novel experiences he is always interested. Making a collage with small boxes is one which will interest a young artist. The boxes can be almost any kind or size provided they are manageable for him. As before, the paster covers part of a sheet of cardboard with the thick flour-and-water paste and presses his boxes in place. As each section is covered to his satisfaction, he moves on to another part until all is finished. It may be he will want to paint it the next day, when it has dried, before he allows his newest creation to be exhibited. Pieces of wood of all sizes and shapes can also make interesting collages for an enterprising artist, who may decide to pile some of the pieces one on top of the other for a truly three-dimensional effect.

Hopefully, among your treasures are some of those stationery and Christmas-card boxes that have clear plastic tops. These can be used to make attractive three-dimensional pictures. A garden collage is beautifully made with flower petals of all colors and shapes, leaves, twigs, tiny pine cones, and seeds pressed into the paste covering the bottom part of the box. The creator uses what he wishes to make his scene the way he wants. When finished and dry, the plastic cover is glued in place and a pretty piece of ribbon is used to hang the miniature. A seascape can be made the same way. You have to provide the cut-out fishes, but your cohort can paint each one if he wishes. When they have dried press them into the paste along with the shells he gathered the last time the family was at the beach. Adding a bit of blue food coloring to the paste makes the scene even more appealing. Using this type of box to make a collage of whatever materials are available and fashioned in whatever way the preschooler wishes may be the most fun of all. The finished product is bound to be interesting and is well worth displaying for all to see. The plastic covers from coffee cans can also be used to make collages in a similar way and they are especially attractive when hung in a sunny window. The plastic top of a Christmas-card box makes an exquisite window picture when fashioned this way.

Those left-over odds and ends of tissue paper are a natural for another colorful collage. A piece of cardboard, the kind that comes with dad's shirts from the laundry, is just right. The cardboard is covered with paste by the child—this is great fun in itself —and then bits of twisted paper are pressed in with gay abandon. Of course, you have the job of getting the pieces of tissue twisted beforehand so that they will stand out from the backing. Sometimes the artist decides he is going to flatten each piece of paper and perhaps even pile several pieces of tissue one on top of the 241 other. No matter what he does, if he is enjoying himself that is what is important, and the mosaic produced will be his creation.

For additional variety you can cut the cardboard cylinders from paper toweling or toilet paper into various lengths for him. When pasted onto cardboard they make a delightful presentation. If the preschooler is interested he may want to paint this collage when it is completely dry. Occasionally the rolls are not too firmly embedded and when painted become dislodged. To avoid this it may be more practical to have him paint them before they are cut and pasted. With all the paste and cutting materials already assembled, it is lots of fun for the preschooler to make paper chains. Strips of fairly sturdy paper about ¾″ wide and 3″ long are prepared by you. Each strip is looped around the next and then the ends are pasted together. Brightly colored strips of material can be used as well as all kinds of attractive paper. This makes a lovely crown or necklace, and can be used as an attractive decoration for a party or Christmas tree.

Play dough should not be overlooked as a vehicle for creative expression. Up to this point the hands and fingers of the child have not been able to utilize this material to its fullest, although you may have offered him bits of pastry for modeling when he was younger. Chances are there was more eating than manipulation at that point, but, no matter, it was probably an enjoyable experience whatever happened to the dough. But with greater strength and dexterity, play dough really seems to come into its own. A recipe for making this can be found in the Appendix. When the dough is being prepared, a little more interest can be injected if the water is colored with food coloring before it is mixed with the flour and salt.

If the budding sculptor has not had much experience with dough, show him how it can be employed to make an interesting shape—after you have covered the work area with lots of newspaper, and protected your child's clothing if need be. Rolling it into long wiggly worms or perhaps into just a round ball gives him the idea and he is launched into a new career. It is fun for you to do your own sculpturing too—you may be surprised at your own talent. Rolling the dough with a small rolling pin is interesting, especially if you then offer cookie cutters for "cookie" and shape making. Potato mashers, worn-out sieves, and forks can also be used to make interesting designs on the rolled dough. Salt and flour beads (see Appendix for making) are fun for the preschooler to make and even more fun to paint and string into a fancy necklace. For an imaginative child with a helpful companion (that's you) the possibilities for enjoyable play-dough activity are extensive.

Some children of this age seem ready for modeling with clay, and if this seems to be the case it is worthwhile to purchase a small amount of clay for a trial run. Art-supply stores usually stock wet clay or the dry powdered clay which needs only sufficient water to permit easy handling. The fun of holding, feeling, and shaping the material is a unique sensory experience and while the finished piece may again be a snake, a ball, or a blob, it has been a great experience.

Play dough can make the foundation for a stabile, which is a simple stationary sculpture. Pipe cleaners, twigs, some with leaves and some without, toothpicks, straws, small pieces of plastic cutlery, coffee scoops, Q-tips, Popsicle handles, discarded ball-point pens, old used toothbrushes, especially the child's size, mascara brushes that have lost their usefulness, and empty tubes of lipstick can all be used with imagination for a magnificent creation. And what an excellent place for dad's no longer used pipes (he has given up the habit) to add real flavor to the stabile. Styrofoam packing, which comes in many parcels, is also practical, although its versatility is a bit more limited than the dough, which permits a wider variety of material to be used. A left-over cooled baked potato, sliced lengthwise, makes an interesting base for a stabile. Colored toothpicks, pipe cleaners, and straws in various lengths can all be pushed into the soft potato, and, 243 in the case of the pipe cleaners, in unusual shapes. Sponges may be used to make a base, provided only slender objects are used.

Play dough can be used as the foundation for a hand or foot print. The dough is placed in a box large enough for the child's hand—a little oil or shortening or flour is rubbed on the hand so the dough won't stick and the hand is pressed down to make the imprint. If a more permanent impression is desired the box is filled with slightly moistened sand so that it will make a mold when the hand is pressed in. Plaster of Paris is gently poured into the freshly made mold and allowed to harden. If the proud parents want to be able to hang it up, a very short piece of straw inserted at the wrist end before hardening will provide the opening for the silver ribbon which is really the only suitable cord for such an important memento.

It is not too early to introduce papier mâché, and while the first productions may not be too elaborate it will be worth the time and mess. This kind of activity is best done when both of you have extra time, since it is not the kind of thing that can be initiated on the spur of the moment like ball playing or working on puzzles. Shredding newspaper into thin strips 6″ to 8″ long is the first step—one, incidentally, that most children engage in with some glee. There seems to be great satisfaction in tearing, particularly when it is for an appropriate purpose. Tearing newsprint just for the sake of tearing does not seem too productive and may in fact give the child the mistaken idea that tearing things anytime, anyplace, is quite acceptable. Papier mâché gives the child the opportunity to tear for a worthwhile goal. Once the paper is shredded it is a simple matter to mix flour and water until there is a mixture about the consistency of thick gravy. After work area and child are well covered with suitable protection, the work can begin either with the preschooler digging right in or with a little preliminary demonstration if that seems indicated. Show him how to run a strip of paper through the paste and then fasten it around a carton, a plastic bottle, or whatever is to be covered. Javex bleach bottles with the tops cut off are nice since they can be used as planters when the artist has completed his handicraft. Painting the dried papier mâché the next day is something to look forward to. What colors should be used? Should it be all one color or several colors? Would stickers add to its beauty? What a lot to think about for tomorrow! It may be that the child will not be interested in covering an object. He prefers to make up his own shapes, and what could be better—he is doing his own thing.

Cognitive activities

Simple matching tasks have been mentioned in an earlier chapter, but now that the preschooler's third birthday is rapidly approaching, more complex matching tasks may interest him. Whether or not he is successful in completing the task is not nearly so important as is the time spent with an accepting parent. Some beginning understanding of the concept presented, the excitement of trying a new problem, and the language practice are also important components of the interaction. Whatever the experience provides, it can be a productive one if the adult involved understands these important priorities.

In the matching task a number of pictures are gathered together so that each picture can be matched with another on the basis of a certain concept. In the earlier section the match was exact similarity—a collie to a collie, a cow to a cow, a rose to a rose, and so on. A further extension was possible when the match was made on the basis of a similar plant or species of animal, but without the exact characteristics. For example, both pictures would show dogs but one would be a collie and the other a French poodle. The species is the same but the characteristics are quite different. This concept can be used where a picture of an animal is matched with a picture of the same animal presented in a more abstract form. For instance, one picture

245

may be a simple line drawing and the other a photograph or colored picture. The Halloween cat sitting on a fence is a good example of abstraction, and with its prominent whiskers and long tail, its identification as a cat is not too difficult. What a lot of fun for mom and dad if they are talented artists able to make instant pictures!

The presentation of the problem is the same as always. You have a pile of pictures which you show your companion and which you label, emphasizing a specific idea, while he is looking them over. "That's a cat looking the other way, isn't it? Here's a picture that looks like an elephant, but it's a little hard to tell because there isn't too much to it. You can see his long trunk. Do you think it looks like an elephant?" When all the pictures have been carefully scrutinized, at least to the child's satisfaction, you introduce the task. "Let's play a game. I'll mix all the pictures together and after I have picked one out you can look at the others and see if you can find one that is the same kind of animal. Let's see now, how about if I pick this one? Hey, that's right, it is an elephant and you have found a picture of another elephant. That's great."

Matching pictures where there are only slight differences can also be a challenge. A series of faces, each one slightly different but each one having an exact corresponding match, is really quite easy for an adult to make. Inexpensive small paper plates left over from summer picnicking are excellent for this. But any piece of cardboard that can be cut into several circles about 4″ in diameter will really do just as well. Four or five faces are drawn, one without a nose, one without an eyebrow, one without an eye, one without a mouth, and one without the curl in the middle of the forehead. Exact duplicates of the faces are made. In making this problem, it is important to make the variables constant, that is, every feature in every picture is exactly the same: the mouth in each set is the same, the eyes are the same, and so on. It's confusing if there are too many differences. The only thing that should be different is the missing part. Coloring the eyes and mouth help with the discrimination. One blue eye missing is more noticeable than an eye that is only an outline. When a red mouth is missing its absence is easily noted.

The same idea can be used to match emotions. That is, a sad face to a sad face, a happy face to a happy face, a surprised face to a surprised face, and an angry face to an angry face. Again the basic features in each picture should remain the same. Exaggerating the smile or the frown maximizes the possibility of success.

The introduction to the task is the same. You encourage your child to look at the pictures and while doing so point out certain aspects that will help clue him in when faced with the actual problem. "Your picture has a face without a nose. What a funny face! I have one without a mouth. Whoever heard of a face without a mouth? Can you find a picture like mine?"

The matching task depicting emotions is excellent for lots of conversation. "Why do you think that face looks so happy?" If no answer is forthcoming, you continue, "I know, his mother has just told him they are going to have ice cream for lunch."

Another challenge is one where matching social roles with certain objects helps make the child more aware of the people in his environment who perform certain functions. The picture of the doctor's bag or stethoscope naturally goes with the picture of the doctor, the mailbag or mailbox goes with the mailman, the tractor with the farmer, the nurse's cap with the nurse, the fireman's hat with the fireman, and so on. Of course, all these tasks require pictures, but hopefully that is no problem because you have continued to collect good pictures and catalogues for many months and are now finding out how very worthwhile this collection has become.

Understanding about opposites is a bit more complicated, but with the right approach it can provide another kind of matching activity. In this task opposites such as an open door and a closed door, a smiling face and a sad face, an empty spool of thread and a full spool of thread, a rainy day and a sunny day, are mixed together. After the customary examination and explanation elaborate what you mean by opposites and then encourage him to begin the game by holding up a picture and asking for the opposite one. Always remember to take a positive position whatever the response from your child. "Oh, you gave me a picture of a happy face, now can you find one that shows a face that is not very happy. Good boy, you found the opposite to the happy face." It may be that an enterprising child, while doing his preliminary looking, has already noticed that each set is made up of different objects and proceeds to match on that basis—door to door, face to face, spool to spool, and so on—without any regard to the concept of opposites. You always have to be a couple of jumps ahead and you can soon make things more difficult by adding several nonmatching pictures, some containing one or two of the objects, for example, or maybe a face without any particular expression. This is bound to add sufficient perplexity to whet the intellectual appetite of the problem solver.

Pictures of different kinds of fabric can also be used for an intriguing mental exercise. In this situation a certain design is matched to a similar but not necessarily identical design; a plaid with a plaid, a check with a check, stripes with stripes, a polka dot with a polka dot, a flowered pattern with another flowered pattern, and a solid color with another solid color. The lucky mother who has lots of different fabrics can make an even more attractive matching task along with a tactile component. You can glue pieces of fabric onto cardboard figures and ask your child to "find another dress almost like this one." Naturally you continue to label and provide information as requested.

One concept that is bound to enchant a young child utilizes parents and offspring. A baby definitely goes with a mother or father, a chick with a chicken, a calf with a cow, a kitten with a cat, a puppy with a dog, a foal with a mare. For a little complexity other combinations not so easily recognized can be added: a caterpillar goes with a butterfly, a tadpole with a frog, a seed with a plant. Along with this task is another where the match is the home of the animal to its inhabitant: a house is the home for a little boy, a hive for a bee, a web for a spider, a tree for a squirrel, a nest for a bird, a barn for a cow, a stream for a fish, an ant hill for ants, and a cave for a bear. After your child has made a thorough examination of each picture pick one and say, "Oh, I have a picture of a nest. Who lives here? That's right, the bird lives in a nest, doesn't she?" You might volunteer more information if your child seems interested. "Some birds build nests in trees, some just on the ground in the weeds, and some build in the spaces under the roof of our house."

Not to be forgotten is the task where two objects frequently found or used together must be matched: salt and pepper shakers, cups and saucers, bread and butter, tea and coffee, ice cream and cake, bacon and eggs, pancakes and syrup, table and chair, ball and bat, doll and doll carriage, paper and pencil. There are lots more combinations and you are sure to think of many others. In each instance, the key, of course, is the location of suitable pictures to start the whole thing, and this alone may limit the range of possibilities.

A more complicated matching task is one where the concept being depicted is function. Many different objects have similar functions. For example: crib-bed, cup-glass, plate-bowl, stove-barbecue, lamp-candle, carriage-stroller, plane-helicopter, train-streetcar, horse-donkey. It might be a good idea here for you to label and explain the function of each object as your child is doing his preliminary examination. When he has finished, pick one up and ask him to find a picture of an object which is used for the same thing or in the same way.

Not to be overlooked is a matching game using objects that identify the season of the year. Ice skates, skis, a snowmobile for winter; swimsuit, sailboat, sandpile, picnic for summer; budding trees, tulips, crocuses for spring; autumn leaves, Thanksgiving turkey, black Halloween cat, and pumpkin for fall.

In much the same way, catalogue reading can provide a wealth of spontaneous matching tasks. You and your child are looking through the latest Sears' or Eaton's edition and as you come to a certain section capitalize on the situation by making queries. "Here's a page of nice shoes, let's see if we can find some other things which could go on feet. Hey, that's great, you found a pair of rain boots, they sure go on feet. Can you find anything else? That's right, socks go on feet. You have red socks on today, don't you?" Other objects can be categorized in the same way. Rings, gloves, and mittens go on hands; curlers, hats, bobby pins, clips, bows, and ribbons go on hair. Many objects are found only in the kitchen: stove, refrigerator, pots, pans, and toaster. Many others are found in the dining room, bedroom, and the bathroom. The possibilities for fun and games with catalogue reading are almost endless and worth repeating many times over. For the end of the day, a quiet time just looking at the catalogue together, labeling interesting objects and talking about the various things on each page is very satisfying.

A natural extension of the matching game is the domino game. The principle is exactly the same, except that pictures of objects rather than numbers are to be matched. A flower and a dog make one card (domino), a dog and a cup another, a cup and an orange yet another, and so on. After your child has had a chance to familiarize himself with the cards and you have labeled the objects, explain the point of the game. To make it interesting you provide lots of combinations, some with two or three objects that have to be matched to one end of a domino card that has the same objects, in the same number. This does add a bit of spice to the challenge. With many cards you might just be lucky enough to be invited to participate. If more complications are indicated you can add similar but not identical objects. For example, one dog might be a collie, the other a terrier, but the match is still dog to dog. A glass might be a match for a cup and a rose might be a match for a violet. In each instance, similarities have to be understood in order to have the game proceed.

Another extension of the matching game is that old favorite "bingo." Again, instead of numbers, pictures of objects are used. You make a simple bingo card 9" x 9" with nine 3" squares each containing a picture. Stickers are excellent for this. You also make a number of cards, several but not all of which correspond to the ones on the bingo card. The aim of the game is explained. When you hold up a picture of an object which your child also has on his card, he gets to put a marker on his picture. When he has enough markers to cover one line he has won the game. The 251 prize might be having the roles reversed with you becoming the bingo player and he the caller. No doubt you have lots of ideas for little prizes. A more thought-provoking bingo can be manufactured just as easily by making some of the pictures so that they contain more than one object, and the card held up must show the same number. The preschooler may have a picture of a dog, but your card shows a picture of two dogs. He has to wait for another picture showing two dogs. By adding more objects, you continue to emphasize the concept of numbers, something which you undoubtedly have been doing all along whenever appropriate.

Incidentally, there is no reason why the other matching concepts could not be used for both the domino and bingo games if the child has found them interesting. If the concept of animal to home is being used, then in the domino game a bird card would legitimately be placed next to a card showing a nest, a bee next to a hive, and so on. With the bingo game, when you hold up a bird card, the player has to find its home, which is a nest; when you hold up a little child, he has to find a house; and when you hold up a spider, he has to find its web. Planning more cards both for bingo and domino in the event a little playmate appears on the scene and wants to join in the fun may be advantageous. This all takes time and not a little work for parents, but the playing together is beautiful and the learning extensive, especially if both parents understand that the object of the task is fun and stimulation for their child. If these matching tasks seem too advanced they can easily be introduced at a later date when he seems more ready.

Sorting colors was introduced when the toddler was close to two; now that he is a year older, a new kind of sorting may tempt him. Paper is very different from metal and these are a good combination to start with. Take a quick look around the house and find a piece of Kleenex, a paper bag, a paper napkin, a paper jewelry box, some fancy wrapping paper, an old Christmas or playing card, an envelope, and a paper plate. You put all in a pile and add some metal objects such as a set of measuring spoons, a hair clip, a fork, a tart tin, a pie plate, nail clippers, and a large safety pin. Before beginning the game encourage your child to examine this mound of odds and ends and as he does emphasize the material each is made of. "That's a paper plate but that pie plate you are holding is made of metal. Let's put all the paper things in one pile and the metal things in another." If the young sorter isn't quite sure what to do you can start the ball rolling. "This lunch bag is made of paper so I'll put it here. Can you find something else made of paper? That's right, Kleenex is made of paper." If the object he has selected is metal respond positively with, "Oh, you want to start your own pile of metal objects. Here's a metal fork to add to it." Wooden and plastic objects are just as much fun to sort. Sometimes the task is mastered quickly and if so additional difficulties can be introduced by mixing together a variety of objects, some wooden, some plastic, some metal, some fabric, with each sorted into the correct category.

Gathering objects that are just used for cooking and mixing them in with several other noncooking utensils provides another challenge. You invite your preschooler to look at the pile of objects and while he is doing so you note all the ones that are used for cooking. "This frying pan cooks bacon and eggs very well. This is the pot I use to cook your vegetables." When the observations and labeling are finished suggest that he put all the cooking things in one pile and everything else in another. If the second pile, by the way, has objects which could be sorted in another way, you might seize the opportunity to bring this to the sorter's attention. "Let's see, how many plastic things can we find in this pile? Oh, you found a big plastic spoon, that's great. Is there anything else that is plastic? You're right, my measuring spoons and that cup are plastic." Other categories such as gardening, carpentry, and sewing can be sorted in this way.

A natural extension of this game is one where you collect objects that belong to a certain category: an orange, a lemon, a carrot, a potato, an apple, a banana, and a pickle. Include as well one that does not belong, for example, a rubber ball. As always during the initial scrutiny label each one, pointing out in the process the ones that are food. With this concluded pose the question. "Oh, oh, something doesn't belong in this pile. What doesn't belong?" Doll clothes, cars, and trucks are just a few of the many other categories that can similarly be used for this "odd-man-out" puzzler.

Blindfold tasks do not really require the child to be blindfolded. Many children object to this and would be unhappy if coerced into it. But the challenge in this game necessitates one participant not being able to see what is happening. In other words, he must rely on his other senses to determine the appropriate responses. It is a simple matter for you to sit behind a chesterfield or large chair, anyplace where you can be heard but not seen. First gather together a number of objects that make a specific and distinct sound. Any of your child's musical instruments will do—a drum, xylophone, toy piano, or whatever is available—in addition to an alarm clock, an egg beater, two pot lids, two wooden spoons, a long-forgotten baby rattle, and a bell. Tempt him into looking your treasures over and to experiment with the sounds each makes. When that is completed, ask your companion to join in a guessing game. "After I am hidden, listen to the sound I make and tell me what is making it." Just clapping your hands is a good start and not likely to be too much of a problem. With his own musical instruments already familiar to him, one of these is probably a good sound producer to introduce next. It will ensure a high degree of success that will provide an incentive to continue. Naturally you do not forget to reverse the roles so that you are the guesser and your preschooler the doer.

In much the same way the tactile box, previously mentioned,

can be used for a more complex problem, again where the object to be identified cannot be seen. First gather up a few of your child's favorite small toys which have fairly obvious characteristics, for example, a dump truck, a racing car, and an oil tanker; or a small doll, a plastic animal, and a series of small plates and cups from a toy tea set. After the usual play period three objects are placed in the box and the guesser is asked to get a specific one. Once the idea is clearly understood, you can add other trucks and cars, or objects with less noticeable differences. Various clearly distinguishable grades of sandpaper can provide another interesting problem using the tactile box. Little things, middle-sized things, and big things (dolls are great for this particular task) take careful manipulation before a correct choice is made. Long things, short things, wide things, narrow things also lend themselves well to this kind of problem. But whatever the choice respond positively, because you are more interested in sharing an activity and having a good time with your child than you are in teaching him concepts solely so that he will become a "bright child." In a warm accepting environment that is gently stimulating, the child will develop his full potential emotionally as well as intellectually. In a high-pressure environment this is not likely to happen.

If your child has not objected to being blindfolded then you can play that old favorite "pin the tail on the donkey," only this time make the donkey so that several parts can be removed and replaced: ears, legs, nose, as well as the tail. The body and head of the donkey, and all the other parts except the nose, can be made of cardboard; the nose can be made of vinyl, since it is flexible and easily managed. The nose can also be made out of a large button and all the parts pinned on with adhesive tape. The body and various parts are outlined in paste and then in cotton batting or fabric so that the shapes of the various parts of the body are outlined and emphasized. A cardboard easel will make the backdrop and will also determine the size of the donkey. The larger the better. A too-small donkey really means only the tail can be pinned on since it is far too difficult for the young child to determine where the parts go. But with a large animal the game can be more expansive. The donkey is taped on the board in its complete form and your child gets a chance to touch and examine it. During this time offer some helpful information. "When you feel his head here, you find his two ears, and farther around this way is his nose." As he proceeds, you remove parts and let him replace them. With all the information apparently noted ask your preschooler if he would like to play a game. Then blindfold him, give him the tail and tell him to find the place where it belongs and put it on the donkey. Successful or not, it is still fun, and the fun is increased if more than one child can participate. If no large cardboard box can be found, taping the donkey to the refrigerator door works quite well.

Working in sand has always been satisfying and sand drawing is a nice variation. For this you collect a number of objects that make a specific mark when drawn through the sand, for example, a fork, a pencil, a car, a sieve, a ruler, a pastry cutter, and a potato masher. With baby's old plastic bath retrieved and enough damp sand in it to fill the bottom, all is ready. After examining this conglomeration the preschooler can either close his eyes, turn around so that he is not facing the sandbox, or leave the room so that you can make a drawing in the sand with one of the articles. The fork leaves several straight parallel lines, the sieve a sort of checkered pattern, the pencil one thin line, and so on. When he turns around, he is asked to pick out the object which made the mark and then experiment to see whether or not his choice was correct.

Tasting foods while unable to see is great fun. You assemble a number of fruit bowls and put in some left-over pudding, some mayonnaise, ketchup, prepared mustard, a squirt or two of whipped topping, a little cooked cornstarch, and anything else that is handy in the kitchen which has a similar consistency. After the usual perusal and labeling the examiner is blindfolded if he is unable to resist opening his eyes, but only if he consents willingly. He is then offered the opportunity to feel, taste, and identify the food. The same problem can be presented by using dry flour, icing sugar, baking powder, and cornstarch. Spices also can be used in this way. Smelling and identifying different kinds of foods such as fruits and vegetables can be equally puzzling.

Sometimes you overlook what is in effect a veritable gold mine in the kitchen for imaginative problem-solving activities.

Games where memory plays a part are usually quite intriguing for an enterprising youngster. One which can be easily arranged requires only a few objects, each quite different; a spoon, a potato, and a small square of cloth. After these items have been examined and labeled, ask your child if he would like to play a guessing game. With a positive response, you cover up all the objects and ask, "Tell me all the things you remember seeing before I covered them up." If there seems to be a bit of difficulty in getting started, give him another look or reduce the number of objects. That does the trick and he soon rattles off all the names. On the other hand, if he has found the initial game easy and it seems appropriate, other things can be added for more complexity. Of course, the roles should be reversed once in a while, giving you a test of how good your memory is. Another memory game is one where a few articles are provided, a ball, an orange, and a cup. Again after the preliminary examination and labeling are taken care of, cover the objects and, unnoticed by your child, carefully remove one. The cloth is removed and the query made: "I took something away, what is missing?" This task can be made more difficult if warranted by using more of the many household odds and ends. A rather nice reversal of this task occurs when one or two objects are added instead of being removed.

Placing a number of objects in a specific order sets the stage

257

for another kind of memory task. Once everything is in place and examined carefully, you cover them and without your companion seeing rearrange the order. The question is posed: "I have moved things around, what did I move?" This game is best started, as with all the others, in low key. Not too many objects should be used in the beginning—about three is right— and only the position of one is changed. Once your child gets the hang of it, more difficulties can be introduced by using more objects and changing the position of more than one of them.

Another interesting memory task for the child who has been enjoying these little challenges is one where two distinct boxes are used. That is, they are of different colors, sizes, or shapes. Two objects are placed in each box and after the usual looking you cover both. One item is removed from one box and placed in the other without your child being able to see the switch. The cover is removed and the question asked: "I changed one of the objects, which one did I change?" A little more complexity can be arranged by changing two of the items so that while there are still two things in each box, they are not the same two things that were previously there. The preschooler soon realizes, if he hasn't already, that this task requires a good long look in order to detect the change.

Tapping a dish, a plastic container, and a metal pot in a certain order unseen by the child is another intriguing problem where he is invited to duplicate the exact order. Tapping a certain beat on a pot with a request for a similar performance by your child is no easy matter. But it can be arranged if the first beats are quite simple. Once the idea is comprehended it can be expanded for more complexity if your child seems ready and interested.

Sequencing tasks are sometimes a real pleasure for the child who has become an inveterate problem solver. Empty spools of thread (you knew you would find a use for them one day) make a good beginning since you only need to use three or four of varying size to get the purpose of the task easily across to your companion. Show him how to arrange them according to size and then turn the job over to him, adding a few more spools of different sizes for more sustained involvement. Different lengths of cardboard about an inch in width can be arranged in the same way. Paint color cards from the hardware store can also be used for sequencing activities. Start off by using only three or four shades of one color at first, and line them up in order of dark to light. This gives your companion the "aim of the game" and he is soon at it. Naturally other shades of the same color can be quickly added. A really tough problem can be introduced where several colors, each with its own set of graded shades, are mixed together. The sorting task must be mastered first before the sequencing of each set of colors can begin. Even partial success with a multiproblem is a real accomplishment for this youngster.

Sequencing a story in its proper order of events is a special game for the preschooler. For this you need to develop a story line and find pictures to portray the plot. For example, the story shows mother and child going for a walk. The first picture would show a mother and child, the second the mother looking for clothes (it is cold outside), the third the mother dressing the child and herself, and the fourth and last one would show the mother and child outside walking. There is not much doubt that being able to draw would be a tremendous asset for this particular activity. Sometimes one can find very inexpensive little books which after being read many times can be made into a task using the sequencing principle. The pictures, of course, have to be cut out and as few or as many are used as seem indicated at the time. Whatever is used, you place each card in front of your listener as you tell the story, then after quickly rearranging them ask your companion to tell you the story using the pictures.

A discrimination task in a fairly simplified form has been mentioned in a previous chapter. Now that your child is well into his third year more complex discrimination tasks can be provided because his ability to note differences is at a more sophisticated level. The reader may recall the earlier task where all the cups except one were red and the odd one was blue. A little toy was placed under the blue cup and the baby encouraged to look under that cup. Eventually after several play sessions and over a period of time the baby would begin to understand that the blue one meant the one that was different from the majority— and ultimately, of course, that blue meant a certain color. Still using color, another kind of discrimination task can be provided. In this case gradation of color provides the setting and the verbal clues given will refer to the lightest or darkest shade of color. For this activity several small boxes are needed, ideally very much the same size. Little jewelry boxes are very nice for this. Take your paint color cards and select one color—say, blue —and glue several of the cards on the bottom of each box so that you have a series of each with a different shade of blue. At first use only three or four so that there is a noticeable difference between the various shades. Others can be added later as your child gains competence. After the child examines the boxes, during which time you point out the lightest and darkest shade of blue, the preschooler is invited to participate in a hiding game. Explain that you will hide something under one of the boxes and then give him a clue as to where to look to find it. The boxes are placed in order of gradation as a first step and, unseen by your child, place a small treasure under the box with the lightest shade of blue. A hint is given: "I put it under the box with the lightest shade of blue. Look there." When that has been retrieved successfully you place it under the next lightest with the appropriate clue and continue on until it is finally put under the darkest one. If the game has been found fairly easy, continue by mixing the shades up and perhaps starting with the darkest shade. It should not be continued, however, if both participants are not enjoying it. This will happen if you become anxious about your child's achievements and if you become somewhat negative about some of his less successful attempts. If this has happened, forgetting about discrimination tasks for a while and reintroducing them at a later date, with some different "treasures," may rekindle interest.

Using this same principle, boxes of different sizes can be used to reinforce the concept of biggest and smallest. The procedure is the same with the initial examination and labeling and only three or four boxes are used at the beginning so that the size differential is very apparent. As understanding increases and if interest prevails (as well as the supply of boxes), more boxes of different sizes can be added to make the game increasingly complex. Longest and shortest is another concept which can be used in the discrimination tasks. Rough and smooth is another. With this latter problem you can use the same kind of jewelry boxes with an interesting surprise for hiding under the box, and glue various kinds of sandpaper on each box. A little more difficult variation of this problem can be offered using different kinds of textured material from rough burlap to smooth satin. All these tasks are excellent too for lots of language as well as wonderful togetherness.

An interesting extension of these tasks is one where the position of the box is the determining factor. That is, the object will be found in a box or container which is in a certain order of position. For example, place several of your boxes in a horizontal line. The little toy is placed in the first box on the right side of your companion. The second time it is placed in the one beside the first, moving to the left. The third time it is in the box third in line, still moving from right to left. Eventually, of course, the toy is found in the last box on the left. The procedure can be reversed so that the object is found in the boxes (sequentially) going from left to right. Placing the boxes in a vertical line is another change. Putting two sets of boxes together both vertically and horizontally in a cross formation poses a real problem, but if the idea has been developing correctly the child will understand that he needs to keep looking until he finds the object and then he will be able to proceed in the correct direction on each succeeding try. If, for example, it is found in the top position of the vertical line, he should assume with each successive try that he will find it in the box nearest to it going in a downward direction. If he finds it in the bottom box of the vertical line the second time around, then he will perceive that he must seek his find in the box adjacent to the first one going in an upward direction. In the beginning he may have to do quite a bit of looking before he locates the object. That position should give him the information as to where he must look following each "find." If the time seems right you begin the procedure in the usual way by permitting examination and labeling where you emphasize the position of the key boxes and explain the aim of the game. "I'm going to hide this little car under one of the boxes for you to find." When it has been discovered you can explain further, "You found your car in the box at the top of the line. I'm going to hide it again, see if you can find it." Too much frustration is the signal that this task is not quite suitable and it should be discontinued and introduced at a later, more appropriate time. It is no fun if the young problem solver is not ready for it and he should not be urged to continue.

Verbal puzzles can be lots of fun too. Here you give your child some information about an object or animal you are thinking about and ask your companion to guess what you are thinking. This is a sort of "I-spy-with-my-little-eye" game only on a more simplified level. With your child interested in participation it goes something like this. "I'm thinking of an animal that sounds like this—meow, meow. What animal am I thinking about?" Starting with a sure-fire easy one gets the idea across and you can proceed to more difficult ones. "I'm thinking of a green animal which hops on lily pads and goes croak, croak." If more information is needed it is quickly supplied. "He lives near the water, swims well, and likes to eat flies. That's right, I was thinking of a frog, wasn't I?" This game is a natural for "turns" with you becoming the guesser once in a while. With rather vague clues from your preschooler you may have a rather hard time to guess just what he is thinking about, but no matter, it's yet another challenge for you.

Summing up

Romping, running, and gentle roughhousing have become an integral part of the preschoolers repertoire of behaviors along with piggyback rides, peek-a-boo, and playing chase with mom and dad. Though his appetite may have decreased, his level of energy never ceases to amaze as he goes about the business of everyday living. Not only has he shifted into high gear in all spheres of his development, but his gears have become more complex and refined, honed by the various experiences he has had. Having received love, he loves; having felt security, he blossoms in his independence; having received praise, he has developed self-esteem; having experienced failure, he knows he can overcome his difficulties with persistence; and having known parental guidance, he feels safe in his explorations.

Language is well established and lucky parents may find their youngsters full of fanciful and imaginative stories. Often parts of favorite songs and rhymes will be recited or anticipated as mom and dad read them. Key words and phrases of well-known stories will be added and the preschooler may even "read" on his own, leafing through the book and explaining each page in an abbreviated form—leaving parents amazed at how precisely their child has picked up their intonations and speech patterns.

During the first three years of life the child has taken giant steps forward in his preparation for the school years. With good experiences, consistent discipline, and lots of love, care, and interaction with his parents and friends he will continue toward developing a healthy personality.

8　A Few

Last Thoughts

The early years, the magic years, the years of innocence—call them what you will—are years of tremendous growth and change in the young human individual. From the time he was a tiny creature, making his presence known in his mother's body, through the time span of this book, he has been influencing his environment as well as being influenced by it. Actively seeking information about his world, often frustrated and unhappy, but equally as often successful and joyous, he has made a unique impact on his immediate surroundings. Not only has he had to adapt to his parents, but also they have had to adapt to him, changing their environment in response to their child's rapid growth and increasing mobility, mentally, physically, and emotionally.

The title of this book, *Loving and Learning*, reflects the authors' philosophy that it is the emotional component, the love, the warmth, and the simple joy of interacting with their baby at his pace and at his level of competence, that will foster his curiosity and enable him to make use of the learning situation. The child does not need to be taught how to learn, he has been a master at that from the time he drew his first breath. This is so clearly demonstrated by his self-initiated explorations, his persistence in working through problems that arouse his curiosity and his pleasure at mastering these various problems, be they the triumph of his first steps, or the realization that a

265

certain shaped block fits into a certain shaped hole. The activities we present are but vehicles through which we hope that the family will get to know and understand one another in a pleasant way.

Many psychologists today are expressing some concern about the focus, structure, and ultimate outcome of the current approach to preschool education and "cribside academics." Dr. Jerome Kagan, who is a specialist in early childhood development, maintains that we, as parents, are "losing our common sense," searching for a fancy recipe to ensure academic success. He feels that in the early years, the best things parents can do for their child are to play with him, teach him songs, take him to the zoo, bounce him on their knees—in short, anything that parents enjoy doing. Since the parent-child relationship is so important in the early patterning of a child's personality, the child who grows up knowing he is a source of joy to his parents will most likely develop a healthy self-image. And parents who are enjoying and having fun with their child can be reasonably sure that their child will flourish and succeed in his future endeavors.

As we observe and study babies we learn more about them, their strengths, weaknesses, and vulnerability to the environment. In the past some psychologists have taken very strong stands on child-rearing and educational practices, but as we observe the results of these practices, we realize that a method that works for one parent does not necessarily work for another. There is so much diversity in the human personality and the modes of human interaction, and so many ways to successful parenting and teaching. Despite this diversity, however, certain basic tenets seem to hold universally in terms of the needs that children have.

Aside from their need for food, shelter, and love, healthy, happy babies have or develop other needs that provide the motivation for their learning. As anyone who has watched babies knows, they tend to be quite *active*. In the beginning much of this activity seems to be random as the baby practices using his muscles, but very quickly it becomes purposeful and movements become smooth, precise, and goal-oriented. Not only are babies active but they seem to have a strong need to do things with their hands, to *manipulate* objects endlessly until they are thoroughly familiar with their properties. They also have a need to *explore* and satisfy their insatiable curiosity, bit by bit familiarizing themselves with the intricacies of their environment. And very important in their environment are other people. The desire for *social interaction* starts very early as babies delight in being talked to, played with, held and cuddled. Finally, children seem to develop a need to *produce*, which appears later than the other needs. This need differs from manipulation in its focus on the end product. For example, a two-year-old is primarily interested in feeling, sifting, patting, and pushing sand around, but a three- or four-year-old likes to build roadways, castles, and all sorts of things with the sand. As the child grows older he becomes more involved with what he is producing and less concerned with the sheer pleasures of the actual movements involved.

Because of the manner in which the activities have been presented, it is a concern of the authors that parents might think "time is of the essence." That is, certain activities have to be done at a certain age, in a certain sequence, at a certain time every day. While we do encourage parents to try to have regular times set aside when they play, read, or simply pass the time exclusively with their child, we also encourage parents to be spontaneous and do things when the right moment and mood come along. By having regular playtimes, the child knows that even though his parents are terribly busy right now, he can count on some of their time later on.

It may seem that many of the activities we suggest are too complicated for babies at the specified age ranges. But if you remember that any given activity is only a *suggested* approach, and that babies have a wide range of abilities, moods, and levels of readiness for any given activity, then you can gear the activities to the particular level of your individual child. We feel that a child should have the *opportunity to try* various activities and that his interest, competence, and pleasure will guide parents in their choice of activities. If neither parent nor child enjoy the activity they are engaged in, then the time spent together will be frustrating for them both. The name of the game is to make the interactions a time for exploration, experimentation, and fun. Some will be quiet and relaxing, others boisterous and exciting, but always enjoyable.

Inasmuch as children should have the opportunity to experience new things with their parents, to explore new games and go to new places, they should also have lots of opportunities to explore, experiment, succeed, and fail all by themselves from their earliest months. It is one thing to be *shown* how to succeed at a task and quite another to experience this success *all by one-self*, just as it is one thing to always have things pointed out to you and to discover things all by yourself. It is important that parents let their child take the initiative rather than always being the initiators. Children have a marvelous capacity for discovering all sorts of things all by themselves without the benefit of parental guidance. Often the discoveries are wonderful for the baby, but require careful supervision and a quick reaction on the part of the parents. New discoveries in the house are frequently heralded by a sudden silence as a toddler has stretched to reach a higher shelf in the kitchen cabinet (one that mother was sure he couldn't reach for quite a while), gotten down a package of spaghetti which he opened with some difficulty and then spilled its contents all over the floor. But what discoveries! The spaghetti is brittle, makes a snapping sound when broken, doesn't taste too bad, kind of pricks if he pokes himself, is slippery if he stands up and tries to walk on it, and is very difficult to get back into the cellophane wrapper, but fits beautifully through the slats in the hot-air register. He could spend quite a long time playing with it if his mother wasn't just a bit discouraged by his latest discovery.

While interacting with their child, or standing back and observing him, parents are learning not only about their child but also about themselves. They learn all sorts of interesting things about their ability to tolerate the new sounds, smells, and sights of a growing baby. They may discover hidden talents in all kinds of creative endeavors, from painting to story telling, from building things to singing songs. They also appreciate discovering things through the eyes of their child, taking him places that they would never have gone on their own (as adults) without a child. They learn that having a child in the house makes a big difference.

Not only are the early years important ones for the child, but they are also important for his parents, for it is during this time that the patterns of interaction are established. How much is lost when a father all of a sudden discovers he has a son who would like to be taken to hockey practice, but he really doesn't know very much about his son. Or perhaps a daughter who all of a sudden is no longer a baby but a teenager who needs her parents' guidance but who does not know how to talk with them. Each plays a part in contributing to the kind of exchange that parents and children experience with each other as they grow up *together*. Parents who have made an effort to interact with baby when he was very tiny will find it much easier to interact with their toddler, teenager, and grown man as he progresses through time.

It would be unrealistic to suggest that every moment the family spends together will be happy, tension free, and rewarding. A comfortable routine and good relationship can often be interrupted by minor caretaking problems that baffle and annoy parent and child alike. All seems to be going well when suddenly the baby no longer sleeps through the night, refuses to eat meals, 269 at times may throw temper tantrums and become reluctant to go on the potty. The toddler wields his powerful "no" and insists on doing things his way or not at all. While these behaviors may seem somewhat arbitrary to the busy parent, or even the not-so-busy one, with a little thought and soul-searching a reason for the behavior can usually be found. Often restlessness and loss of appetite are caused by teething problems or a cold that has not yet manifested itself. These upsets in an established routine, provided the baby is generally happy and healthy and on a good basis with his parents, are most often of short duration. If the problem is one of teething, for example, once the baby has been made comfortable or the tooth has popped through the gum, his regular routine should be re-established. Naturally an upset baby needs to be comforted and must be comforted, but our smart babies quickly figure out which of their behaviors get a response and they may start manipulating parents after the original cause of discomfort is over. This is the time for calm, consistent handling on the part of parents. If redirection has not been successful, then the baby may cry for a short while until he realizes his ploy no longer works. A baby who is secure and trusts his world, who has had lots of positive attention and loving care, will quickly readjust and return to a comfortable routine.

Many a time parental behavior must seem rather arbitrary to a child. For example, a mother may oblige her child's request for a biscuit at midafternoon but refuse a half hour before suppertime. To the child, his hunger state is the same, but his mother just does not seem to understand that he needs that biscuit now. Mother, of course, has good reasons for her nonacquiescence to various requests but they are not always apparent to her child. Parents often act on an intellectual level while their child responds purely on an emotional level, guided by his immediate needs and perceptions. Children tend to think on a

different qualitative level from adults since they have fewer experiences with the subtleties and complexities of past and future events.

With consistent, calm handling each problem is solved until the next one comes along. Transition times are often hard for both children and parents: changing from two naps to one a day; changing diet; changing from being immobile to crawling to walking; from a nontalker to a talker; from being fed to feeding oneself; from soiling diapers to being "dry," and so on. As the baby grows and changes parents develop expectations for what will come next, and what they feel their baby should be doing in his new phase of development. However, as baby passes from one stage to another he may actually regress for a while into the security and comfort of a behavior that he knows how to do well—the walker will all of a sudden start crawling again, the very independent toddler will need lots of extra cuddling and comfort, perhaps resorting to tears instead of words to announce his discomfort. Most children delight in their new-found skills but find that once they express some expertise in them, parents may have too high expectations and not realize that they are still babies, needing the warmth and security of being rocked, held close, and sung to. The precocious baby, one who is tall for his age and has started walking and talking earlier than some of his peers, is especially prone to unrealistic expectations on the part of others. The reverse, of course, is also true. A very small, "cute" baby may be babied because of his size and appearance and not given the opportunities and encouragement to try things for himself. Fortunately, most babies have the strength to set their own patterns, and most parents are sensitive enough to respect their child as an individual and give him opportunities and encouragement to progress at his own pace, be it slow and steady, fast and erratic, or any combination of fast and slow.

By hook or by crook, we as adults cannot but help influence young children, especially if they have learned that theirs is a warm, trusting world because of the adults in it. A baby will be responsive to the kind of environment that adults provide, watching and learning from what they do and say. Parents, because they are in such intimate contact with their young ones, and because they are loved by them, are perhaps among the most influential and important teachers in the early years. Unless the baby has older brothers and sisters or spends considerable time with other adults and children (in day-care centers, for instance), his parents provide him with his major learning experiences through their example and the kind of environment they provide. Parents who love music, for example, will probably provide their child with lots of opportunities to participate in music experiences, while others find different avenues of interest and expression. Thus every child gets exposed to a unique combination of sights, sounds, and emotions, examples, and feedback from those he loves the most.

In an article in *Woman's Day*, April 1973, Eda LeShan, a family-life specialist, talks about the most important things parents can teach a little child as he approaches his school years. She feels, as we do, that early concentration on academic tasks, to the exclusion of other important kinds of growing, can inhibit normal development into a fully functional person. If we can instill in our children feelings of happiness, self-confidence, optimism, curiosity, and friendship, then they will probably be eager to learn. However, if they are nervous, angry, frightened, and preoccupied with unmet needs they will not be able to take advantage of the intellectual stimulation available to them. Ms. LeShan pinpoints ten skills or attitudes that parents should try to teach their child in preparation for dealing with the wider world that the school years bring. They are: (1) To love himself—by loving him and giving him feelings of self-worth; (2) To read behavior—by helping him understand his own behavior as well as that of others; (3) To communicate with words—so that he may explain feelings that his behavior does not always show; (4) To understand the difference between thoughts and actions

—by helping him understand that thoughts are not the same as actions, that feelings never hurt anyone, and that it is natural to feel scared when hurt or worried; (5) To wonder and ask why —by not squelching his natural instinctive intellectual curiosity; (6) To risk failure as a necessary part of growing up—by helping him learn through his mistakes and giving him the courage to try again; (7) To understand that complicated questions do not have simple answers—by gauging our answers to the child's level of understanding and helping him look deeper for the solution; (8) To have a mind of his own—by giving him realistic choices and then respecting his decision; (9) To trust grownups—by being honest and trustworthy ourselves; (10) To know when to lean on adults—by showing him that we understand his world and that we can be his friends.

While the authors started this book with some trepidation, we finish it with some reluctance. So much has been said, yet so much still remains unsaid. As we stated at the beginning, we hope that parents will use it as a guide, an idea book, rather than a definitive statement of what must and should be done with babies. We hope that through reading the book, parents have become a little more aware of the varied abilities and tremendous complexity of their little child; that this awareness has helped them relish the rewards and simple pleasures of watching their child discovering himself and his world. We have learned much in writing this book, in being with and enjoying children—their intricacies, complexity, imagination, and honesty have never failed to amaze us. And so, in conclusion, we urge our readers to enjoy their children for what they are, and above all to cherish them and the special moments that pass so quickly in the early years.

Glossary

Bibliography

Appendixes

Index

Glossary

CHILDPROOFING: is a thorough safety check of the house to spot and correct all possible hazards to the child. Parents can get down on all fours to explore the house as their inquisitive baby would, checking closet floors, low cupboards, latches on cupboards, undersides of raised furniture, dangling cords and light sockets, to name only a few. In addition there are all the collected treasures that parents may have and cherish. These are going to be extremely tempting to the child and when handled by little hands run the risk of being broken. Attention to childproofing is not limited just to this young age. Parents must be aware of their continuing responsibility to protect the growing child from all kinds of environmental hazards, even until adolescence.

COGNITION: is the name for all the various ways in which the baby learns about his world. It includes the building up of knowledge through such things as perceptions, memories, images, concept formation, judgment, and reasoning.

CONCEPT: refers to the way a child classifies his experiences. It is how he thinks about the qualities, common elements, and relationships between objects. Comparing, generalizing, abstracting, and reasoning are all part of concept formation. It is understanding the principles that lie behind and support all the separate bits and pieces of information that babies learn about their world. Language plays a large part in the learning of concepts.

DEVELOPMENT: usually refers to the gradual natural and spontaneous unfolding of all aspects of a baby's physical, mental, social, and emotional being. The progress of his development is directed from within, fostered and nurtured by caring people in his environment. While there is a general pattern in the way all children develop, the rate and the specifics of growth are unique for each child.

DIMENSION: is basically the length, width, and depth of an object, three special properties of objects that the baby gradually notices and comes to understand.

DISCIPLINE: comes from the Latin, meaning to instruct and to learn. Unfortunately it is often thought of as being synonymous with punishment. It really means the training of the baby's mental, moral, social, emotional, and physical abilities through loving instruction by parents. By setting firm, consistent, and realistic limits and praising him for acceptable behavior, parents help give him the idea of what is expected of him. Discipline is part of the process of socialization through which the child learns to become a member of his society. He is eventually guided by his own inner controls as he gains maturity. (See also EXTERNAL CONTROL.)

DISCRIMINATION: is the ability of the baby to perceive differences in similar objects, sounds, and situations through his various senses. Discrimination tasks are useful for helping him to observe his world more precisely and note differences that are increasingly subtle.

DISTRACTION (also called redirection): is a technique that can be used to shift a child from a negative activity (for example, pulling leaves off a house plant) to a positive one. Distraction encourages him to behave in a way that is acceptable to him and to his parents. The reasoning behind this method stems from the fact that a child can go from an unacceptable activity to an acceptable one much more easily and happily than just being told to stop and given no alternative.

EGOCENTRIC: refers to the time when a baby feels that the world revolves around him and should cater exclusively to his needs. It is part of the baby's growing awareness of himself as a unique individual and is part of the normal personality growth.

EMOTIONAL GROWTH: is a term that describes the natural growing pattern of the baby's feelings. At birth the baby experiences his feelings as a simple alternation between comfortable and relaxed and uncomfortable and tense. Gradually all the rich shades of emotional tones, such as smiling, differentiated crying, laughter, frustration, sadness, anger, fear, jealousy, joy, loneliness, and so on, are elaborated with growth.

EMPIRICAL: in the general sense means based on experience. In psychology it means based on observation and experiment as opposed to deduction from general philosophical principles.

ENVIRONMENT: generally refers to all the external experiences, such as living conditions and family circumstances, objects, people, and pets, which make up the surroundings of the baby. Environment has a significant influence on his growth and development.

EXTERNAL CONTROL: refers to behavioral guidance given by parents who act as a combination policeman and teacher, directing and modifying the behavior of the baby. Parents initially monitor and control his behavior in order that he may learn to control his own behavior later on (this is called internal control). (See also DISCIPLINE)

EYE-HAND CO-ORDINATION: is the synchronization of the eyes, the hands, and fingers enabling the baby to reach for, grasp, and manipulate objects. Learning how to do this is a gradual process in which the baby's skill improves with time and practice. (See also FINE MOTOR CO-ORDINATION)

FACILITATOR: is any thing, person, situation, or experience that happens in the baby's life that will make present and future learning and growth easier for him.

FEEDBACK: is the positive or negative information the baby gets from his parents and the objects in his environment when he says or does something. This information is utilized by the baby in whatever way he chooses. Positive feedback encourages and negative feedback discourages.

FIELD OF VISION: is the area to the front and sides of the baby's face which he can take in visually.

FINE MOTOR CO-ORDINATION: refers to the movements of the small muscles, especially of the hands and fingers, which enable the baby to pick up and handle objects. Fine motor co-ordination often requires both the co-ordination of these small muscles and his vision. (See also EYE-HAND CO-ORDINATION)

GROSS MOTOR CO-ORDINATION: refers to the baby's use of his large

279

muscles, as in the arms, legs, and trunk. The movements of these muscles gradually become smooth, rhythmical, and co-ordinated, enabling the baby to engage in such necessary activities as reaching, walking, running, and so forth.

HABIT: is an automatic response to a specific situation established through repetition and learning over a period of time.

HEREDITY: is the name for the genetic transmission of various characteristics from parents to their children. Many physical characteristics are obvious (hair coloring, height, and so on), and others are still unknown quantities (intellectual and emotional traits).

IDIOSYNCRATIC: refers to the special ways babies have that make them unique. Some of these characteristics may be slightly unusual or even amusing to the parents but they are expressive of their own child's individuality.

IMPULSE CONTROL: (also referred to as inner control, self-control, internal control) is an ability which the child gradually acquires enabling him to control his own behavior before deciding that this is something which is or isn't acceptable for him to do. Impulse control is a gradually acquired ability.

INTUITION: is knowing immediately what "feels" right without going through a conscious thinking and reasoning process.

KINESTHESIS: describes the baby's perception and feeling of movement when any part of his body is moved whether he moves it himself or it is moved for him. Another name for kinesthesis is muscle sense.

LOCOMOTION: is a fancy name for the baby's movement from point A to point B, whether it be hitching, creeping, crawling, hopping, rolling, walking, running, or skipping.

MANIPULATION: is the handling and examining of objects that is an essential part of the baby's learning experiences and the satisfaction of his curiosity. It also refers to the managing or controlling of a situation between a baby and his parents.

MATURATION: is a natural process governing the baby's growth and development, including the psychological, the physical, and the intellectual.

NORMAL: means average, what is typical and expected. With reference to babies it can be a rather vague term defining a typical baby who is developing in about the same way as other babies of his age. However, babies grow so quickly and unevenly it is often quite difficult to compare one baby with another, calling the one normal and the other above or below normal.

OBJECT PERMANENCE: is the baby's awareness and understanding that an object still exists even when he can't see it.

OVERSTIMULATION: is the act of bombarding the baby's senses excessively, so that he is unable to take it all in and enjoy and learn from these experiences.

PALMAR GRASP: is the name for the baby's grasping with the palm of his hand. When he is very young he moves all his fingers together against his palm to grasp objects and he continues to use his palm at least partially up to approximately five months of age. Somewhat after this age he grasps objects in an increasingly adultlike manner using his thumb and first finger (pincers grasp).

POTENTIAL: refers to the possible growth of the baby in all areas. A nurturing environment with loving parents encourages the child to strive toward his potential.

PRONE: refers to the placing of the baby on his tummy.

PROPERTIES: refers to the various qualities and charcteristics of objects. For example, size, shape, color, texture, smell, to name just a few.

REFLEX: is a physical reaction by the baby to something that influences him and that is beyond his control to start or stop. For example, the swallowing reflex occurs when food is placed on the back of the tongue.

REGRESSION: is a retreat on the part of the baby to an earlier stage of behavior. Such regression is most often temporary and quite normal and may be expected especially when there has just been a big change in his life.

REINFORCEMENT: is a response to the baby's behavior from mother and father which is either positive or negative. A positive response encourages the baby to repeat a particular behavior and a negative response discourages a particular behavior.

SELF-ESTEEM, SELF-WORTH, SELF-VALUE: are words that describe the good feelings a child comes to have about himself. Through many positive experiences with his environment he learns that basically he is worthwhile and is valued by his parents and others. Such a self-concept is essential to a healthy physical and psychological state.

SENSORY: refers to the baby's principal senses: hearing, seeing, smelling, tasting, and touching.

SPATIAL RELATIONSHIPS: as the young baby's vision becomes more finely attuned he pays increasing attention to the objects he sees around him, to the distance between those objects and to the distance separating him from the objects. Locating objects and understanding their relationships to each other enables him to maneuver himself as well as to reach out, grasp, and handle objects accurately.

STABILE: is a piece of sculpture made up of various attractive materials such as wire, wood, pipe cleaners, and so forth inserted in a stationary base.

STIMULATION: is the provoking of the baby's attention to a particular experience. It can be an internal experience such as hunger or an external one such as music. It arouses in him the desire to become actively involved in that situation.

STIMULUS: is anything that influences the activity of the baby; anything that evokes a response.

SUPINE: is the placing of the baby on his back.

SYMBIOTIC: is the physical and emotional sharing that mother and infant enjoy together. The symbiosis is at first completely physical, as before his birth he is actually attached to his mother in the womb. After birth symbiosis is extended to include emotional closeness as well as such physical sharing as breast-feeding. With his own growing independence the baby and his mother begin to need each other less and the quality of the emotional bond changes, gradually allowing him to widen his emotional ties beyond that with his mother.

TACTILE: refers to the sensations a baby gets by touching and feeling.

TEMPERAMENT: is the baby's own special make-up, his own way of responding to his environment, its joys and its frustrations. For example, he may be placid or explosive, happy-go-lucky or serious.

Bibliography

Books for parents

Bettelheim, Bruno, *Love Is Not Enough: The Treatment of Emotionally Disturbed Children*. Chicago: Free Press, 1950; New York: Crowell Collier and Macmillan, 1965 (paperback).

Bloom, Benjamin S., *Stability and Change in Human Characteristics*. New York: John Wiley, 1964.

Bowlby, John, and others, *Maternal Care and Mental Health*. New York: Schocken Books, 1966.

Brazelton, T. Berry, *Infants and Mothers: Differences in Development*. New York: Delacorte Press, 1969.

Caplan, Frank and Theresa, *The Power of Play*. New York: Doubleday (Anchor Press), 1973.

Chess, Stella, Thomas, A., and Birch, H. G., *Your Child Is a Person: A Psychological Approach to Parenthood without Guilt*. New York: Viking Press, 1965.

Consumer Reports, February, 1973.

Dodson, Fitzhugh, *How to Parent*. Los Angeles: Nash Publishing, 1971.

English, Oliver Spurgeon, and Foster, Constance, J., *Fathers Are Parents, Too*. New York: Putnam, 1951.

Fanz, Robert L., and Nevis, Sonia, "Pattern Preference and Perceptual Cognitive Development in Early Infancy." *Merrill Palmer Quarterly of Behaviour and Development*, Vol. 13, 1967, No. 1, p. 77.

Flint, Betty M., *The Child and the Institution: A Study of Deprivation and Recovery*. Toronto: University of Toronto Press, 1966.

Fraiberg, Selma, *The Magic Years: Understanding and Handling the Problems of Early Childhood*. New York: Charles Scribner Sons, 1965.

Fromme, Allan, *The ABC of Child Care*. New York: Simon and Schuster, 1970.

Gordon, Ira, Cunagh, B., and Jester, R. Emile, *Child Learning Through Child Play*. New York: St. Martin's Press, 1972.

Gordon, Ira, and Lally, J. Ronald, *Intellectual Stimulation for Infants and Toddlers*. Gainesville, Florida: Institute for the Development of Human Resources, College of Education, 1968.

Gwynne Jones, Eurfron, *Children Growing Up*. Harmondsworth, Middlesex, England: Penguin Books, 1973.

Larrick, Nancy (compiler), *The Wheels of the Bus Go Round and Round: School Bus Songs and Chants*. Los Angeles: Golden Gate Junior Books, 1972.

Le Shan, Eda, "The Most Important Things Parents Can Teach a Little Child." *Woman's Day*, Vol. 36, April 1973, p. 44.

Levy, Janine, *The Baby Exercise Book: The First Fifteen Months*. New York: Pantheon, 1974.

Montagu, Ashley, *Touching: The Human Significance of the Skin*. New York: Columbia University Press, 1971.

Montessori, Maria, *The Child in the Family*. Chicago: Henry Regnery, 1970.

Piaget, Jean, *The Origins of Intelligence in Children*. New York: International Universities Press, 1953.

Prudden, Bonnie, *How to Keep Your Child Fit from Birth to Six*. New York: Harper and Row, 1964.

Ribble, Margaretha, *The Rights of Infants: Early Psychological Needs and Their Satisfaction*. New York: Columbia University Press, 2nd ed., 1965.

Salk, Lee, and Kramer, Rita, *How to Raise a Human Being: A Parent's Guide to Emotional Health from Infancy through Adolescence*. New York: Random House, 1969.

Sander, L. W., "The Longitudinal Course of Early Mother-Child Interactions: Cross-Case Comparison in a Sample of Mother-Child Pairs." In Foss, B. M. (editor), *Determinants of Infant Behaviour IV*. London, England: Methuen, 1969.

Simont, Marc, and Boston Children's Hospital Medical Center Staff, *A Child's Eye View of the World*. New York: Delacorte Press, 1972.

Spitz, Rene A., "Hospitalism. An Inquiry into the Genesis of Psychiatric Conditions in Early Childhood." In *Psychoanalytical Study of the Child*. New York: International Universities Press, 1945.

Spock, Benjamin, *Baby and Child Care*. Des Moines, Iowa: Meredith Press, 3rd. ed., 1968; Toronto: Simon & Schuster of Canada, 1968.

Craft books for parents and toddlers

Banet, Barbara, and others, *The Scrap Book*. Ann Arbor, Michigan: Perry Nursery School, 1972.

Cole, Ann, and others, *I Saw a Purple Cow and 100 Other Recipes for Learning*. Boston: Little, Brown, 1972.

Craft "How To" Create Books. Temple City, Colorado: Aleenes.

Fletcher, Helen Jill, *The Big Book of Things to Do and Make*. New York: Random House, 1961.

Gregg, Elizabeth, and Boston Children's Hospital Medical Center Staff, *What to Do When There's Nothing to Do: 601 Tested Play Ideas for Young Children*. New York: Delacorte Press, 1968.

How to Make Sock Toys. Park Ridge, Illinois: Clapper Publishing Company.

Make It with Milk and Cream Cartons. Chicago: Graff Publications, 1966.

Marshall, Leslie, *Book of Things to Make and Do*. Leicester, England: Brockhampton Press, 1973.

Philpott, A. C., *Let's Make Puppets*. London, England: Evans Brothers, 1972.

Saeger, Glen, *String Things You Can Create*. New York: Sterling Publishing Co., 1973.

Wickers, David, and Finmark, Sharon, *How to Make Your Own Kinetics*. New York: Van Nostrand-Reinhold, 1972.

Pets

Buck, Margaret Waring, *Pets from the Pond*. New York: Abingdon
    Press, 1958.
The Pet Library includes the following titles:
Enjoy Your Canary
Know Your Parakeets-Budgies
Know Your Aquarium
Planting Your Aquarium
Enjoy Your Goldfish
Enjoy Your Guinea Pig
Enjoy Your Hamster
Enjoy Your Gerbils, Rats and Mice
Enjoy Your Snakes
Enjoy Your Terrarium
This series is published by
        Sternco Industries Inc.
        Box D
        Harrison, N.J. 07029

Nursery songs and finger play

Bone, Margaret Bradford, *Fireside Book of Folk Songs*. New York:
    Simon and Schuster, 1947.
Dean's New Gift Book of Nursery Rhymes. London, England: Dean
    and Son, 1971.
Fletcher, Margaret I., and Denison, Margaret Conkay, *The New
    High Road of Song for Nursery Schools and Kindergarten*. Scar-
    borough, Ontario: W. J. Gage, 1960.
Fowke, Edith, *Sally Go Round the Sun: 300 Children's Songs,
    Rhymes, and Games*. Toronto: McClelland & Stewart, 1969; New
    York: Doubleday, 1970.
Graham, Mary Nancy, *50 Songs for Children*. Whitman Publishing
    Co., 1964.
Grayson, Marion, *Let's Do Fingerplays*. Washington: Robert B.
    Luce, 1962.

Lloyd, Norman (arranger), *The New Golden Song Book*. New York: Golden Press, 1966.

Matterson, Elizabeth, *Games to Play with the Very Young*. New York: McGraw, Hill, 1967.

Montgomerie, Norah, *This Little Pig Went to Market*. London, England: The Bodley Head, 1966.

Panabaker, Lucile, *Lucile Panabaker's Song Book*. Toronto: Peter Martin, 1968.

Paulson, Emilie, *Finger Plays for Nursery and Kindergarten*. Boston: D. Lathrop, 1963.

Pointer, Priscilla, *Ten Little Fingers*. New York: Wonder Books, 1954.

Wilkin, Esther, *Play With Me*. New York: Western Publishing Company, 1967.

Winn, Marie (editor), *What Shall We Do and Alee Galloo*. New York: Harper, 1970.

Books for infants, 1–18 months

Allen, Robert, *Numbers*. New York: Platt & Munk, 1968.

Battaglia, Aurelius (illustrator), *This Is My House*. Racine, Wisconsin: Western Publishing Company: Playskool, 1963.

Bill Bunny's Surprise. New York: Golden Press, 1968.

Bryant, Dean (illustrator), *ABC Book*. Chicago: Rand McNally, 1959.

Cansdale, George, *The Ladybird Book of Pets*. Loughborough, Leicester, England: Wills & Hepworth, 1957.

Gagg, M. C., *Puppies and Kittens*. Loughborough, Leicester, England: Wills & Hepworth, 1966.

———*The Zoo*. Loughborough, Leicester, England: Wills & Hepworth, 1960.

Giannini (illustrator), *Brownie and Puff Paint the Doghouse*. New York: Golden Press, 1972.

Hall, W. N., *Whatever Happens to Puppies?* New York: Golden Press, 1965.

Izawa, T., *My First Book of Numbers*. Rappongi Minato-ku, Tokyo: Zokeiska Publications, 1971.

Kaufman, Joe, *Words*. New York: Golden Press, 1968.

Kunhardt, Dorothy, *Pat the Bunny*. New York: Golden Press, 1962.

Matthiessen, Thomas, *Things to See*. New York: Platt & Munk, 1966.-

A Picture Book of Aeroplanes. Froebel-Kan Co., 1970.

A Picture Book of Ships and Boats. Forebel-Kan Co., 1968.

Porter, Bertha Morris, *The Wonders of the Seasons*. New York: Golden Press, 1966.

Sherman, Diane, *My Counting Book*. Chicago: Rand McNally, 1963.

Rison, Ole, *I Am a Bear*. New York: Golden Press, 1969.

———*I Am a Bunny*. New York: Golden Press, 1963.

———*I Am a Kitten*. New York: Golden Press, 1970.

———*I Am a Mouse*. New York: Golden Press, 1964.

Rojankovsky, Feodor, *Animals in the Zoo*. New York: Alfred A. Knopf, 1962.

———*Animals on the Farm*. New York: Alfred A. Knopf, 1967.

Scarry, Richard, *Best Storybook Ever*. New York: Golden Press, 1968.

———*The Great Big Car and Truck Book*. New York: Golden Press, 1951.

———*What Animals Do*. New York: Golden Press, 1968.

Wagner, Ken, *From One to Ten and Back Again*. New York: Golden Press, 1972.

Wingfield, Ethel and Harry, *A Ladybird First*. Loughborough, Leicester, England, Wills & Hepworth, 1970.

———*A Ladybird Second*. Loughborough, Leicester, England: Wills & Hepworth, 1970.

———*A Ladybird Third*. Loughborough, Leicester, England: Wills & Hepworth, 1973.

———*A Ladybird Fourth*. Loughborough, Leicester, England: Wills & Hepworth, 1971.

———*A Ladybird Fifth*. Loughborough, Leicester, England: Wills & Hepworth, 1973.

———*Learning with Mother*, Book I. Loughborough, Leicester, England: Wills & Hepworth, 1970.

Witte, Pat and Eve, *Who Lives Here?* New York: Golden Press, 1961.

Books for toddlers, 18 months to 3 years

Bedford, Annie North, *Frosty the Snowman.* New York: Golden Press, 1950.

Berenstain, Stanley and Janice, *Inside, Outside, Upside Down.* New York: Random House, 1968.

Berger, Knute, *A Visit to the Doctor.* New York: Wonder Books, 1960.

Browner, Richard, *Everyone Has a Name.* New York: Henry Z. Walck, 1961.

Clure, Beth, and Rumsey, Helen, *Little, Big, Bigger.* Glendale, Calif.: Bowmar Publishing Corp., 1969.

DeCaprio, Annie, *The Bus from Chicago.* New York: Wonder Books, 1965.

Eastman, Philip D., *Are You My Mother?* New York: Random House, 1960.

———Go, Dog, Go. New York: Random House, 1961.

Farley, Walter, *Little Black Goes to the Circus.* New York: Random House, 1963.

Flack, Marjorie, *Angus and the Cat.* New York: Doubleday, 1931.

Francis, Sally R., *Scat, Scat.* New York: Platt & Munk, 1940.

Freud, Rudolf, *Animals Every Child Should Know.*

Giannini (illustrator), *Willy Learns a Lesson.* New York: Golden Press, 1972.

The Giant Walt Disney Word Book. New York: Golden Press, 1971.

Hazen, Barbara Shook, *Rudolph the Red-Nosed Reindeer.* New York: Golden Press, 1958.

Joyce, Irma, *Never Talk to Strangers.* New York: Golden Press, 1970.

King, Patricia, *Mabel the Whale.* Chicago: Follett, 1958.

Krauss, Ruth, *The Carrot Seed.* New York: Harper, 1945.

Landis, Dorothy Thompson, *My Flower Book.* Chicago: Rand McNally, 1962.

Lenski, Lois, *The Little Fire Engine.* New York: Henry Z. Walck, 1946.

Le Sieg, Theodore, *The Eye Book.* New York: Random House, 1968.

Let's Go Shopping. New York: Playskool, 1964.

Long, Ruthanna, *Ten Little Chipmunks*. New York: Golden Press, 1971.

McClintock, Mike, *A Fly Went By*. New York: Random House, 1958.

McCloskey, Robert, *Blueberries for Sal*. New York: Viking Press, 1948.

Miller, Howard, *Little Bunny Follows His Nose*. New York: Golden Press, 1971.

Munn, Ian, *Johnny and the Birds*. Chicago: Rand McNally,

Palmer, Helen, *I Was Kissed by a Seal at the Zoo*. New York: Random House, 1962.

Pearson, Wanda Lynn, *Buttons and His Sunday Coat*. Austin, Texas: The Steck Company, 1959.

Piers, H., *Five Little Pigs*. London, England: Methuen, 1969.

Potter, Beatrix, *The Tale of Benjamin Bunny*. London, England: F. Warne, 1904.

Potter, Marion, *The Red Caboose*. New York: Golden Press, 1953.

Rockwell, Anne F., *Sally's Caterpillar*. New York: Parents' Magazine Press, 1966.

Scarry, Richard, *The Great Big Air Book*. New York: Random House, 1971.

———*The Great Big Schoolhouse*. New York: Random House, 1968.

———*Nicky Goes to the Doctor*. New York: Golden Press, 1972.

Seymour, Dorothy Z., *Big Beds and Little Beds*. London, England: Initial Teaching Publishing Company, 1965.

Wildsmith, Brian, *Circus*. New York: Franklin Watts, 1970.

———*Mother Goose*. New York: Franklin Watts, 1964.

Zion, Gene, *All Falling Down*. New York: Harper, 1951.

———*Harry the Dirty Dog*. New York: Harper, 1956.

———*Harry by the Sea*. New York: Harper, 1965.

———*No Roses for Harry!* New York: Harper, 1958.

Appendixes

Recipes

Salt and flour beads

1/4 cup salt
1/4 cup flour
1/8 cup water

Mix salt and flour together and then add water. Shape dough into beads 1/2″–3/4″ in diameter. Place "beads" on wax paper and turn several times until they start to harden. Grease a skewer with vegetable oil and pierce each bead carefully. Allow to harden. (This takes more than one day.) When hard, paint and string.

Squirt paint

1 cup flour
1/4 cup salt
1/8 cup sugar
Food coloring, powdered fruit drink, or dry tempera paints

Mix dry ingredients together and then add enough water to get the consistency of light cream. Place in plastic bottle which can be easily squeezed.

Starch base for finger paints

2 tbls. cornstarch
2 tbls. cold water
1 cup boiling water

Mix cold water and starch together until smooth. Add boiling water and stir.

For colors: Add powdered fruit drink to 1 oz. of starch base, starting with 1 tsp. until the desired depth of color is obtained. Soya sauce added to 1 oz. of the starch base until the desired depth of color is obtained will produce a most acceptable brown. 1 tbls. prepared mustard added to 1 oz. of the starch base will produce a beautiful canary yellow.

Flour base for finger paints

2 tbls. flour
3 tbls. water

Mix to smooth paste. Add powdered tempera paints, powdered fruit drink, or food coloring.

Collage paste

2 tsp. flour
2 tsp. water

Mix until smooth. Use immediately.

Modeling dough

1 cup flour
1/3 cup salt
1/3 tsp. lard
Enough water to give right consistency

For colored dough add food coloring to water before mixing in with dry ingredients.

Things to Make

Table and chair

The secret of making a suitable table for a young child lies in the height from the floor. It should not be too large, nor should the chair be too large. The child should be able to rest his feet on the floor, as this is more comfortable and gives him a feeling of security. The actual working area of the table is not important but how high it is from the floor is important. If dad makes the legs no higher than 14″ he is probably on safe ground. As the child grows, longer table legs can replace the shorter ones.

Sometimes cutting out an insert about 4″ in depth and 10″–12″ long in the middle of one side will permit the child to move right in and thus maximize his working space.

Cube chairs are safe, and easy to make. Four pieces of 1/4″ plywood are cut into 12″ squares. Three are attached to make the sides and the back. The fourth piece is fastened in the middle, about 6″ up from the floor, for the seat. As the child gets bigger the seat can be raised. For extra safety the ends of the side panels can be rounded off and well sanded to avoid splinters. If the table surface is painted a solid color it helps emphasize the artist's work.

Bolster pillow

Find a sturdy piece of fabric 22″ x 22″ which can be easily laundered. Hem and place Velcro on two edges so that two sides can be easily fastened when placed together. A pillow or several sturdy bath towels can be made into a roll, covered with the prepared piece of fabric, and fastened securely. In a pinch the edges can be fastened at each end with a sturdy safety pin if Velcro is not easily obtainable. As the child grows older the bolster pillow can be enlarged by using a larger square of material.

Book case

Take a sturdy piece of fabric approximately 3 feet long and 2 feet wide and hem the edges. Cut and hem three strips of fabric 2 feet long, making one 8″ wide and the other two 6″ wide. Sew the 8″ strip onto the large piece of material so that it makes a pocket 4″ from the top. Sew on the other two strips each below the other. Two seams 12″ apart from top to bottom will provide nine slots for books of various sizes. This is just an oversized shoe bag.

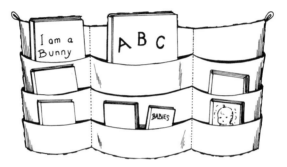

Painting holder

Opened medium-sized cardboard box with ends of the bottom extended outward for support.

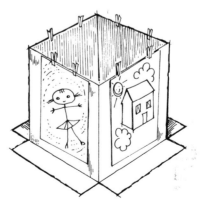

Easel

Medium-sized cardboard carton cut in half diagonally. The picture can be attached with small strips of Scotch tape.

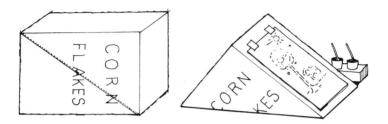

Stamps

Take empty wooden thread spools and glue onto each of them one of the following: a piece of heavy cord; a bottle cap; bits of fabric; small pieces of pipe cleaner formed into geometric shapes or any other design. The innovative parent can add a wide variety of other objects that will make interesting stamps.

Drum

Made from the bottom halves of two large plastic bottles. A small cut is made in the edge of one to facilitate the attachment. Glueing keeps them in place. For different-sized drums, longer or shorter sections of the plastic bottles are used. Pieces of doweling become sticks but wooden spoons can also be used.

Drum

The potato-chip carton provides the drum and a dish mop covered with a small piece of cloth makes a very interesting stick.

Drum

Large potato-chip container with pieces of doweling for sticks. Again wooden spoons can be utilized.

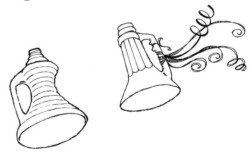

Horns

Made from the ends of large plastic bottles. Can also be used to make a telephone by attaching the two together with a fairly long piece of discarded plastic garden hose.

Shaker

Any small plastic bottle with an elongated neck for a handle and filled with beans, rice, or pebbles also makes a suitable shaker.

Shaker

Made from a plastic lemon or lime-shaped container for concentrated lemon or lime juice. Rice, beans, or small pebbles are inserted first. Then a piece of graded doweling is pushed into the opening. The handle of a wooden spoon works equally well. A little glue added to the stick will keep it attached. Brightly colored ribbons add to its attractiveness.

Shaker

Take a paint stirrer and fasten to it two or three smooth-edged disks from frozen-orange-juice cans. Nailing them so that they are not too close to the stick will permit the disks to shake freely and so will make the jingle sound. If a little glue is used on the nail, it will keep it firmly attached to the paint stirrer. If the end of the nail protrudes it can be clipped off with a wire cutter.

Shaker

Take two aluminum tart tins and "sew" them together with heavy cord in such a way that there is a small opening at the top and bottom. Place some beans, small pebbles, or rice inside and then insert a flat smooth stick 6″ long and 1/4″ wide through the two openings. If the openings are a bit large and the stick does not fit snugly a few extra stitches will close the gaps and prevent the beans from falling out. The shaker is ready.

Discrimination task

One-pound or two-pound coffee cans with two different-shaped openings, each opening permitting only one object to be passed through. For more choices the larger coffee can is excellent. Tobacco tins and cottage-cheese containers can also be used for this discrimination task.

Eye-hand co-ordination task

The one-pound coffee can or tobacco tin can be used for this along with several smooth-edged disks from frozen-orange-juice cans. Cut a slot 2″ x 1/2″ in the lid and if it is metal protect the edge with adhesive tape so there is no possibility of cuts. The task is now ready to be mastered.

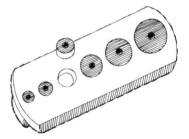

Sequencing form board

This is made in the same way as the geometric form board shown on the facing page except that the shapes are all the same except for size. It can be made easy or more complex by using a few circles or many.

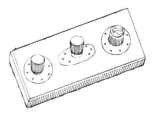

Simple threading board

Cut and sand a small piece of wood 8″ x 4″. Attach with small nails the necks of several detergent bottles with their tops and the board is ready.

Complex threading board

Take a sturdy piece of wood 12″ x 8″ and partially cut several holes the size of each of the nuts into the wood but not through it. The various kinds of nuts used should be of quite a large size. Glue each in place in its hole and with the bolts the board is ready for use. Adapters of different sizes can also be used for more novelty.

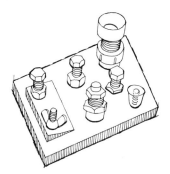

Geometric form board

Three-piece geometric form board requires one piece of 1/4″ plywood 9″ x 3″ and one piece of 1/2″ plywood the same size. Each shape is cut out of the 1/2″ plywood and sanded so that it fits easily into the appropriate opening. A small knob screwed and glued into the top makes it easy to handle. The piece of 1/2″ plywood is then fastened to the 1/4″ piece of plywood and the form board sanded until free of rough edges. It can be painted a bright color for additional interest. If geometric pieces are going to be painted, each should be painted the same color, otherwise the task may become a mixture of memory and discrimination. This is a little too complicated for the very young child. More complex form boards for a later time can be made with the addition of more shapes and in this case each piece can be painted a different color.

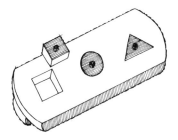

Latch board

Cut and sand two pieces of 1/4" plywood 20" x 10". In one board cut and sand several small doors and fasten with one part of each latch set. Attach each door with a hinge in the appropriate place on the board and then nail the two boards together. Attach the other part of the latch sets in each corresponding place and the board is ready for use. It's important to use sets that can be operated fairly easily by little hands, otherwise it becomes too frustrating and not much fun. When each door is opened it adds to the interest if an attractive picture is glued inside. Colorful stickers are excellent for this purpose.

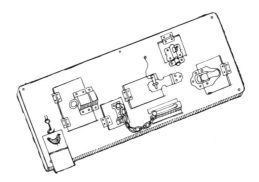

Picture Credits

Index